THE COMPLETE

Kylie

THE COMPLETE
Kylie

Simon Sheridan

Reynolds & Hearn Ltd
London

For Linda Morris, my 'little' big friend x

First published in 2008 by
Reynolds & Hearn Ltd
61a Priory Road
Kew Gardens
Richmond
Surrey
TW9 3DH

A CIP catalogue record for this book is available from the British Library.

ISBN 978 1 905287 60 4

Designed by Peri Godbold

Printed and bound in Great Britain by MPG Books Ltd, Bodmin, Cornwall.

Contents

'I awoke one morning and found myself famous.'
Lord Byron (1812)

'I just want to do everything!'
Kylie Minogue (2006)

Acknowledgments

My sincere thanks to Jonny Davis plus Mark Berry, Luke Evans, Peri Godbold, Marcus Hearn, Derek Kinsley, Martin McDowell, Gennie Nevinson, Noel Price, Richard Reynolds, John Sartain, Darren Willison, Richard Wyatt and James Blair at Project K. Extra special mentions to my wonderful family and Sue Chick, John Clements and Robert Vickers for their continued support.

With fond memories of Rebecca Collins and 'Especially for You' on the jukebox in St Matt's bar, 1989. Those were the days.

Thank you Elsie Snixx, you were invaluable!

To my very own showgirls, Charlotte Watts, Katie Holt, Liz Davies, Rachel Jones and Hilary Arnott. I need to buy you sequins and feathers...

And, as always, I couldn't have done this without Mark Powell.

'Round like a circle, caught up in a spiral...'

Disclaimer:

Introduction

'Being an entertainer and living my life like this is the only thing I know how to do. I don't have any form of CV. I'm not trained to do anything useful!'

Kylie Minogue (2007)

Bonsai sex goddess, sex siren, pop puppet, pop moppet, pop goddess, pop tart, pocket Venus, pint-sized pop princess, perennial pop child, midget gem, mini-sparkler, bottle-top beauty, little stick of dynamite, little sparrow, show pony, singing budgie, diminutive diva, disco diva, disco bunny, disco doll, living doll, pop's true chameleon, pop pixie, pop madam, the gay forces' sweetheart, gold-plated gay icon, impossible princess, indie kid, clever girl, award-winner, hot pants hottie, Aussie hot-bot, world's most wanted arse, Aussie bombshell, Australian Shirley Temple, soap queen, dancing queen, homecoming queen, queen of reinvention, bubbles in the champagne, pink fairy, green fairy, one-take wonder, space vixen, sexy alien, girl-next-door, artist's muse, provocateur, pin-up, cover girl... the hardest working woman in pop.

There are few international entertainers who have been bestowed with as many nicknames as Kylie Minogue. She is journalist Paul Morley's 'fantasy creature' and stylist William Baker's 'immaculately primed canvas', but to those who know her intimately, she's just called 'Min'. She is idolised by teens, worshipped by queens. She is a singer, an actress, a charity worker, a sex symbol, a style icon, a businesswoman, a showgirl; the ultimate 'star' in the most authentic sense of the word.

Kylie Minogue was born on 28 May 1968 in Melbourne, the daughter of Carol, a dancer from Maesteg, Wales, and Ron, an Australian accountant. She has long since dispensed with her unusual surname. To millions of people around the world she's just 'Kylie', no further introduction is required. It seems like everybody feels on first-name terms with her – Kylie's all ours. But this global pop brand name wasn't always destined to be famous. It was younger sister Dannii who was initially the performer in the family; Kylie was merely on stand-by.

Everybody's favourite showgirl, Sydney, November 2006

9

Kylie (right) and
sister Dannii, 1980

'I never had any pressure from my parents to get up to the front and smile,' admitted Kylie in 2004. 'I don't consider myself a stage school kind of kid. I was quite shy, actually, and I didn't go in the school plays.'

However, something of her sister's stardust rubbed off on Kylie and at the age of 11 she gingerly went in front of a TV camera for the first time in an Australian soap called *Skyways*. Even though nobody knew it at the time, Kylie's cuddles with a stuffed koala were the beginning of something very special. But even the year before she left school and the careers advisor asked her what she wanted to be, Kylie still came up a with a blank. 'I honestly didn't know I wanted to be an actress,' she admitted. 'I certainly had no overwhelming desire to be a pop star. It just came accidentally. My brother Brendan took some publicity photos of me and everything just took off from there.'

Worldwide fame in the long-running *Neighbours* came relatively quickly, but it was her virtually overnight reinvention as a pop star, and the gift of 'I Should Be So Lucky', which took her to a landscape she'd never dreamed of. The girl-next-door sitting pretty at #1 in over a dozen countries was still that same girl-next-door, painfully self-conscious, often awkward, overcome by the insatiable pop machine. 'When I became famous, and that happened very quickly, I didn't know how famous I was, or how big a deal it was to have a number one single,' she revealed many years later. 'I'm not Madonna. She was surrounded by the right people. I wasn't. People growing up in New York just have a better chance of being cool than some girl growing up in the suburbs of Melbourne.'

The *Smash Hits* generation embraced Kylie immediately; she was their sort of girl. Others were not so kind. 'In the early days I don't think I was ever taken seriously,' she has said. 'People thought I was a gimmick. I had to put up with so many criticisms over the years and one of those was 'she can't sing'. And it all ended up with me being labelled 'the singing budgie', which even then I embraced. And so I always felt the need to prove them wrong basically and to do it for myself.'

In a half-joking introspective moment, Kylie once described herself as a 'purely manufactured product' – and she has sometimes been content to let others mould her public image, although it can occasionally be an alarming experience. In May 2003 she got the chance to see how others view her. Kylie's face, projected onto a giant screen, appeared as the backdrop to Rafaela Bonochela's new dance piece '21'. Sitting in the audience at Sadler's Wells Theatre Kylie absolutely hated what she saw. 'It made me feel really uncomfortable,' she said. 'I was the main subject, used to represent celebrity as a whole. I was huge. That was the point, but it was awful.'

Kylie has managed, relatively successfully, to keep her public and private personae very separate. In an era where grisly confessional interviews are expected of everyone, Kylie has made an art of keeping mum. She's dignified to the point of being frustrating, but that's all part of the Minogue mystique. Even her potentially purgative fly-on-the-wall documentary *White Diamond* was more quietly spoken than revelatory. Kylie freely admits to being more circumspect the older she becomes, especially since fighting breast cancer, an experience which cemented her iconic status. However, this is the woman who's still tempted to type her name into Google to see what trivia pops up, although she notes that the resulting stories get 'further and further away from who I really am.'

Kylie is also lucky enough to have the luxury of submerging herself in the best dressing-up box in showbusiness. 'I'm like an eight-year-old! I change characters when I do a photo shoot,' she once said. 'It's

kind of me avoiding being me ... which I've become very good at!' When stories leak into the press about troubles in her life our collective heart bleeds for her. Our feelings towards Kylie are more protective than lustful; we worry about her health and disapprove of all those vain boyfriends who've been ghastly to her.

Kylie is the real deal. It really would be impossible to put up a false front for three decades for, as Kylie has recognised, 'You can't fool the public.' She possesses a warm-hearted accessibility, uniting herself with her audience yet always maintaining an intrinsic glamour and 'special-ness'. She is dazzling yet down-to-earth, sensuous rather than overtly sexy; an icon whom you can't help but admire as well as wanting to snuggle up to. She provides inescapable escapism not only for her legion of fans, but also for herself, so that dressing-up box is probably here to stay.

After there was some public apathy towards her music in the mid-1990s, and she had her fingers burnt after the reaction to the 'Impossible Princess' album, Kylie has been understandably reluctant to revisit the dark side of her character. The tortured diva is a romanticised notion, appealing and disconcerting in equal measure. More usually the public demands 'smiley Kylie' and that, for the most part, is what she excels at.

I remember seeing Kylie perform at Wembley during her *KylieFever* tour in 2002 and being amazed at how remarkably natural she was. Early on in the concert she came to the front of the gigantic stage, a tiny, fragile, shimmering figure almost lost in the darkness. She crouched down and spoke to the little children sitting at the front, almost squealing with delight at the fact such young fans were in attendance. 'I am so glad you have all come to see me tonight,' she said. 'It's so fabulous to see all you grown-ups and all you little kiddies too. Thank you. I honestly couldn't do this job without you.' I remember thinking how legitimately thrilled she looked, even for someone famous for flashing the biggest smile in the business. How many other international stars would engage like this with their audiences, and be genuinely excited by it? As Kylie once said: 'For me, live performance is the ultimate performance.'

Kylie's talent lies in the fact she is enduringly likable; the public are endlessly fascinated with her life, despite her giving away very few juicy secrets. This enigmatic pop maven projects such a bona fide sweetness that people seemingly want to see her succeed. As a result there is little public hunger to see Kylie portraying anybody other than herself; we are quite content with Kylie the pop star, the warm personality. Post-*Neighbours* Kylie has only dipped tentative toes into the acting world and her movies have been few and far between. Aside from her impressive debut in 1989's *The Delinquents* she has not accepted another leading role, understandably reluctant to headline again after that film's mixed critical reception.

But Kylie always bounces back from the lean times; her name means 'boomerang' in Aboriginal after all. Kylie's massive popularity is, apparently, infinite and the awards and accolades continue to stack up from all over the world, probably none more prestigious than her OBE, one of the surprise announcements in the New Year Honour's list of December 2007. 'I feel deeply touched to be acknowledged by the UK, my adopted home, in this way,' she said. 'This last year I have felt so much love and support from everyone.' Australia is rightly proud of Kylie but it is Britain which has claimed her as one of their own.

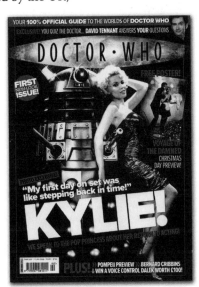

Kylie freely admits to having an 'appalling' memory, so perhaps this unashamedly nostalgic retrospective of her public life will jog a few memories for her. Naturally, when you bring out a book with 'complete' in the title you are immediately asking for trouble, but enclosed herein you will find all Kylie's singles, albums, movies, TV acting roles and tours, plus a whole lot more besides.

Kylie once complained that when people write about her they only concentrate on four aspects of her life: *Neighbours*, Michael Hutchence, cancer and her delectable bum. Obviously there are mentions of all of the above, but this isn't a tabloid trawl through Kylie's private life. This is a celebration of her incredible professional achievements: selling 60 million singles and 40 million albums is no mean feat. This is Kylie's story told through her career from the first time she acted in an Aussie soap right up to her box-office busting KYLIEX2008 tour nearly 30 years later. Kylie might claim not to own a CV, but hopefully *The Complete Kylie* is the nearest thing to a glittering résumé she'll ever have.

The Complete **Kylie**

Once upon a time there was a little Australian girl who became an international pop singer, but all global megastars have to start somewhere. How about we begin Kylie's career in an airport departure lounge in Melbourne ... ?

Skyways

Episode #58 'Kristy'

Seven Network / 1979-1981 / A Crawford Production / 188 x 50 minute episodes / Series first broadcast (Australia) 11 July 1979

Created by Jock Blair and Terry Stapleton / Produced by Graham Moore / Executive Producers Ian Crawford and Jock Blair

Principal cast: Tony Bonner (*Paul MacFarlane*), Tina Bursill (*Louise Carter*), Bruce Barry (*Captain Doug Stewart*), Bill Stalker (*Peter Fanelli*), Ken James (*Simon Young*), Bartholomew John (*Captain Nick Grainger*), Deborah Coulls (*Jacki Soong*), Brain James (*George Tibbet*), Kris McQuade (*Faye Peterson*), Gaynor Martin (*Mandy MacFarlane*), Andrew McKaige (*Alan MacFarlane*), Joanne Samuel (*Kelly Morgan*) with Kylie as *Robin Simpson* and Jason Donovan as *Adam Simpson*

Languishing at the bottom of the Aussie soap filing cabinet, beneath the well-oiled drawers marked *Neighbours, Sons and Daughters* and *Home and Away*, sit 188 episodes of *Skyways*. Full of high-flying histrionics, wobbly sets, quick cutaways and actors forgetting their lines, *Skyways* could well be the lowest point in Australian TV history – lower even than the infamous 'Bouncer's dream' episode of *Neighbours*. Nearly 30 years after it was first broadcast on Australian screens, it is now only remembered for one thing – Kylie's very first professional acting role, filmed in 1979 and broadcast early the following year. 'There was this bit where I'm hugging a toy koala bear,' Kylie recalled two decades later, grimacing at the memory. 'An actor asks me to do something and you can see I have no idea what I'm supposed to do!'

Australian soap operas have not always been about tanned young bodies on white sandy beaches or meddling neighbours in quiet cul-de-sacs. Back in the early 1970s Australian TV execs were producing some

Australia's most valuable overalls, safe behind glass during Kylie: The Exhibition, 2005 of the raunchiest adults-only drama seen anywhere in the world. Most infamous was *Number 96* (even the title was a double entendre), first screened on Network Ten in 1972, featuring the bed-hopping antics of the residents of a Sydney apartment block. Striving to break taboos from the very beginning, *Number 96* made its debut with full-page newspaper advertisements proclaiming 'Tonight at 8.30pm television loses its virginity!'

Throughout the 1960s and 70s Crawford Productions, one of the most prolific production companies in Australia, had dominated the TV market. A family-run organisation headed up by Hector Crawford, the company specialised in police dramas, but in a direct response to the success of *Number 96* it premiered *The Box* in 1974, a sex 'n' scandal soap set against the background of a commercial TV station. Initially trading on flashes of nipple, extra-marital shenanigans and Australian TV's first ever lesbian kiss, *The Box* later had its salacious content toned down by its concerned network and the show was finally axed in 1977. Going back to the drawing board Crawfords realised there was only one place to go, and that was up.

Skyways premiered in July 1979, promising to take soaps where they'd never been before, namely the mile-high club. 'You won't believe what they get UP to!' the publicity material gushed. 'This is where adult TV drama takes off!' Set at the fictitious Pacific International Airport, *Skyways* concerned itself with the lives, and complicated loves, of the airport's pilots, security team, airline staff and management. The new soap was an ambitious project, featuring real Jumbo Jet props, but thanks to some appalling special effects, abysmal acting and outrageous scriptwriting it ultimately stalled on the runway. Tony Bonner played Paul McFarlane, the reluctant, and rigid, head of Pacific International Airport (exterior scenes were actually filmed at Melbourne Airport in Tullamarine). Friction arose as McFarlane was often at loggerheads with his ruthlessly ambitious assistant manager Louise Carter (Tina Bursill), *Skyways'* resident blonde super-bitch.

Skyways' impressive John Barry-esque theme tune promised plenty but the series continually overstretched itself on a very limited budget. Despite accompanying publicity for the show promising an action-packed series based at an airport terminal which 'five million passengers pass through every year', you'd be hard-pressed to spot even five walking past the camera in *Skyways*. Most scenes were strictly studio-bound, so, using technology called 'chroma-key', empty windows were superimposed with shot of Boeings taking off and runways bustling with traffic. *Skyways'* distractingly bad visuals, coupled with the continual roar of dubbed plane noise in the background, made the series virtually unwatchable. Even the impressive uniforms, dishy pilots and pretty lesbian air hostesses proved less appealing than TV's usual round of doctors, nurses and coppers.

Viewers were distinctly lukewarm about the set-bound action and, when planes actually did take off, like the explosive-laden flight to Tasmania which ended up in a fireball, the results just looked ludicrous. On terra firma the pilots regularly knocked back vast quantities of whiskey before taking to the skies ('Emergency with the 152 from Adelaide! It's 20 minutes late and the captain's had a heart attack!'), and an endless parade of potboiling storylines about armed robbers, drug traffickers and teenage stowaways clogged up departures with terrible clichés. Viewers had been warned to fasten their seatbelts for a bumpy ride, but this really was one trip not worth making.

Amazingly, into all this chaos dropped two cute, cherubic faces making their debut on television. Seven years before they started snogging on *Neighbours*, Kylie and Jason Donovan appeared as the special guest stars in episode #58 of *Skyways*, playing a couple of mini-tearaways, initially caught by airport security mucking around on the escalators (which being low-budget Aussie soap, we never actually get to see). Named Adam and Robin Simpson, the tiny, grinning siblings are awaiting the arrival of their father Charles (Matthew King) whose light aircraft is experiencing engine traffic. ('He's a beaut pilot,' boasts Kylie.) Assistant airport manager Louise has to keep them amused for a while, even getting a fright from Jason's big, ugly rubber spider. When Louise starts screaming Kylie counters, 'Now show her your mouse!', but she declines the offer.

The young actors were paid $300 each for their two days' work. Of the two Jason probably had fractionally more acting experience, albeit restricted to school plays. His actor father, Terence Donovan, had encouraged him to audition for the role after hearing about it from a contact at Crawfords, for whom he was starring in primetime police drama *Cop Shop*.

Jason actually looks positively evil in this episode (and sounds suspiciously like his voice is breaking), and Kylie whines throughout while continually clutching her toy koala Kristy ('my very best friend'). The pair end up irritating the entire airport staff including namby-pamby admin assistant George Tibbett (Brian James) and his fussy cousin Madge, who just happens to be hanging about the departure lounge. When Jason's character accidentally knocks over an overflowing ashtray with his energetic yo-yo, Madge intervenes in the most over-the-top fashion. 'Now you just clean that up. Go on! Clean it up. Every bit of it,' she scolds, making the poor kid pick up dirty dog ends and ash with his fingers. 'Don't they teach you manners at school?' She then chides Kylie for slouching: 'Oh, *do* sit up dear!'

Cleanliness freak Madge is played by wooden character actress Jessica Noad, who coincidentally became Kylie's equally awful maternal grandmother in *Neighbours* a decade later. After some inconsequential dialogue about pizza ('The cheese was fantastic. It was stretchy, just like slime, except it was yellow,' pipes Kylie), the children are collected by their father, but not before Kristy the stuffed koala is left behind at the airport! There's further excitement when the children's plane undergoes an emergency landing on a golf course, necessitating a spell in hospital for the family. Thankfully, effete air-traffic controller Simon Young ('Alpha Tango Quebec do you read me?') whisks the koala over to the hospital in a mercy dash.

With material like this it's no surprise that *Skyways* was yanked from the schedules barely two years after it started. 'It didn't last long,' Kylie confessed to *Smash Hits* magazine many years later, 'because it was dreadful. Both Jason and I looked pretty terrible. He was really chubby with a bowl haircut and I was really small with long straight blonde hair and big buck teeth.' Jason's lasting memories of *Skyways*' co-star weren't any more favourable. 'After filming was wrapped and we said our goodbyes I didn't give her a second thought,' he said in 2007. 'I was far too young to be interested in girls and if anything I remember thinking she was a little skinny.'

The Sullivans

Episodes #637 to #644

9 Network / 1976-1982 / A Crawford Production / 1,114 x 25 minute episodes / Series first broadcast (Australia) 15 November 1976

Created by Hector Crawford and Jock Blair / Produced by Henry Crawford and John Barningham / Theme tune composed by Geoff Harvey

Principal cast: Lorraine Bayley (*Grace Sullivan*), Paul Cronin (*Dave Sullivan*), Andrew MacFarlane (*John Sullivan*), Steven Tandy (*Tom Sullivan*), Richard Morgan (*Terry Sullivan*), Susan Hannaford (*Kitty Sullivan*), Norman Yemm (*Norm Baker*), Michael Caton (*Uncle Harry Sullivan*), Maggie Dench (*Aunt Rose Sullivan*), Vivean Gray (*Ida Jessup*) with Kylie as *Carla*

Arriving like a wholesome breath of fresh air in Australian living rooms, tainted by the shocking sights and sounds of a rash of permissive 1970s soaps, *The Sullivans* was a back-to-basics family serial with a historical twist, a teatime soap set during World War II. Running from 1976 until 1982, *The Sullivans* gave Crawford Productions the biggest hit in its long history. The episodes began in 1939, just before the outbreak of war, and followed one family as they struggled with life-changing events both at home and abroad.

Although initially only commissioned for a 13-week run, such was the popularity of *The Sullivans* that it eventually ran for over 1000 episodes, its broadcasting history approximately mirroring the true length of the conflict it was set against. Set in the Melbourne suburb of Camberwell (coincidentally the same name as Kylie's high school), the series exuded a warmth and charm so frequently absent from Australian television drama and the public immediately took the family to their hearts. Even the critics were almost uniformly won over by the series' attention to historical detail and the performances of the cast.

Actor Paul Cronin (best known for his part as a hard-nosed copper in long-running Aussie series *Matlock Police*) played the moral head of the family, Dave Sullivan, but it was his sympathetic and attractive wife that most inspired audiences. One-time-*Playschool* presenter Lorraine Bayly was Grace Sullivan, the quiet, highly principled Catholic mother, loyal to her husband and loving to their three sons John, Tom and Terry and daughter Kitty. As the matriarch of *The Sullivans*, Bayly rapidly became the most popular member of the cast, mobbed by fans wherever she went and pursued by the press. She twice won an Australian Silver Logie TV award (named after John Logie Baird, the British inventor of television) for 'Best Actress in a Leading Role'.

Storylines gradually moved away from the family household, local pub, general store and guest house, the latter owned by the waspish Ida Jessup (Vivean Gray – later to become *Neighbours'* legendary busybody Mrs Mangel), and shifted to war scenes in Crete, Holland, Greece, the deserts of North Africa and the jungles of South-East Asia. Several plotlines followed young Tom Sullivan (Steven Tandy) and family friend Norm Baker (Norman Yemm) as they fought across Europe, enduring hardship and tragedy. It was their partnership which provided most of the series' heart-wrenching cliffhangers.

More than any other Australian TV series, it was *The Sullivans* that helped to whet the British appetite for Australian soaps. The series was often slow and sentimental, and rather too studio-bound (especially when the lead characters were purportedly abroad), but *The Sullivans* also provided dollops of romance, cosy familiarity and tense drama over its six years. In Britain the series became a staple of ITV's daytime schedule from the late seventies, although it was broadcast at different times in different regions, meaning viewers in Yorkshire could quite easily be watching storylines years ahead of their counterparts in the south of England. *The Sullivans'* shambolic scheduling made it the butt of television jokes, but there is no denying its fanatical popularity. It was the first Australian series to make a serious dent in the international TV market, eventually selling to 45 countries worldwide.

Because it was Kylie's younger sister Danielle who had the real aspirations to be a performer, Kylie often accompanied her and mum Carol to TV auditions, and this was how the relatively shy Kylie initially got noticed by casting directors. It happened for *Skyways* and it was the case again for *The Sullivans*. Dannii (as she later became known) was up for the part of a crudely realised Anne Frank-type character named Carla in a forthcoming storyline set in Holland. However, the show's casting director thought Dannii far too young for the role and asked Kylie whether she might like to have a read-through of the script instead. After the audition the elder Minogue was offered the job, but for Dannii her rejection may well have been a blessing in disguise. Kylie ended up playing the bedraggled Dutch girl complete with a dirty face, greasy hair and ragged clothes.

When Kylie became a star in Britain in the late 1980s she often claimed *The Sullivans* had been her very first acting role. This was mainly to cut cultural corners, since the series was familiar to UK viewers, whereas the dubious delights of *Skyways* had yet to be screened in Britain.

The character of Carla first appeared in *The Sullivans* in episode #637. The poor little soul is so weak from hunger that in Kylie's opening scene she collapses like a rag doll right in front of globe-trotting Norm Baker. She is quickly befriended by Norm and his mate Tom Sullivan, and although the men are initially wary of her (fearing that she may be a miniature Nazi spy), Carla starts chattering like a canary when offered a juicy radish to chew on. 'You are Engleesh pilots, not?' she asks the bemused Aussie soldiers in her faltering accent. 'Papa and Mama knew many Engleesh people. Papa used to go to London for his business. Sometimes ve vent vere for holidays. That is vere I go to school – vere I learn Engleesh.'

Just like the real Anne Frank, her Jewish family have been hounded by the Nazis and when the police come to cart them away Carla's mother stows her tiny daughter in a hidey-hole behind a cupboard. It is from here that she falls into the basement where our Aussie heroes are secreted. After finishing her radish she immediately reveals she has plans for them. 'Now I am here,' she tells them defiantly, 'you vill save me!' Carla develops an increasing dependence on Norm, who tries his best to shield her from the harsh realities of war. Forced to part, he gives the girl a coin as a token of his affection.

For an 11-year-old with little acting experience Kylie equips herself with the best European vowels she can muster. However, the young actress sounds more like she heralds from downtown Berlin rather than uptown Amsterdam. 'I had to try and learn a Dutch accent,' Kylie recalled in a British interview for *TV-AM*. 'I had a man called Mr Muskins who'd come round and go through my script with me and cross out letters and put in the letters I was supposed to say.'

Over the space of eight episodes (all set in the summer of 1944), Kylie displayed considerable acting talent, even more so in a role that was extremely challenging for a young child. Indeed, Kylie's brief tenure in *The Sullivans* was memorable enough for the character of Carla to 'return' a couple of years later. After the war ends, Norm makes enquiries about adopting the Dutch orphan and Carla miraculously turns up in Melbourne. However it subsequently emerges that the girl is an impostor (played by a *totally* different-looking, and much older, actress, Saskia Post) and that the real Carla tragically died. It transpires that the new girl met Kylie's character in a children's home and pinched her coin. Norm takes pity on her and, this being a good-natured Australian soap, he adopts her instead.

In reality Kylie was too busy at school to reprise her role as the timid Dutch girl and it would be another four years before Kylie stepped in front of a TV camera again.

The Zoo Family

Episode #23 **'Yvonne the Terrible'**

9 Network / 1985 / A Crawford Production / 26 x 25 minute episodes / Series first broadcast (Australia) 4 May 1985

Created and based on the book by Robert Klein / Produced by Gwenda Marsh / Written by Alison Niselle and John Reeves / Directed by John Reeves

Principal cast: Peter Curtin (*Dr. David 'Mitch' Mitchell*), Kate Gorman (*Susie*

Mitchell), Steven Jacobson (*Nick Mitchell*), Rebecca Gibney (*Julie Davis*), John Orcsik (*Ken Bennett*), Maciek Staniewicz (*Harry*), Gennie Nevinson (*Peta*), Jon Finlayson (*Colonel Archibald Spencer*) with Kylie as *Yvonne*

The Zoo Family, as the title suggests, concerned the adventures of veterinarian David 'Mitch' Mitchell and his two children, Nick and Susie, who live and work at a large city zoo. Filmed entirely on location at the Royal Melbourne Zoo, each episode involved itself with specific animals and the problems they encountered. A comedy element was prevalent throughout as individual episode titles testify – *Going Ape*, *Monkey Business*, *Rotters and Otters*, as well as the heartbreaking *Reptiles Can't Cry*. It was that kind of show. 'It was fabulous fun to work on,' recalls *Zoo Family* actress Gennie Nevinson, 'although working with animals created its own problems at times. I played a keeper in charge of the giraffes and elephants. I hasten to add I knew *nothing* about giraffes *or* elephants!'

Against this backdrop of domestic drama and the plight of poorly animals arrived Kylie as troubled kid, Yvonne, or more specifically 'Yvonne the Terrible', as the episode title has it. 'She was only about 16 when she came to join the cast,' says Gennie, 'but she impressed us all. She was incredibly sweet and competent in quite a difficult role. I think she surprised a lot of people with how good she was.'

Playing a girl four years her junior, Kylie excelled as an abused child given refuge by the zoo caretaker. Truculent and abrasive, Yvonne struggles to adapt to zoo etiquette and sets about unlocking cage doors and letting the furry and feathered inmates go free. Realising it's a cry for help, the Mitchell children try to help her and when Kylie's character sees a battered baby kangaroo returned to her mother's pouch she suddenly realises where she's been going wrong.

Although only present for a few days' shooting, Kylie fitted right into the show and struck up a friendship with Kate Gorman, who played the vet's daughter Susie. In yet another coincidence of Australian television, Kate was the first actress to audition for the part of Charlene in *Neighbours* in late 1985. Kylie got picked instead and Kate was awarded the part of her nemesis, Erinsborough High School's bitch Sue Parker. As for *The Zoo Family*, it never returned. Filming at a working zoo created any number of headaches for Crawfords and the series failed to attract big enough viewing figures. 'It was a charming little series, very much in line with other Crawfords shows,' says Gennie Nevinson, 'but it wasn't a huge success. It was maybe just a bit too cute for viewers.'

The Henderson Kids (series 1)

24 x 25 minute episodes

Network Ten / 1985 / A Crawford Production /
Series first broadcast (Australia) 11 May 1985

Produced by Alan Hardy / Written by Roger
Moulton, Galia Hardy, Peter Hepworth and John
Reeves / Directed by Chris Langman

Principal cast: Nicholas Eadie (*Mike Henderson*),
Nadine Garner (*Tamara Henderson*), Paul Smith
(*Steve Henderson*), Diane Craig (*Alice Henderson*),
Mark Hennessey (*'Cowboy' Clarke*), Kylie Minogue
(*Char Kernow*), Ben Mendelsohn (*Ted Morgan*),
Bradley Kilpatrick (*'Brains' Buchanan*), Peter
Whitford (*Ashley Wheeler*), Annie Jones (*Sylvia
Wheeler*), Antoinette Byron (*Pat Edwards*), Michael
Aitkens (*Wal Mullens*), John Larking (*Sgt George
Budd*)

The first Australian soap aimed
squarely at children, *The Henderson
Kids* was the latest small-screen success for
the ever-prolific Crawford Productions. It
also provided Kylie with her first regular,
long-running role as a spunky, provincial
punk – a part awarded to her after
impressing Crawfords with her scene-stealing turn in *The Zoo Family*.

The Henderson Kids was a brave attempt to bring adult themes
to a teenage audience, touching on issues of isolation, grief, anger,
poverty, rejection and the angst of young love, punctuated with good
humour, slapstick and action. The titular Hendersons are brother and
sister Steve (Paul Smith) and Tamara (Nadine Garner), 'happy, *normal*
teenagers' as the ham-fisted publicity continually stressed. However,
the normality of the siblings' lives in suburban Melbourne is shattered
when their mother is killed in a tragic accident, squashed under the
tyres of a truck while trying to save a toddler. With their biological
father presumed missing in England, the kids are shipped off to quiet
Aussie seaside town Haven Bay ('Population 300') and their legal
guardian Uncle Mike (Nicholas Eadie), the dishy local policeman. On
the outskirts of the town Steve and Tamara inherit a huge stretch of
land overlooking the sea called Henderson's Point, but the picturesque

idyll, complete with a secret aboriginal cave, is no match for the hustle and bustle of city life.

The kids' adjustment from a busy metropolis to a sleepy, depressed backwater is central to the series' early episodes. 'I need pollution,' opines Steve, 'I'll suffocate without it!' For Boy George-fixated Tamara it's even worse. 'There's no hot water,' she screams, 'and there's a frog in the toilet!' Feeling depressed after the death of their mother, the kids' unhappiness is compounded by a feeling of alienation in their new home. The children's awkward, over-sensitive uncle finds it difficult adapting to his new role as parent and encourages Steve and 'Tam-Bam' to makes friends in the town. Mercifully Haven Bay is over-run by hormonal teenagers. 'Is this whole town owned by people under 18?' asks one bemused visitor.

The Hendersons enrol in Haven Bay Consolidated School but their arrival is initially met with hostility by the local kids, who resent their new 'city slicker' classmates living with the local copper. 'You better watch out,' one of the kids warns Steve. 'We don't like Hendersons round here.' After some name-calling and idle threats ('I'm gonna fix your face, mate, over there behind the dunny!'), a potentially fatal cliff fall brings the youngsters together, making them realise they have more in common than they originally thought.

Heading up the local kids is Haven Bay's resident 'super-spunk' and professional layabout 'Cowboy' (actor-turned-stuntman Mark Hennessy), squirrel-faced glutton 'Brains' (Bradley Kilpatrick) and cocky, scowling bad boy Ted (an early role for much-loved Australian actor Ben Mendelsohn). Kylie plays Cowboy's girlfriend Charlotte 'Char' Kernow, the town totty and local clothes horse. Char's only family is her elderly father, a local trawler man who lives on the breadline and struggles to keep his daughter in the latest city fashions.

If Kylie later cringed about some of the outfits Pete Waterman's stylists made her wear while promoting her first album she must have despaired of the concoctions dreamt up by *The Henderson Kids'* wardrobe mistress. Over-emphasising her role as a punky, rebellious young woman attempting to make her mark, Kylie's fashions veer from the bizarre to the downright eye-popping. Over 24 episodes Kylie sports a variety of lime green tops with polka dots, sailor hats, skin-tight Day-Glo jeans, red woolly tights and even a bright pink fairy godmother's outfit – all of these topped off by big plastic earrings, make-up and startling red hair. 'We didn't want two blondes in the first and second roles,' recalled director Chris Langman, 'so we decided to dye Kylie's hair red to make her look a bit different. Kylie was shy and the other actress Nadine Garner definitely wasn't, so Kylie took a back seat for a while.'

Kylie's character reaches the peak of horrendousness when she starts work at blowzy Mrs Weston's blue rinse hair salon, where she has to dress in a shapeless polyester smock accented by a gigantic Margaret Thatcher bow. When interviewed on TV's *Young Talent Time* in June 1985, Kylie expressed her embarrassment at the clothes her character wears. 'She likes to dress up in all the latest fashion and she thinks she's the trend of the town,' she explained, 'but it's only a small country town, so of course she's not really!'

Char is a dreamer who fantasises about becoming 'Hairdresser of the Year' and loves leafing through the latest style magazines. 'Look at this new hairstyle,' she says excitedly. 'It's called 'house-on-fire'!' Two years before she finally locked lips with Jason Donovan on *Neighbours* she also enjoys her first screen kiss with actor Mark Hennessy.

Kylie's performance in *The Henderson Kids'* early episodes seems quite self-conscious, but as the series progresses you witness the moving portrayal of a young girl helplessly watching her father face bankruptcy and her break-up with Cowboy, who has been tipping his Stetson in the direction of doe-eyed Tamara. Alongside her more touching scenes, Kylie exhibits a livelier side, dancing energetically to the jukebox and giving fashion advice to her mates ('You look *grouse*, mate!'). It was this engaging versatility in Kylie's performance, and her obvious popularity with viewers, that first brought her to the attention of *Neighbours* casting director Jan Russ. 'She was like a quiet little mouse when I first met her,' admitted Russ later, 'but she had this terrific quality just to light up the screen.'

Although it was to be Nadine Garner who got the prestigious Silver Logie TV award for her part in *The Henderson Kids*, it is Kylie who really dazzles on screen. She's particularly impressive in her scenes with Mark Hennessey and Bradley Kilpatrick as they make the best of the limited social life Haven Bay offers them. The gang spend most of their time playing pinball at the perpetually deserted Marine Milk Bar, which only seems to have one song on the jukebox – unfortunately the series' anodyne theme tune, 'Carry on together – sharing every day!'

Slurping milkshakes, the teenagers unite in their hatred of ruthless local businessman Ashley Wheeler (Peter Whitford), Haven Bay's slimy sawmill owner, who is desperate to get his sweaty hands on Henderson's Point so he can build a hotel complex on it with the help of a bunch of sneaky Japanese investors. After an interminable series of mishaps involving near-drowning, punch-ups, runaway bicycles, tumbling motorbikes, tripping down mineshafts and cowboy boots full of porridge, the kids finally defeat evil Wheeler, but not before Steve Henderson dangerously falls in love with the treacherous property developer's pretty daughter Sylvia (played by future *Neighbours* schoolgirl, Annie Jones). Other pre-*Neighbours* actors causing predictable mayhem included Stefan Dennis as a pimp's associate and Peter O'Brien as a vindictive cattle drover.

Filmed in the small town of Birregurra, Victoria, in the summer of 1984, but not screened in Australia until the spring of the following year, *The Henderson Kids* proved to be a huge ratings hit for Channel Ten. Although the series came to a satisfactory conclusion after 24 episodes with the Hendersons' errant father, Wal Mullens (English actor Michael Aitkens), turning up to take them back to the city, producer Alan Hardy made the decision to recommission the show late in 1985. However, *The Henderson Kids II* suffered from the fact it was wholly Melbourne-based, effectively dispensing with the 'fish-out-of-water' premise which made the original such a success.

With the most interesting members of the cast axed for the second series, the show suffered and Hardy has since admitted it was not the cleverest of moves. 'I think the biggest mistake I ever made,' he said, 'was to sack Kylie. But for her own career it was probably the biggest boost I could have given her. I like to think I made Kylie famous by not casting her in any more episodes of *The Henderson Kids*!'

Fame and Misfortune

6 x 25 minute episodes

ABC Network / 1986 / An ABC-Revcom Production / Series first broadcast (Australia) 15 May 1986

Produced by Noel Price / Directed by Karl Zwicky, Noel Price and Bill Garner / Written by John Jones / Music by Ben Hocking

Principal cast: Myles Collin (*Tim Hardy*), John Flaus (*Mr Hardy*), Marie Redshaw (*Mrs Hardy*), Kylie Minogue (*Samantha Hardy*) with Ben Mendelsohn, Martin Sharman, Peter Hosking, Syd Conabere

Kylie's most obscure TV series and one rarely seen since its original broadcast is *Fame and Misfortune*. A co-production between the Australian Broadcasting Corporation and now-defunct French company Revcom, the series was a quirky six-part comedy-drama about a 15-year-old boy called Tim (Myles Collin) and his grand ambition to own his very own piano. Tim's amusing, and sometimes hazardous, journey sees him desperately trying to raise the necessary cash in order to realise his dream.

Actor and writer John Flaus plays Tim's father, while his mother is played by veteran actress Marie Redshaw (at the time best known for recurring support roles in *Matlock Police* and *Prisoner*). Kylie, in a role removed from the streetwise, sympathetic Char in *The Henderson Kids*, took the role of Tim's irritating, but cute, younger sister whose main purpose in life was to be a source of continuous torment for her older brother. The series was screened in the UK by the BBC in 1989. The *Sun* reported; 'Kylie hoped her fans in Britain would never see it. She wants to create a new adult image!'

Fame and Misfortune's award-winning producer Noel Price recalls what it was like working with the young Kylie. 'She was only about 15 or 16 back then, but I instinctively knew what a talented kid she was,' he says. 'Considering she'd been acting for a while already she was extremely sweet natured and unaffected. I know it's a cliché to say it, but here was a young girl with real warmth and a very sunny disposition. Kylie always took a conscientious approach to her acting and had a nice sense of comedy and lots of enthusiasm.'

Between takes Noel remembers sitting with Kylie and talking to her about her other passion, aside from acting. 'Honestly, the main thing I think of when I recall making *Fame and Misfortune* is her big smile,' he says. 'She seemed to be most happy when we talked about music. She absolutely adored music, even then, and this was years before she had a pop career. I was really impressed that she could actually remember the lyrics of songs in the charts – most people remember the odd bits of a chorus but she actually knew the verse lines and could sing them back to me. Funnily enough I didn't pick up on her amazing ability and I certainly had no idea that this might be a precursor of things to come!

'Kylie really was a delightful teenager who was incredibly lively, optimistic and fun to work with,' adds Noel, 'but our series rather fell by the wayside compared to her next project. Everybody associates Kylie with *Neighbours* nowadays. Back then I had no idea I was working with a soon-to-be international superstar!'

AUTHORISED VERSION

Neighbours

AS SHOWN ON BBC TELEVISION

RAMSAY STREET

Written by Valda Marshall and Ray Kolle

THE RAMSAYS A FAMILY DIVIDED!

READ ABOUT THE PAST LIVES
OF YOUR FAVOURITE NEIGHBOURS!
Based on the Grundy Television Series

No. 1

Neighbours

Episodes #234 to #777

7 Network (1985), Network Ten (1986-ongoing) / A Grundy Television Production / Series first broadcast (Australia) 18 March 1985 / Series first broadcast (UK) 27 October 1986

Created by Reg Watson / Originally Written and Produced by Reg Watson / Original Script Supervisor – Ray Kolle / Theme tune composed by Tony Hatch and Jackie Trent / Originally performed by Barry Crocker

Principal cast (1986-1988): Alan Dale (*Jim Robinson*), Anne Haddy (*Helen Daniels*), Stefan Dennis (*Paul Robinson*), Peter O'Brien (*Shane Ramsay*), David Clencie (*Danny Ramsay*), Paul Keane (*Des Clarke*), Elaine Smith (*Daphne Clarke*), Myra de Groot (*Eileen Clarke*), Anne Charleston (*Madge Mitchell*), Craig McLachlan (*Henry Mitchell*), Jason Donovan (*Scott Robinson*), Kylie Minogue (*Charlene Mitchell*), Guy Pearce (*Mike Young*), Annie Jones (*Jane Harris*), Kylie Flinker (*Lucy Robinson*), Ian Smith (*Harold Bishop*), Vivean Gray (*Nell Mangel*), Geoff Paine (*Dr Clive Gibbons*), Joy Daniels (*Rosemary Daniels*), Anne Scott-Pendlebury (*Hilary Robinson*), Lisa Armytage (*Dr Beverley Marshall*), Ally Fowler (*Zoe Davis*), Fiona Corke (*Gail Lewis*), Charlene Fenn (*Nikki Dennison*), Kate Gorman (*Sue Parker*), Gloria Ajenstat (*Susan Cole*), Mark Little (*Joe Mangel*), Lucinda Cowden (*Melanie Pearson*), Scott Wealands (*Baby Sam*) and Bouncer as *himself*

Kylie's first appearance (episode # 234)
17 April 1986 (Australia), 28 September 1987 (UK)

Kylie's last appearance (episode # 777)
26 July 1988 (Australia), 1 November (1989) (UK)

Would Kylie have become such an international star without the help of *Neighbours*, and would *Neighbours* ever have become such a global hit without Kylie? Nobody can be certain, but there can be no denying that both exploited each other, but while Kylie used the series as a springboard to great things *Neighbours* has always remained in her shadow. Kylie's supernatural influence still permeates every corner of the show, even 20 years after her departure from Australia's most famous fictional street.

Neighbours was created by Reg Watson, one of the most experienced and successful entrepreneurs in British television. The man behind

ATV's long-running, although much-derided, *Crossroads* (1964-1988), emigrated to Australia in the 1970s and started work on a string of other populist serials, including *The Young Doctors, Prisoner* and most notably *Sons and Daughters*, his glossy twins-separated-at-birth soap. By the early 1980s Watson was head of drama at Grundy Productions, one of Australia's most successful TV companies and birthplace of *Sons and Daughters*. The 7 Network was looking for another serial and Watson had the idea of a wholesome suburban soap, focusing more on family values and running along the lines of *Coronation Street* but with more international appeal.

Initially the BBC was approached in the hope that the corporation would co-produce the new series. They passed, little knowing what an important part of their daytime schedule the series would eventually become. Back in Australia the 7 Network knew it was a risk commissioning a new soap for the channel, but knowing Watson's track-record for high-rating shows they stumped up the majority of the Aus $8 million budget and the new series went into pre-production in the autumn of 1984. Originally rather bleakly titled *One Way Street* it eventually morphed into the more positive-sounding *Neighbours*. 'I wanted to show families living in a small suburban street who are friends,' Watson explained, 'and humour has to play a big part in it.'

Neighbours centred on the fictional Melbourne suburb of Erinsborough, and more specifically a leafy cul-de-sac called Ramsay Street. From the outset *Neighbours* was a world away from the melodramatic *Sons and Daughters*. The soap's gentler, more homespun approach to family affairs was at odds with its stablemate's histrionic parade of accidental deaths, bomb plots, bitching and plastic surgery, all played out against sets uniformly painted brown and beige. Watson's sunny new series preferred to concentrate on everyday matters, the resolution of domestic issues and the ongoing neighbourly feuds between Ramsay Street's two most prominent families – the working-class Ramsays (after whom the street was named) and the middle-class Robinsons.

Heading up the cast was popular ex-*Sons and Daughters* actress Anne Haddy as the series' sympathetic matriarch and amateur portrait painter Helen Daniels, her straight-as-a-die, widowed son-in-law Jim Robinson (played by former *Young Doctors* pin-up Alan Dale) and his scheming eldest son Paul (Stefan Dennis). Across the street lived pig-headed plumber Max Ramsay (Francis Bell), his high-strung wife Maria (Dasha Blahova) and their two teenage sons.

Bizarrely, considering Watson's insistence that his new series would have 'down-to-earth appeal', *Neighbours*' debut episode opened with a wild fantasy sequence featuring young Danny Ramsay (David Clencie) running through the neighbourhood in the middle of a stormy night wearing just his pyjama bottoms, while being dazzled by car headlights and taunted by the rest of the Ramsay Street residents, who laugh maniacally. Suddenly he sees his Speedo-wearing brother Shane (Peter O'Brien) diving to his death. All this is set to a disturbing sub-zombie movie soundtrack. From this rather unexpected start *Neighbours* settled into far more humdrum soap opera clichés.

Early storylines included a tragic car crash, bank robbery, attempted murder and the consternation caused by the arrival of a stripper in Ramsay Street (played unconvincingly by the very un-stripper-like Elaine Smith). Despite some noteworthy performances by the cast, Anne Haddy in particular, and a super-catchy theme tune co-written by *Crossroads*' composer Tony Hatch, *Neighbours* was seriously underwhelming to soap fans. Traditionally, serials set in Melbourne are unpopular with audiences in Sydney and *Neighbours* was no exception. The more lurid shenanigans of *Sons and Daughters* were wiping the floor with the new soap upstart and although *Neighbours* was holding its own in Melbourne, 7 Network pulled the plug on its expensive new soap in July 1985, after just 170 episodes had been shot. The final episode was screened in Australia on 8 November that year.

The cast were stunned at the news, but even more so when they learnt that Ian Holmes, their then-boss at Grundys, seething at what he saw as 7 Network's betrayal, offered *Neighbours* to rival commercial TV station Ten Network, who, after little persuasion, re-commissioned the series. Up to that point it was unprecedented for an axed Australian TV series to jump channels.

Network Ten ordered a raft of immediate changes to *Neighbours* before it went before the cameras again. Sets were redesigned and rebuilt (7 Network had 'accidentally' burnt the old ones), unpopular storylines were dropped and several cast members had their contracts terminated. One such casualty was actor Darius Perkins, who played Jim Robinson's youngest son Scott. Perkins was allegedly released from his contract due to his unreliability on set, coupled with a desire by Grundys to recast his character as a more 'fun and romantic' teenager.

The actor chosen to bring new vitality to the role was Jason Donovan, a handsome, blond 17-year-old who made mullets almost fashionable again. Jason had recently appeared in Aussie gold rush series *Golden*

Pennies (1985) and had originally been earmarked for the Danny Ramsay role. But on the advice of his actor father Terence Donovan (later a *Neighbours* star himself), he decided to finish his schooling first. Now he was free to accept.

Network Ten were certain that they had amassed a cast that would win viewers and spearhead a bright new beginning for *Neighbours*. The revamped series returned to Australian screens on 20 January 1986 with a charm offensive designed to finally win over viewers in Sydney. This literally involved several actors promoting the series door-to-door and hanging off the back of trucks festooned with advertising.

Neighbours' core cast members also included the adenoidal Lucy Robinson (Kylie Flinker), schoolboy hunk Mike Young (Guy Pearce), gorilla-gram entrepreneur Clive Gibbons (Geoff Paine), jug-eared bank manager Des Clarke (Paul Keane), his meddling mum (Myra de Groot), pompous fuddy-duddy Harold Bishop (Ian Smith) and Ramsay Street's resident spiteful busybody, and erstwhile church organist, Mrs Mangel (played with relish by the wonderful British-born actress Vivean Gray). Rounding off the cast was lovable golden retriever Bouncer, who was passed around the house-hopping cast members with astonishing regularity.

One of Network Ten's new additions to the cast was veteran actress Anne Charleston as Madge Mitchell, the fiery sister of soon-to-depart Max Ramsay, who moved into 24 Ramsay Street. Hot-tempered Madge, with her unmistakable smoker's voice, was an immediate hit with viewers, so much so that Grundys decided to gradually introduce her onscreen offspring, whom she had abandoned back in Coffs Harbour. Fans were eventually introduced, therefore, to tomboy Charlene and, later, dippy, muscle-bound Henry (Craig McLachlan).

Watson knew that young actors were key to *Neighbours'* success. He had seen Network Ten's market research which proved his series was appealing to a strong teen demographic. Watson also knew if there's anything teenagers like it's attractive actors having a love affair; it was time to give Scott Robinson a girlfriend to get his lips around.

When Kylie originally auditioned for *Neighbours'* casting director Jan Russ, her future in *The Henderson Kids* still hung in the balance. The second series had been commissioned, but it seemed likely (and was eventually the case) that Kylie's character of Char would not be reappearing. Several young actresses were going for the role of Madge's headstrong daughter, including Annie Jones (who eventually got the role of Mrs Mangel's granddaughter, 'Plain Jane Superbrain'), but it was

Kylie who most impressed Russ. 'She just had something intrinsically *special*,' she recalled.

Kylie initially signed for just 12 weeks, but despite her big break in *The Henderson Kids* she was still better known to viewers as 'Danielle's Big Sister'. Dannii Minogue (born 1971) had achieved considerably more TV fame than Kylie. For six years from 1982, Dannii was one of the 'team members' on the long-running *Young Talent Time*, a popular comedy variety series which showcased teenage kids singing and dancing and was presented by avuncular host Johnny Young. While appearing on *The Henderson Kids* Kylie was invited onto the show for an interview followed by a cringe-worthy singsong of 'My Old Man's a Dustman'. Although Kylie later made several more appearances on *Young Talent Time* Dannii was definitely the big star in the Minogue clan. Everything was about to change, however.

Kylie started filming *Neighbours* at Grundy's Nunawading Studios on the outskirts of Melbourne on 24 February 1986, not knowing the sheer magnitude of the impact she would eventually have. The character of Charlene Mitchell was envisaged as a headstrong, slightly wayward teenager, emotionally scarred by her parent's bitter separation and her own pregnancy, and subsequent abortion, aged 15. In episode #234 rebellious and fiercely independent Charlene turns up at number 24 only to discover nobody's home. Deciding to enter the house through an open window she is spotted by eagle-eyed Scott, who assumes she is a burglar, and a male burglar at that. Charlene rewards his heroics with a swift punch to his face and when she pulls off her cap her long curly locks tumble out. 'As slight and petite as she is, let me tell you, Kylie certainly knows how to throw a mean punch,' Donovan admitted 21 years later. 'She had quite a swing on her and a good aim too.'

In a predictable bit of soap opera back-story, viewers were reminded that Charlene and Scott were not, in fact, total strangers. Back in the 1970s Madge's daughter would visit her Uncle Max in Erinsborough and she and Scott would play games in the Robinsons' back yard; presumably 'Doctors and Nurses'. The obvious appeal of the handsome boy-next-door meeting the pretty girl-next-door was instantaneous. Within weeks Australian viewers were talking of nothing else. The characters' on-off relationship would keep fans hooked for the best part of three years (1986-1989). The introduction of Jason Donovan, and then Kylie, marked the golden age of *Neighbours* and it is remarkable that, despite running for over 20 years, the series is still primarily remembered for a only tiny portion of its broadcasting history.

Compared to the grim reality of British soaps, *Neighbours* seemed to display a disproportionate amount of buff, tanned flesh, big smiles, white teeth and blue eyes. If ever there was an advert to encourage people to emigrate Down Under, *Neighbours* was it. And the relationship between naïve, blustering Scott and confident out-of-towner Charlene captivated viewers from the outset. The fact that both actors were incredibly easy on the eye didn't hurt either. 'They were lovely to look at, both of them,' recalled actress Joy Chambers, who played Rosemary Daniels. 'They had the vulnerability of youth and the audience took them to their hearts.'

It was nearly seven years since the pair last acted together on screen, in *Skyways*, and the chemistry between Kylie and Jason was obvious to viewers, although perhaps not as obvious to the actors themselves, if a *Smash Hits* interview from 1988 is to be believed. 'When I joined *Neighbours* I don't think he even remembered me from *Skyways*,' recalled Kylie. I said, 'Don't you remember we did that show together?' I had to remind him. I must have made a really lasting impression!'

Within a fortnight of Charlene's first appearance it was clear to the series' producers that the public wanted more. Kylie's 12-week, $4000-a-month, contract was extended until the end of 1986, but filming five episodes a week could be a gruelling experience. Kylie often rose at 6.00 am, was in make-up by 6.45 and was in the studio an hour later. A normal *Neighbours* week consisted of two days of rehearsals, three days of recording and a further two days of location filming, with episodes shot six weeks in advance. Invariably the most popular cast members would be working a 60-or 70-hour week.

On top of learning scripts Kylie also tried to catch up with her fan mail. By the summer of 1986 the actress was receiving more than 1000 adoring letters a week, more than the rest of the cast's mail combined. One question dominated her post – 'When are Scott and Charlene going to get together?'

Reg Watson knew there could be absolutely no messing about in terms of where this particular storyline was heading. Even in their first scene together – immediately after Charlene has socked Scott on the jaw – she watches his bum as he walks away from the house, smiles broadly and says 'Mmmm!' to herself. After Charlene enrols at Erinsborough High School the flirting between the pair intensifies; she just can't stop ogling him in his Speedos at the school pool and he confesses to best friend Mike that he's mad about her big curly perm. The burgeoning love between Scott and Charlene was the big hook *Neighbours* had been looking for. Even after the series' move to Network Ten viewing figures hadn't been exactly scintillating, but the 'Kylie and Jason Effect' was suddenly hitting paydirt.

Kids across Australia became obsessed with the couple and instinctively related to their adolescent love affair as the characters struggle to be taken seriously by their disapproving parents. Jim Robinson is outraged to find the youngsters snogging on the sofa when they should be babysitting little Lucy. 'We're in love,' Scott protests. 'People in love kiss each other!' And Charlene didn't have it much easier from her interfering mum Madge. 'My mother treats me like a half-wit,' she screams. 'According to her she's worried about my morals. She's never going to understand that I'm an adult and I can make my own decisions!' The teenagers' struggle to express their desire for each other and the generation gap conflicts exposed by their families' objections was to be *Neighbours*' masterstroke; suddenly nothing else mattered on Australian TV. Viewing figures for the once-top rating *Sons and Daughters* dwindled and the series was axed by a furious 7 Network in 1987. First the channel had seen *Neighbours* rise from the ashes on a rival station and now it was crushing all competitors as its ratings continued their meteoric rise.

It didn't take long for Aussie teen magazines to realise the commercial benefits of placing Kylie on their cover. In something akin to the appeal of Princess Diana, one magazine regularly added 40,000 readers each time Kylie graced its front page. 'I suppose people like Charlene because she is an average teenager growing up, having difficulties with her mother,' Kylie explained in 1987. 'She is a bit of a rebel and kids relate to that, and while she has her problems she will always come out on top. Charlene is much more tomboyish and outspoken than I am. If Charlene has trouble she punches someone, but I would get flattened if anything like that happened to me.'

It wasn't long before Charlene's fists were flying again in *Neighbours*. In one of the most daring storylines the tea-time series had yet screened, Scott starts pressurising his girlfriend for sex. Charlene goes for contraceptive advice at the home of kindly Dr Clive Gibbons and then she and Scott start sneaking around looking for privacy. They decide to slope off to a hotel room at Lassiter's, the Erinsborough 'leisure complex' managed by Scott's big brother Paul. Scott takes Charlene, looking adorable in her school dress and white socks, back to the room, boasting that he's made love several times 'but it meant nothing.' In reality he's still a virgin, but when she confesses that this isn't her first time immature Scott goes all moody and storms off. Charlene rewards him with another punch to the face. Boy, that girl's got a mean right hook. 'It's all right if you wanna sleep with me,' screams Charlene, 'but if somebody else does, I'm a slut!'

While estranged from Scott, Charlene starts knocking back the Castlemaine XXXXs and going to all-night parties. Madge is understandably furious and, in a totally ridiculous storyline, her daughter moves into a caravan by Lassiter's lake, which later blows up. Scott and Paul save Charlene from near-death, but it's only after further disaster – when Scott is hospitalised with three broken ribs, a punctured lung and temporary paralysis to his legs, having crashed his car in a near-miss with a runaway pram, coincidentally containing Charlene's baby half-brother Sam – that Charlene suddenly realises she should get back with her clean-cut blond beau. *Neighbours*' storylines were nothing if not dramatic. Charlene also finds a responsible job. In a slightly surprising move she becomes an apprentice mechanic at Rob Lewis' garage, finally ditching her knitwear (decorated with West Highland terriers) for more sensible khaki overalls.

Viewers were fiercely resistant to any rocky patches in Scott and Charlene's relationship and fans demanded they remain an item. By late 1986 Kylie and Jason couldn't go anywhere without being mobbed. Location filming for *Neighbours* often had to come to a halt as kids swarmed the actors. During public appearances at shopping malls the couple were overrun with hysterical fans, generating big news stories in the tabloids. Fans speculated whether Kylie and Jason's on-screen romance was spilling out into real life. Donovan later recalled that it had been his on-screen father, Alan Dale, who had encouraged him to make a move. 'She's mad about you,' he told Jason, 'anyone can see that!'

Jason and Kylie finally got together in a Travelodge while filming in Sydney; not the most auspicious of locations but from there the romance snowballed. Thereafter their on-screen flirting was for real; the kisses lingered a little longer and the hugs were tighter than the script specified. 'We wanted to keep our relationship private and hold something back for ourselves,' Donovan recalled in his shockingly honest 2007 autobiography *Between the Lines*. 'Our fans had the romance between Scott and Charlene to get on with, after all. And we both realised that we had nothing to gain by going public with it.'

In interviews the actors only gave the vaguest of answers about how close they really were behind the scenes. For Grundy Productions this continual gossip was priceless marketing; the rumours kept viewers glued to the screen and kept the young actors' faces continually in the newspapers. In particular, Kylie's popularity knew no bounds. In March 1987 she became the youngest ever performer to win the Silver Logie for 'Most popular actress in Australia'.

Back on screen Scott and Charlene decide to shack up ('We are going to live together and nobody can stop us!'), but their respective parents are aghast at the idea. They figure the only solution is to get hitched and Scott pops the question while Charlene is flat on her back under a Ford Escort. Hypocritical Jim Robinson is incandescent with rage at the news. ('They're a couple of kids,' he rages. 'It's an insane idea!') When wise old Helen Daniels quietly reminds him he was about the same age when he went up the aisle he instantly mellows. The romance kept viewers gripped, but the soap's scriptwriters, tiring of the characters' endless on-off shenanigans, and wary that fans might be getting frustrated, made the snap decision to marry them off quickly and be done with it. Executive producer Reg Watson demanded a romantic wedding with 'a fairytale dress' to replace Charlene's permanently greasy overalls.

The wedding episode, screened in Australia on 1 July 1987, remains *Neighbours'* defining moment, where fantasy and reality merged and Aussie soaps finally found their place on an international stage. Eventually broadcast in over 50 countries, *Neighbours* has never bettered this episode's winning mix of anxiety, suspense, comedy and romance. Jason Donovan overacts throughout, as he had a tendency to do in his early acting days. Scott is convinced that he'll mess up the vows, or worse still Charlene will stand him up. 'I'm gonna muck this up, mate,' he says with a perpetually pained expression on his face. Things aren't much calmer over at the Ramsay residence, where Madge hasn't quite got round to ironing her dress. Charlene, however, is slouching round the house, hair in unflattering rollers, face smeared in cream and her gob stuffed with Danish pastry. 'She's got a ladder in her pantyhose!' screams her hysterical grandmother.

The wedding ceremony itself (filmed on location at the 135-year-old Holy Trinity Anglican Church in Doncaster, on the outskirts of Melbourne) goes off without a hitch. Twitching Scott, dapper in his grey

1987's Wedding of the Year

coat tails, finally calms down when he sees his-bride-to-be glide through the church door, on the arm of big brother Henry. Kylie, having a Princess Diana moment, innocently gazes up from behind her curly fringe and there isn't a dry eye in the house. 'It felt quite surreal seeing my girlfriend trussed up like that,' recalled Donovan two decades later. 'We had to suppress our giggles as we stood at the altar and delivered our vows.' The entire cast seem to be welling up, even Mrs Mangel, who is secretly lusting after her lodger Harold.

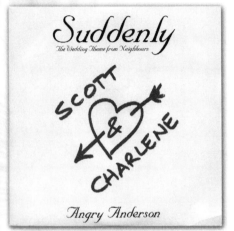

Cleverly, the producers decided against filming the sequence with dialogue, opting instead for a soundtrack of Angry Anderson's rock ballad 'Suddenly' played over the soft-focus visuals. On the radio Anderson's abrasive song may have seemed largely unpalatable, but it slotted in here just perfectly. After the vows are swapped, Scott swoops down for a prolonged snog with his new bride. At the reception – done on the cheap, since it takes place in the Robinson family lounge – *Neighbours*' trademark comedy streak takes centre stage with Mrs Mangel accusing Charlene's granddad of being 'a pervert', a mouse being set loose, creating predictable chaos, and the newly married couple sneaking off to Scott's room so they can start 'pashing off'. For Kylie, filming the episode was memorable for all the wrong reasons. 'It was a really tiring day,' she recalled later. 'I must have walked up and down that aisle 20 times while we were trying to capture the right mood. And I had that dress on for ten hours!'

The wedding made the front cover of *TIME Australia* ('Aussie Soaps Capture the World!') and earned itself more press coverage than any other home-grown TV series, before or since. The day before broadcast, Grundys had promoted the event (not like it needed promotion, since the whole of Australia was waiting with bated breath) by sending Kylie and Jason to the Parramatta Shopping Mall in Sydney. Almost 4000 screaming fans turned up to watch them cut a replica wedding cake, but pandemonium broke out and in the surge to the stage several fans were crushed and fainted. *Neighbours*' teenage stars made desperate pleas for calm and the event's hysteria made front-page headlines across Australia. 'TV Wedding Stampede!' screamed the front of the Australian *Daily Mirror*.

It proved beyond a shadow of a doubt that Kylie and Jason were now bigger than the show that created them. 'I had people coming up to me and thinking I really was getting married,' Kylie told reporters. 'They were so excited and their whole lives seemed to be revolving around it. People look up to you so much, but I stop and think why? I'm just an actress.'

Over in Britain BBC1 was looking to revamp its daytime schedule, which until that point had seriously lagged behind ITV's output. The head of programme acquisitions was told to scout around for a daytime soap, buoyed up by the success of primetime *EastEnders*, launched in 1985. The corporation was offered six serials, five from America and one from Australia. Appalled by the glossy excesses of the American soaps, the execs found that the series from Down Under immediately pressed all the right buttons. Michael Grade, then controller of BBC1, considered *Neighbours* to be the perfect daytime antidote to the grim reality of *EastEnders*. He also felt that an Australian soap would be easier for viewers to relate to, just as *The Sullivans* and *The Young Doctors* had when screened successfully by ITV previously.

Neighbours debuted on British screens on 27 October 1986, running each weekday at 1.25 pm with a repeat the following morning at 9.05 am. BBC1 heavily trailed the series with clips of Max Ramsay moaning about Daphne ('Look Jim, if a stripper moves into the street property values will go down...') and the plummy continuity announcer promising 'the everyday story of Australian folk.'

Neighbours was a slow-burner for BBC1, regularly attracting a couple of million viewers each day but, just as had been the case in Australia, it didn't start pricking the consciousness of the masses until the introduction of Jason, and then Kylie, to the cast. 'They were young, fresh, attractive and vibrant,' remembered casting director Jan Russ. 'They were what we needed in Australia at the time and obviously what England needed at the time as well.'

Kylie's first *Neighbours* episode was screened on 28 September 1987 (Britain was still lagging 18 months behind the Australian broadcast) but, prompted by the huge buzz generated in Oz and massive media coverage in the British tabloids, her breaking-and-entering debut was a foregone hit. It was nothing short of love at first sight. Just like their Australian counterparts British kids were mesmerised by the Charlene and Scott romance. Seeing Kylie in a yellow bikini and Jason in his orange Speedos frolicking on a beach and savouring every kiss was unlike anything seen in an episode of *Crossroads* or *Coronation Street*.

The beautiful Australian weather coupled with an attractive cast and a central storyline about flowering young love appealed to every idealistic dreamer in Britain. One journalist wrote that *Neighbours* owed much of its success to the fact that the sunshine 'shone outdoors *and* indoors'. *Neighbours* offered British viewers something unique to British TV; for the first time youngsters took centre stage in a soap opera, something that *EastEnders*, in particular, was quick to imitate.

The huge teen appeal of BBC1's import meant viewing figures started nudging the five million mark, unheard of for a daytime show. *The Sun* reported that kids were turning up late to class after watching the 9.05 am screening, or worse still bunking off at lunchtime to watch the 1.25 pm screening and then not bothering to come back. It seemed Double Geography just couldn't compete with the wholesome appeal of Kylie and Jason. Things came to a head in the autumn of 1987 when Michael Grade's teenage daughter admitted that kids in her class were sneaking off to watch *Neighbours* in the school common room. Wisely listening to his family, Grade shifted the show's repeat broadcast to a 5.35 pm slot. Within one month *Neighbours* had an astounding 16 million viewers per day.

As soon as *Neighbours* became a cultural phenomenon in Britain – and a phenomenon it really was – the press were desperate to get to the truth behind Kylie and Jason's romance. Viewers confused the on-screen lovers with the actors off-screen and for a while everybody was happy to play cat-and-mouse with the British tabloids, even after the youngsters were photographed by the *News of the World* cavorting on a beach in Bali. ('Keep 'em guessing,' an ecstatic Grundys told its brightest young stars.) On a joint appearance on Terry Wogan's BBC1 chat show in December 1988, the genial interviewer tried to get to the bottom of the rumours.

'So you're just pals, are you?' he asked.

'Yeah,' replied Jason, smirking.

'Depends on what paper you read during the day,' added Kylie.

'Not a hint of romance?' Wogan persisted.

There followed an awkward silence when Kylie and Jason looked at each other and giggled.

'You see, nobody's going to believe all this!' concluded an exasperated Wogan.

Smash Hits magazine, which by 1988 had adopted the pair as semi-permanent cover stars, was debating whether they were now 'the most famous couple in the world'. Then, on 8 November of that year, *Neighbours* mania reached its peak in Britain with the screening of Scott and Charlene's wedding. An incredible 23 million viewers watched the occasion, more than the entire population of Australia. Not only did the episode give BBC1 its highest ever viewing figures for 1988, it also provided the springboard for Angry Anderson's first solo British single. Capitalising on the wedding, the sleeve for Angry Anderson's 'Suddenly' featured Scott and Charlene's names and a red love heart on the front. It reached #3 and remained in the charts for nearly three months, selling 250,000 copies.

Back in Australia coach parties of British fans were besieging *Neighbours'* real-life cul-de-sac location (Pin Oak Court in the once-quiet Melbourne suburb of Vermont) and knocking on the Robinsons' front door, much to the consternation of the actual inhabitants, but fans hoping to catch a glimpse of Kylie filming were to be sorely disappointed.

In March 1988 Kylie won an unprecedented four Logies, including a Gold Logie for 'Most Popular Television Personality in Australia', presented to her by veteran Hollywood star Mickey Rooney. The Australian *Daily Mirror* dubbed her 'Queen of the Logies' and commented that the awards may have to be renamed the 'Minogies' [sic] in her honour. 'I hope I can do the industry proud in some way,' Kylie told the audience. 'Maybe I will be back here in a few years' time. I hope so.'

What British fans didn't know at the time was that Kylie had already decided to quit the show. In February 1988 she hit UK #1 with 'I Should Be So Lucky' and four months later she was filming her final scenes for *Neighbours*. 'I'm not leaving because I think I'm too good for the job,' she told journalists, some of whom had accused her of turning her back on Australian television. 'I feel I have to devote my time to other things now. After all, I can't hang onto *Neighbours* forever.'

Kylie's final episode was screened in Australia on 26 July 1988. However, because of the time delay in broadcast, British viewers still had another year and a half of Kylie episodes to savour. Incredibly, by the time Kylie's last UK *Neighbours* appearance was screened on 1 November 1989 she'd already had seven Top 3 hits and was just about to have another massive hit with 'Never Too Late'. There can be little doubt that Kylie's regular weekday appearances on British television boosted her pop career in the early days. *Neighbours* kept Kylie on telly, her records kept her on the radio and her romance with Jason continually kept her in the press. 'She just transformed from this innocent, non-worldlywise little girl into a star,' recalled Pete Waterman, her music producer. 'She was a tiny 18-year-old girl with a huge workload and was exhausted half the time, but as soon as she had to work her whole personality would transform.'

Grundy Productions never contemplated 'killing off' Charlene Robinson; she was far too valuable to them. Bosses were forever hopeful that if Kylie's pop career faltered they could tempt her back to the role that had made her an international star. One Australian tabloid alleged that *Neighbours* had offered her $15,000 per week to stay in the show. Instead Charlene just packed her bags and moved to Brisbane to live in a house her grandfather had bought for both her and Scott. The promise of a semi-detached home and a new job servicing cars under the tutelage of her hot-headed Uncle Max (now also living in Queensland) was just too hard to resist.

In episode #777 Charlene said a tearful farewell to Ramsay Street for the very last time. She departed alone; Scott ostensibly couldn't abandon his cadetship as a trainee journalist for the internally renowned *Erinsborough News*. In reality, Jason Donovan had another ten months of his *Neighbours* contract to run and Grundys were reluctant to lose the other half of their money-making double-act. 'I thought my last day filming would be emotional,' recalled Kylie, 'and it was. I bawled my eyes out. At my farewell party I tried to make a speech and I burst into tears again!'

The void left by Kylie's departure was almost immediately filled (in episode #780) by dumpy poodle-permed runaway Sharon (played by Jessica Muschamp). Perhaps Kylie really was irreplaceable, for to try to cast a similar actress would have patronised the audience. So poor Jason Donovan was left in limbo for the next 187 episodes. Without his sweetheart, Scott's subsequent storylines dragged on endlessly, only perking up when he started flirting with a buck-toothed model named Sylvia (she invited him back to her place to show him her 'portfolio') and then fellow journalist Poppy, whose Mediterranean passions compromised him on the back seat of her car.

Grundys knew they were just treading water with Jason's character since audiences couldn't stand to see him paired up with anybody but Kylie. Magazines and newspapers endlessly debated whether *Neighbours* could survive the loss of one half of its most beloved couple. The remaining cast got heartily sick being asked whether they thought the series' days were suddenly numbered. In one British interview the inevitable 'post-Kylie' question caused Alan Dale to haughtily retort, 'You've got to remember that *Neighbours* is more than just Kylie Minogue!'

Dale was partly right. *Neighbours* has certainly created other stars who have gone on to greater things, but there has been only one bona fide superstar, and that's Kylie. Several other *Neighbours* actors have tried to emulate her musical success. Natalie Imbruglia has enjoyed a modest pop career, and both Delta Goodrum and Holly Valance have had brief brushes with the Top 40. Even Stefan Dennis charted in the UK with his unintentionally hilarious 'Don't It Make You Feel Good' in May 1989. His laughably bad vocal style was mimicked in classrooms across the country, but it didn't stop his song hitting the Top 20.

Stoical Scott Robinson was finally reunited with Charlene after he transferred to a Queensland tabloid ten months after his young bride had flown the coop, freeing Jason Donovan from *Neighbours'* Australian run in May 1989. By this stage Jason had already followed in Kylie's footsteps and had secured a recording deal with Pete Waterman. Donovan scored his first hit with the less-than-convincing *Nothing Can Divide Us* (#5 in September 1988). 'I didn't really like the song,' admitted Donovan in 2007. 'It was a little high for me. I struggled with a couple of notes.' Far better was the anthemic *Too Many Broken Hearts* (his first solo #1 in March 1989) and his debut album *Ten Good Reasons* also hit #1 in the British charts, two months later.

Ironically, unlike Kylie, it was only after his exit from *Neighbours* that his career started to take a tentative nosedive. At the time of Donovan's departure Grundy Productions really must have felt another lucrative lifeline for the show had been ripped away. The real tragedy of *Neighbours* is that it peaked too early. Never again did the viewing figures scale the meteoric heights of Scott and Charlene's nuptials, nor did any of the series' young leads ever achieve fame comparable to Kylie's. Off-screen Scott and Charlene have enjoyed an idyllic life in Brisbane and now have two children, son Daniel (born in 1990) and daughter Madison (born 1993). Presumably Scott is now the editor of a sleazy Sunday gossip rag and Charlene is sitting at home teaching the kids about the intricacies of effectively replacing sparkplugs.

In truth Grundys have never allowed their audience to forget their biggest stars. For a decade Scott and Charlene's wedding photo stood prominently on the bookshelf in the Robinson household and to this day long-standing characters like Paul Robinson and Harold Bishop still occasionally mention the loving couple, reminding viewers that it hadn't all been a dream after all. And the enduring appeal of the series' best-loved stars has been plundered relentlessly over the past two decades. In 1989, for instance, Grundy Productions released *The Scott and Charlene*

Love Story on the Virgin Video label in the UK. Kylie's management tried to get the video halted, claiming that the release could have a detrimental affect on her pop career.

Also, in 1997 the increasingly frail-looking Anne Haddy reluctantly suggested that her character, Helen Daniels, be killed off. In episode #2965, therefore, Helen suggests that the feuding Ramsays and Robinsons (or what's left of them) once again put their differences behind them and come together to watch, you guessed it, Scott and Charlene's wedding video. Cynically, or sentimentally, depending on your point of view, scenes from the ceremony were intercut into the episode's narrative. 'Oh look, it's the wedding. I haven't seen that for ages,' shrieks Madge, unconvincingly. It's not such a joyous occasion for Helen, however. Obviously finding the strain of re-watching great *Neighbours* moments from a decade earlier too much, she promptly falls asleep on the Robinson couch and dies of a brain aneurysm.

This wasn't the only time Scott and Charlene's wedding was grave-robbed by Grundys. The teenagers' nuptials also provided the centrepiece of *The Neighbours' Wedding Collection* (1990), *Neighbours' 10th Anniversary Celebration* (1995), *Neighbours Defining Moments* (2002) and the limited edition Australian release *Neighbours' 20th Anniversary* DVD (2005), which featured Kylie and Jason grinning on the front cover. Back on television in 2005, *Neighbours* geared itself for a week of anniversary backslapping. In episode #4773 coffee shop waitress-cum-international filmmaker Annalise Hartman (played by *Neighbours'* resident pouting Barbie doll Kimberley Davies) puts together a short documentary to show to the residents of Ramsay Street. The film, celebrating community life in Erinsborough, was an excuse to repeat a few archive clips and get a few new vox pops from 'retired' characters (hello again Jane Harris, Danny Ramsay and Hilary Robinson).

Before shooting the episode the tabloids rumoured that Kylie was going to make a guest appearance as a more mature Charlene. 'We made every effort to accommodate Kylie,' said a Grundy spokesperson, 'and shoot a cameo appearance anywhere in the world at any time. However, the offer was declined.' Instead the celebratory episode re-ran portions of Scott and Charlene's wedding. The now-widowed Harold Bishop bristled with pride at seeing his dead wife's daughter on screen for the umpteenth time.

By spring 2007 *Neighbours'* Australian viewing figures had slumped below a million. In a last-ditch attempt to revitalise the failing show *Neighbours'* new distributors, Fremantle Media, ordered an immediate revamp, including shooting the soap on hi-definition film, brand-new opening titles, new orchestration of the famous theme tune and a 'back-to-basics' approach to storylines, which had drifted alarmingly from the original premise of 'real relationships and family dynamics' and were now straying into *Sons and Daughters* territory with a relentless stream of arson attacks, kidnappings, evil twins and aeroplane crashes.

In a bid to 're-focus' the series Network Ten launched a media offensive with their *'Neighbours – A Change is Coming'* campaign. Unsurprisingly, Fremantle felt compelled to go back to the 1980s to remind viewers just how good the serial had once been. The brilliant goosebump-inducing TV and web trailers presented black and white footage of classic *Neighbours* moments featuring Paul, Madge, Harold, Jim, Des and Daphne brilliantly spliced to the Rogue Traders' spine-tingling electro pop hit '(I'm Falling) In Love Again'. The character they chose to spearhead the campaign was Charlene, naturally, in archive footage from her 1988 wedding. 'These people have changed Aussie drama,' read the marketing strap-line. 'These people have changed our lives.'

Changed our lives? In the world of Australian TV a diminutive curly-haired actress in oily overalls eclipsed everything else; 20 years later she continues to do so. Kylie changed *everything*.

✳ ✳ ✳

The seeds of Kylie's recording career can be traced to one momentous musical 1986 storyline in *Neighbours*. In yet another of the series' interminable plots about being 'competitive', Scott Robinson (Jason Donovan) and Mike Young (Guy Pearce) see an advertisement in the Erinsborough News looking for young talent.

Scott, who's been hopelessly fiddling with his guitar in the soap for some weeks, suggests they enter the competition, especially since Mike has become a bit of a whiz on the Casio keyboard. Their first attempt at songwriting (called 'I Believe') goes down a bomb with Des and Daphne and within hours they think they're going to be as big as The Beatles. Charlene, who has forgone her career of becoming a professional cheerleader, agrees to sing backing vocals for them. The boys know she can hold a tune because previously, in episode #340, she sang a 1930s ballad her grandmother Edna taught her called 'Wanting You, Wanting Me', while dressed like what only can be described as an extra from *The Sullivans*. This episode, broadcast in Australia on 12 September 1986, was Kylie's first serious attempt at singing on primetime TV.

With the help of friendly local doctor, and erstwhile suburban mixmaster, Clive Gibbons (Geoff Paine), Ramsay Street's answer to INXS record a demo tape. In episode #352, after a convoluted plotline involving meddling school bitch Sue Parker, Scott manages to give the homemade recording to legendary real-life Australian music mogul Ian 'Molly' Meldrum, who wrongly assumes Scott is one of his pool-cleaning boys. In a very embarrassing cameo, Meldrum – famous for his trademark cowboy hat and colourful knitwear – listens to the group's tape and offers them an exclusive slot in his recording studio. But there's one very big condition. He only wants to sign up Charlene; the boys are crap. 'That's a great little voice you've got there, Charlene,' he says. 'Tons of potential!' She can hardly comprehend the news. 'I could be a singer?' says a shocked Charlene. 'I don't believe it!'

Predictably Scott starts sulking. However, by the end of the following episode Charlene has made the snap decision not to become an internationally famous singing sensation, preferring to finish her Year 12 at Erinsborough High School. Madge is thrilled to bits, especially when she sees Charlene dressed up in her 'rock chick' outfit (skimpy lace top, white gloves and chunky plastic jewellery). 'No daughter of mine is leaving this house dressed in her underwear!' she croaks.

Like a lot of little girls Kylie had fantasised about being a pop star; acting in Aussie soaps just happened by accident. From the age of four she had started going to rhythm class, learning how to play the violin, and later, the piano. She adored upbeat pop music too, as she revealed to *Smash Hits* in 1988. 'When I was about eight or nine, I used to have pretend ABBA concerts in my bedroom with my friends,' she explained. 'We'd put on dresses and dance to ABBA records. We'd prance about the bedroom or the lounge singing into hairbrushes. I was always the blonde one. I wanted to be Agnetha when I grew up!' The soundtrack album to *Grease* was also one of her favourites and she danced endlessly to the song 'Greased Lightning'.

Musical talent was certainly in evidence in the Minogue family; sister Dannii was easily Australia's most famous teenage singer thanks to her residence on Network Ten's Sunday teatime variety show, *Young Talent Time*. Keen to follow in her younger sibling's footsteps, Kylie had recorded a number of unreleased songs in 1986 – mainly disco standards including 'Dim All the Lights' (originally released by Donna Summer) and 'New Attitude' (by Patti LaBelle). With Dannii she also recorded two duets – the feminist anthem 'Sisters Are Doin' It for Themselves' by Eurythmics and 'Twist My Arm' by the Pointer Sisters.

Following the favourable response she had experienced singing on *Neighbours*, Kylie was invited onto *Young Talent Time* to perform 'Sisters Are Doin' It' in October 1986. The two sisters were filmed in the studio pretending to record the song with a fake producer worrying that Kylie couldn't remember the words. The *Young Talent Time* audience nervously tittered throughout. The pre-recorded insert then cut into a 'live' performance of the two mini-Minogues lip-synching to the song, violently bumping hips while dressed in frightful shiny sequin dresses. It was a frighteningly memorable debut for the sisters and proved popular enough for Kylie to be invited along to sing 'Twist My Arm' at the live *Young Talent Time* anti-drugs concert, where she arrived on stage on the back of a motorcycle to a huge roar from the teenage crowd.

'Locomotion'

Released July 1987 (Australia)
Written by Gerry Goffin and Carole King
Produced by Mike Duffy
Highest chart position #1 (Australia)

Flipside: 'Glad to Be Alive'
Video directed by Chris Langman

In early 1987 Kylie and her *Neighbours* co-stars were invited to a benefit gig in aid of Fitzroy Football Club at the Festival Hall in west Melbourne. 'Some of the *Neighbours* cast were always eager to help out and indulge their musical interests,' recalled Kylie in 2002, 'so we agreed to perform at a football fundraiser. There were about eight of us. We had rehearsed a song at someone's house after work to perform on the night.'

Kylie, along with Jason Donovan, Alan Dale and Stefan Dennis, did a foot-stomping version of Sonny and Cher's 'I Got You Babe'. The crowd demanded an encore and Kylie happily launched into a semi-rehearsed version of a song which unexpectedly was to change her career forever; it was 'The Loco-motion', originally a 1962 hit recorded by American soul singer Little Eva. The *Neighbours* cast's rendition of the song, with Kylie on lead vocals, brought the house down. 'When she finished, silence fell. We looked at each other: we couldn't believe it,' Dale remembered later. 'Here was this tiny little girl who looked great, and who could sing like an angel as well.'

The silence was broken when the inebriated audience of football supporters suddenly broke into rapturous applause. After the show, in what Kylie now remembers as a 'quirky moment of fate', she bumped into family friend Greg Petherick, the musical director on *Young Talent Time*. He congratulated her on her astounding performance and suggested the time was ideal for her to release a record. 'I was immediately dazzled by the prospect of not only recording, but making a video,' says Kylie. Within weeks she had recorded the track in producer Kaj Dalstrom's Sing-Sing studios in Richmond, Victoria, with a live band, a brass section and Petherick overseeing everything; it was rough and rocky, more akin to Lulu's 1960s singalong anthem 'Shout'.

By now Mushroom Records, Australia's premier record label since 1972, had begun taking an interest in Kylie the potential pop star, and in May 1987 they signed her, keen to release her own version of 'The Loco-motion' as soon as possible. Kylie's version of the song was deemed too raw for commercial release so Mushroom's head honcho Michael Gudinski gave the recording to English sound engineer Mike Duffy. Gudinski envisaged the track as a one-off novelty record, not predicting what was later to happen. 'Admittedly I never expected Kylie to become what she became,' Gudinski remembered 20 years later in an interview with Australia's *Herald Sun* newspaper. 'But the closer we worked with her, everyone realised she had a lot more going for her. She's become a great entertainer, not just a star.'

Duffy, who had been imported from producer Pete Waterman's British studios to work on a few projects for Mushroom, was instructed to make 'The Loco-motion' sound more 'like Bananarama'. The English girl group were currently the world's biggest selling female artistes and their hi-NRG dance track 'Venus' was topping the charts around the globe. Duffy took Kylie's vocal and re-recorded the backing track, making it more upbeat, contemporary and teen-orientated.

The single, re-christened 'Locomotion' for the Australian market, was released on Monday 27 July 1987, within weeks of the Scott and Charlene wedding episode of *Neighbours*, deliberately capitalising on the massive popularity of the series and maximum exposure of Kylie. Demand for the single was instantaneous; a week after the song was released it hit #1, selling 200,000 copies and gaining platinum status. It remained at the top for seven weeks, outselling the rest of the Top 10 combined. It also hit pole position in New Zealand, as well as becoming a #1 airplay hit in Hong Kong.

As the weeks went by *Neighbours* fans' hunger for the song remained unabated. Not only did 'Locomotion' eventually become the best-selling Australian song of 1987, it also – amazingly – became the country's best-selling single of the entire decade. So much for Kylie merely being a one-hit wonder.

☆   ☆   ☆

Over in Britain Kylie was still exclusively famous for her role as mouthy teenage mechanic Charlene Mitchell, but word of her new-found Australian musical fame was gradually filtering through to an intrigued BBC *Neighbours* audience. Kylie was conscious that the media might consider her just another actress attempting to climb the musical bandwagon. In a 1987 press release from Mushroom Records she explained her position: 'I love what I do in Neighbours but it's only one thing; one side I want to achieve. In some ways, I feel much more at home singing and dancing.'

In the summer of 1987 Kylie signed up with Terry Blamey Management, who had been recommended to her by Mushroom Records' Michael Gudinski. It is a business relationship which has endured for over 20 years, with Blamey guiding Kylie through every step of her incredible career. It was also Blamey who encouraged her to come to the UK and meet three guys who were to launch her upon an international audience ...

'I Should Be So Lucky'

Released December 1987 (UK)
Written and Produced by Mike Stock, Matt Aitken and Pete Waterman
Highest chart position #1 (UK), #1 (Australia)

Flipside: 'I Should Be So Lucky' (Instrumental)
Video directed by Chris Langman

In London the hottest music producers of the day were hit-making trio Mike Stock, Matt Aitken and Pete Waterman, whose knack for writing and producing one chart-topping hit after another had commanded respect and ridicule in equal measure, depending on whether you were a reader of *Smash Hits* or *NME*. Waterman, the recognisable face of the team and now a celebrity in his own right, started his music career as a club DJ. A lover of northern soul and Motown, Waterman's speciality has always been dance music. He moved into production with hits for Nik Kershaw, Musical Youth and Tracey Ullman, but it was a meeting with Mike Stock and Matt Aitken which led him on the pathway to greatness.

The threesome formed in 1984 when musicians Stock and Aitken approached Waterman with a demo for a track they had written. 'Mike

walked in and played me this track, which was technically excellent but not very commercial,' recalled Waterman three years later. 'I'm not a musician. I'm an ideas man. I know what sells. So I put the commerciality and the money in, and we went out and got a deal.' Waterman promoted the track, called 'The Upstroke', and it was a minor club hit, but the guys soon formed a partnership which was to change the face of British pop forever. 'Pete was the missing piece of the jigsaw,' said Mike Stock. 'Matt and I had been playing in bands for years and we'd run our own studio, but we didn't really have any idea of how to market. As soon as Pete heard our track, he knew what needed to be done to make it commercial.'

The first track the newly created trio worked on was 'You Think You're a Man', sung (or shouted) by cross-dressing American actor Divine. In July 1984 it hit #16, amid much controversy regarding the singer's suitability to perform on family-friendly *Top of the Pops*. Other hits followed, including Hazell Dean's 'Whatever I Do', and it was after the realisation that the gay community could make or break a new artist that they specifically targeted their songs at a predominantly homosexual or teenage audience.

It wasn't until the production team hit #1 in the UK with the unforgettable 'You Spin Me Round (Like a Record)' by Dead or Alive that Stock, Aitken and Waterman, or SAW as they became more commonly known, became a force to be reckoned with. It was their 1986 partnership with Bananarama and their million-selling 1987 album 'Wow!' which sealed their reputation as hitmakers. Later successes with Mel and Kim, Sonia, Donna Summer and Rick Astley gave them gigantic success throughout the world. When Astley's debut single 'Never Gonna Give You Up' hit #1 on both sides of the Atlantic, becoming the biggest-selling record of 1987, the trio were rightly dubbed the 'Hit Factory'. Satirical TV comedy show *Spitting Image* did a sketch where SAW churned out new stars on a factory conveyor belt; it would become the image that followed them everywhere. Suddenly SAW were the new 'Svengalis of pop'.

With Mike Duffy on secondment at Mushroom in Melbourne, Waterman would occasionally receive enthusiastic telephone calls from him explaining how fabulous it was Down Under. Duffy was having his wages paid by Mushroom and Waterman was getting a regular fee for hiring him out, so it worked out well for all parties concerned. One evening Duffy rang Waterman and he could barely contain his excitement. 'I'm number one in Australia,' he gushed. Waterman had no idea what the hell he was talking about, but then recalled a conversation they'd had two months earlier when Duffy had told him about a singer named Kylie Minogue. Waterman has since admitted he didn't have a clue who Kylie was. He'd never even watched an episode of *Neighbours*; Kylie just wasn't on his pop culture radar.

Duffy asked Waterman whether he could help out with a follow-up to the huge success of 'Locomotion'. Duffy was no songwriter and he begged his boss to sort her out with a new tune. Waterman agreed and set up a joint venture between his company and Mushroom. But, up to his neck with Bananarama and Rick Astley, he subsequently forgot all about it. That is until Kylie turned up in the Hit Factory reception one day in October 1987, waiting to record her second single. Her flight back to Melbourne was at 4.00 pm so they needed to get a move on. Panic immediately set in.

Mike Stock claims he wrote 'I Should Be So Lucky' with Matt Aitken in about 40 minutes, while Kylie waited patiently in the corridor drinking coffee. She then memorised the lyrics and the song was recorded in less than an hour. Nobody knew anything about Kylie's personality at that point, so the song was envisaged as nothing more than a simple up-tempo pop tune about being unlucky with boyfriends. Waterman wasn't present at the recording session but Matt Aitken rang him later and said, 'Actually, I've got to tell you, this girl's got a really good voice.' Stock and Aitken had been surprised at how quickly she had learned the lyrics. 'When Kylie went behind the microphone she was pitch perfect,' recalled Stock, 'and her timing was spot on. She was out before 2.15 pm and on her way to the airport.'

For several weeks the tape of 'I Should Be So Lucky' sat forlornly on a shelf gathering dust, until Mushroom Records executives started getting itchy feet, demanding to know where their follow-up to 'Locomotion' was. Allegedly Waterman had forgotten all about it again, so one evening Stock and Aitken sat down and mixed the record. By eight o'clock it was finished, including the extended 12" dance mix. At this stage SAW still didn't comprehend what a potential goldmine they had on their hands. Even then, *Neighbours* still wasn't on the TV at the Hit Factory studios. Waterman now recalls that when the record was first aired on London's Capital Radio the switchboard nearly exploded with fans desperate to know when they could buy it. In the end the DJ had to play it four times in one show and a crowd of kids was growing at reception. It was only when Waterman switched on BBC1, opened his newspaper and listened to what people were saying about Kylie that the penny finally dropped.

In her extended break from filming *Neighbours* Kylie had enjoyed a ten-day working holiday in Britain promoting the soap that had made her a star, but she seemed most concerned about keeping her eyes open. It was her very first trip to Europe and the flight had taken its toll. 'It took me about a week to get over the jet lag,' she confessed to *Smash Hits*, who were already being petitioned by their young readers for articles on their favourite soap actress. 'It was fun to record my single,' said Kylie, 'and I met Rick Astley at Pete Waterman's studio. He's a nice guy.'

Coincidentally her meeting with Astley was to provide the basis for one of the most persistent false rumours of her early career. Already dubbed the 'singing budgie' in her native Melbourne, some British journalists had claimed Kylie's singing voice was like 'Minnie Mouse on helium', hardly original since it was a criticism previously levelled at Madonna several years before. Nobody knows why but tabloid whispers emerged that 'I Should Be So Lucky' wasn't even sung by Kylie at all; it was a Rick Astley track speeded up.

Initially, before his Kylie epiphany, Waterman had tried to license 'I Should Be So Lucky' to three other record companies, but none was even remotely interested. In desperation he used his own label PWL (Pete Waterman Limited) to release the song. Ironically it eventually became the most successful independent record label in the world. Waterman estimates that between 1988 and 1990 he sold in excess of 40 million records, mostly with Kylie's name on them. Two decades on it is difficult to overestimate the massive demand for Kylie's debut British single; there hadn't been a buzz about a song like this since

Frankie Goes To Hollywood's 'Relax' four years previously. Radio stations were swamped with requests to play the track and Virgin and HMV had pre-ordered 800,000 copies.

'I Should Be So Lucky' was released in Britain on 29 December 1987. By the second week in February 1988 it had knocked Tiffany's 'I Think We're Alone Now' off the #1 spot. When the phone rang in the Minogue house in the early hours of the morning a sleepy Kylie moaned to her mother, 'Oh god, this is another one of their journalists...' In actual fact it was a representative from PWL delivering the happy news; a perfect Valentine's Day present, he said. Kylie took residency at the summit of the British charts for five solid weeks, the longest stay at #1 during the 1980s up to that point.

The song subsequently sold 675,000 copies, making it the bestselling single of 1988. In Australia the record also reached #1 – also becoming the year's biggest seller – and Kylie became the first artist to simultaneously hold the top spot in both countries. It also hit pole position in Belgium, Finland, Germany, Japan, Hong Kong, Switzerland, Ireland and South Africa. Throughout the rest of the world it achieved Top 10 placings, all except Canada and the USA, where it stumbled to a halt at 25 and 28 respectively, but even North America wouldn't stay immune from Kylie's charms for long. Back in Britain Kylie's debut eventually hung around the charts for an incredible 16 weeks. Melbourne was justifyiably proud of their most famous daughter's British success and the city's *Sun News Pictorial* splashed 'Our Kylie's No.1' on its front page.

Kylie's joyously infectious song – which considering the sad subject matter should, by rights, have sounded more like Eric Carmen's 'All By Myself' – had become the most loved and loathed single of 1988. Its hard, twangy bassline, stuttering vocals and beguilingly repetitive lyrics (which, incidentally, Chris Lowe from Pet Shop Boys famously called 'a mark of pure genius') made 'I Should Be So Lucky' an instant classic. The song was endlessly parodied and its accompanying video showing Kylie flouncing around an empty flat, having a bubble bath, filing her nails and repeatedly falling backwards onto a four-poster bed, was another triumph of naïve banality. An alternative video was produced exclusively for *Top of the Pops*, in which a perpetually cheerful Kylie is seen being driven around Sydney in an open-top silver Mercedes, causing several surprised motorists to take their eyes off the wheel.

Music appreciation is notoriously subjective, but quite by accident Waterman had helped to create one of the most famous, and iconic,

British singles of all time, even if he's suprisingly modest about his achievement. 'It's simple,' he's been quoted as saying, 'for people like myself, The Beatles and Burt Bacharach, the tune was always the most important thing.'

✫   ✫   ✫

With 'I Should Be So Lucky' topping the charts around the world, including 12 incredible weeks at the summit in Japan, Kylie was requiring more and more time off from *Neighbours* so she could promote her single. Her character, Charlene, was frequently absent from the series, ostensibly on trips to visit her extended family in Brisbane.

For the *Neighbours* producers Kylie's newly discovered pop success was both a blessing and a curse. Kylie's face on magazine covers, her videos on MTV and interviews on chat shows throughout the world had helped raise the profile of *Neighbours* to an unprecedented international level, but the increasing demands of her pop career were taking their toll on her acting. *Neighbours* was desperate not to lose its biggest star and the producers tried to accommodate her other commitments outside the show as best they could, but it came as little surprise to the rest of the cast when she made the momentous decision to finally quit the soap in the spring of 1988.

'Got to Be Certain'

Released May 1988 (UK)
Written and Produced by Stock Aitken Waterman
Highest chart position #2 (UK), #1 (Australia)

Flipside: 'Getting Closer'
Video directed by Chris Langman

Back in London, PWL was under pressure to find Kylie a new song, one which could replicate the two million plus global sales of 'I Should Be So Lucky'. However, there were some concerns that Kylie might not want to return to the Hit Factory after her initial rushed and unenthusiastic introduction to Messrs Stock, Aitken and Waterman. 'So I had to go to Melbourne and crawl,' recalled Mike

Stock in a 2002 interview. 'I went to Kylie's home and apologised for the way we treated her and told her it wasn't my fault and would she please come in the studio again and record some more tracks so we've got a follow-up ... And of course Kylie was reasonable about it, but I think quite logically she didn't think too much of us.'

The British music industry wrongly assumed 'Locomotion' would be earmarked as the new song to follow 'I Should Be So Lucky', but Pete Waterman had other ideas. Kylie needed a brand-new song which would be fresh to all territories, Australia included. The only thing is it wouldn't be *too* fresh. 'Got to Be Certain' had been written by the hit-making threesome in 1987 and subsequently recorded by British model-turned-singer Mandy Smith, an eighties' favourite with the tabloids. Pete Waterman never even got round to releasing Smith's version, however; it sat on a shelf before getting a belated release as a shockingly bad bonus track on 2005's 'Stock Aitken Waterman – Gold' compilation album.

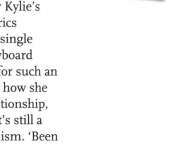
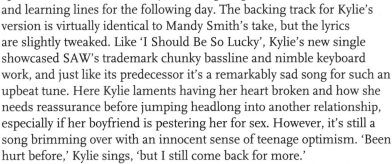

Realising he was getting nowhere fast with Mandy Smith, Waterman earmarked the song as Kylie's next single and it was recorded in Australia in February 1988, sandwiched between Kylie filming *Neighbours* and learning lines for the following day. The backing track for Kylie's version is virtually identical to Mandy Smith's take, but the lyrics are slightly tweaked. Like 'I Should Be So Lucky', Kylie's new single showcased SAW's trademark chunky bassline and nimble keyboard work, and just like its predecessor it's a remarkably sad song for such an upbeat tune. Here Kylie laments having her heart broken and how she needs reassurance before jumping headlong into another relationship, especially if her boyfriend is pestering her for sex. However, it's still a song brimming over with an innocent sense of teenage optimism. 'Been hurt before,' Kylie sings, 'but I still come back for more.'

'Got to Be Certain', with it breezy espousal of hope and quietly memorable 'woah, woah, woah, woah' middle section repeated after the fourth verse, helped make the single one of the most super-catchy hits of Kylie's early career. By the time the song was released Kylie had already filmed her final scenes in *Neighbours* – Charlene Mitchell had folded up her dungarees forever – and the 'Ashes to Ashes' 12" remix of the track was playing to packed dancefloors across Europe.

'Got to Be Certain' hit the Top 10 throughout the continent and lodged itself at #3 in the Eurochart Hot 100. In Britain the single entered the charts at #15 before climbing to #2 and staying there for three weeks, only denied the top spot by Childline's charity record, 'With A Little Help from My Friends'. Down Under the single became Kylie's third consecutive #1, making chart history as the very first single ever to enter the Australian Top 40 in the premier slot.

'Kylie'

Released July 1988 (UK)
PWL / Mushroom Records
Highest chart position #1 (UK), #2 (Australia)
Produced by Stock Aitken Waterman

Track listing:
'I Should Be So Lucky'
'The Loco-motion'
'Je Ne Sais Pas Pourquoi'
'It's No Secret'
'Got to Be Certain'
'Turn It Into Love'
'I Miss You'
'I'll Still Be Loving You'
'Look My Way'
'Love at First Sight'

Released on 4 July 1988, Kylie's eponymous album debuted on the British and Australian charts at #2, the highest placing ever recorded for a debut female. When the album eventually hit #1 on 21 August, Kylie became the youngest female vocalist ever to reach the top of the UK album charts (she was barely 20 at the time). With three massively successful single releases setting the world's charts alight and Kylie teetering on the verge of international superstardom her debut album was never going to fail.

An infectious collection of sugary pop-disco numbers including what would eventually be six global single releases, the album's undeniable highlights are 'I Should Be So Lucky', 'Turn It Into Love' and the surprisingly authentic American pop-soul groove of 'Look My Way', which could quite easily have been recorded by Alexander O'Neal or the SOS Band on the other side of the Atlantic. Incidentally, the album's hyperactive closing track 'Love at First Sight' is not an earlier incarnation of the 2002 Kylie hit of the same name.

'Kylie' became the bestselling album of 1988 and the fifth bestselling of the entire 1980s in Britain, notching up sales of 1.8 million (an incredible sextuple-platinum status) within six months. It eventually sold nearly seven million copies worldwide. In America, where it was released on the Geffen label, it peaked at only #53, charting on the back of Kylie's hit single 'The Loco-motion', but still sold enough copies to be certified gold.

Over in Australia 'Kylie' was briefly re-packaged as 'The Kylie Collection' with five additional remixes, including the 'Made in England' mix of new track 'Made in Heaven'. Dated to today's ears, certainly, Kylie's debut album still provides a perfect masterclass in classic British pop, demonstrating almost effortlessly sublime melodies, faultless vocals and a refreshing happy-go-lucky attitude towards lyric writing. 'A lot of people had a problem with the kind of pop music we were producing with Kylie,' admitted producer Mike Stock in 2004. 'But I knew it wasn't rock 'n' roll!'

'The Loco-motion'

Released July 1988 (UK)
Written by Gerry Goffin and Carole King
Produced by Stock Aitken Waterman
Highest chart position #2 (UK)

Flipside: 'I'll Still Be Loving You'
Video directed by Chris Langman

Prior to the London recording of 'I Should Be So Lucky', engineer Mike Duffy had played Pete Waterman his version of 'Locomotion' down the phone from Australia. Waterman listened to it intently, but wasn't overly impressed. 'It wasn't great but it was passable,' he recalled. 'It sounded roughly, *very roughly*, like one of ours.' Several years later, in another interview, he had slightly modified his view: 'It was rubbish.'

It was agreed that there was enough public demand for the song to be released as a single in Europe. However, Waterman wasn't going to let it loose without a total makeover. In April 1988 Mike Stock and Matt Aitken remixed, or more accurately re-produced the song, re-recording

Kylie's original vocals, adding more trademark stuttering at the beginning, dispensing with Kylie's high-pitched 'yeahs' and smoothing over the backing vocals, as well as removing the electric guitar solo and improving the overall 'tinny' sound of the original take. Kylie fans were already familiar with the SAW version of the song since it had appeared as the second track on her debut album. Pete Waterman, a purist when it came to 1960s and 70s pop music and an inveterate railway fanatic, also corrected the song's name to 'The Loco-motion' and added a train whistle and shout of 'All aboard' at the start of the track.

In Britain the revamped single was released on 25 July 1988 and entered the charts at #2, which, at that time, gave Kylie the record for the highest ever single entry by a female artist, an achievement previously held by Madonna. Although it didn't progress to the coveted #1 spot it nevertheless climbed to the top spot in Ireland, Belgium, Finland, Israel, Japan, Canada and South Africa.

In America, where the appeal of *Neighbours* was still a complete mystery, 'The Loco-motion' debuted on the Billboard Hot 100 at a lowly #80, but within weeks it had climbed as high as #3. Certified 3x platinum it remained Kylie's best-selling single Stateside until 2001, when it was overtaken by the release of 'Can't Get You Out of My Head'. The single also became renowed in America for being the only song to crack the Top 5 in three different decades – 1960s (Little Eva), 1970s (Grand Funk Railroad) and 1980s (Kylie).

It seemed that audiences the world over just couldn't resist that naff singalong quality of 'The Loco-motion' and its accompanying dancesteps. As the lyrics say: 'There's never been a dance as easy to do...' In wedding discos from Helsinki to Cape Town, from Sydney to Swansea, drunken guests were requesting Kylie's song alongside traditional matrimonial standards like 'YMCA', 'The Time Warp' and 'Oops Upside Your Head'.

The worldwide success of the song came as a huge surprise to Australia's Mushroom Records, which had always imagined their rocky singer-songwriter Jimmy Barnes would be the one making international waves. 'Mike Duffy had laid the bed,' recalled Mushroom's former chief publicist Amanda Pelman of Kylie's worldwide hit. 'Then Pete put his incredible magic touch over the top. We had a number 3 song in America. We can't have done all that wrong!'

The track's original video was shot the day after Kylie signed up with Terry Blamey at Strathmore's Essendon Airport, with the singer skipping – Pied Piper-like – followed by an entourage of enthusiastic kids. The interior dancing shots on a black and white tiled floor were filmed at ABC Studios in Melbourne and feature a brief glimpse of Kylie's brother Brendan in a leather jacket. In accordance with the re-recorded version of the song, for a worldwide market the video was also re-jigged and became one of the most requested clips on MTV in America during 1988.

'Je Ne Sais Pas Pourquoi'

Released October 1988 (UK)
Written and Produced by Stock Aitken Waterman
Highest chart position #2 (UK), #12 (Australia)

Flipside: 'Made in Heaven'
Video directed by Chris Langman

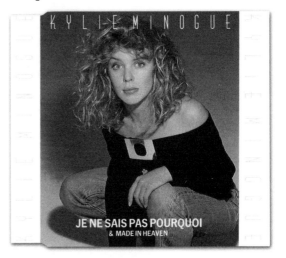

Prior to 1988 the nearest British record buyers had come to clasping a French-tinged pop song to their bosom was the breathlessly saucy 'Je t'aime ... moi non plus', a novelty #1 hit by Jane Birkin and Serge Gainsbourg way back in 1969, and the similarly raunchy 'Lady Marmalade' (with its indelible refrain, 'Voulez-vous coucher avec moi ce soir?') by LaBelle six years later. Kylie was set to change all that with the fourth single from her debut self-titled album.

As a rule, pop songs with foreign titles don't do terribly well in the notoriously xenophobic UK charts, so it was just as well Kylie's single stuck to English for the rest of its lyrics. However, French teachers of the period could be reassured that their pupils had, at least, memorised one foreign phrase. Kylie's broken-hearted lament attests, 'I still love you, je ne sais pas pourquoi' – or otherwise translated, 'I still love you, I don't know why.' Ironically, Britain was considerably more receptive to the French title than Australia, where it was released as the more user-friendly 'I Still Love You (Je Ne Sais Pas Pourquoi)'.

In the UK a brand new SAW composition 'Made in Heaven', an uplifting Donna Summer-style disco stomper, was scheduled to share equal billing with 'Je Ne Sais Pas'. However, the new track wasn't promoted beyond a B-side, despite being listed prominently on the front cover of the 7" artwork. Contrary to legend, the single was never officially listed as a double-A side in Britain, although the plan had been to 'flip' the record over after a few weeks to prolong its commercial shelf life.

Kylie had recorded 'Je Ne Sais Pas' during the sessions for her 'Kylie' album in April, and 'Made in Heaven' over the summer – an experience which had alarming parallels to her acting career. 'Stock, Aitken and Waterman and the Hit Factory weren't that far removed from my role in *Neighbours*,' recalled Kylie. 'Learn your lines, red light on, perform lines, no time for questions, promote the product et voilà!' But by this stage the SAW boys were becoming increasingly fond of their biggest star. 'She has a great voice,' enthused Mike Stock. 'I love working with her because she has a terrific sense of humour, a fabulous personality and she really knows how to sell a song.'

The single, featuring a much more downbeat theme than her previous three hits, sees Kylie in reflective mood, bemoaning the fact she has been let down by her unreliable boyfriend for the umpteenth time, but unable to stop loving him. The gentler, more sophisticated sound of the single is offset by a devilishly unexpected hook where Kylie repeats the 'I' in 'I'm wondering why' three times at the beginning of each chorus.

Despite being an album track the song received extensive airplay on both sides of the world. It entered the UK charts at #11 and climbed to #2, famously being denied the top spot by a shortfall of just 500 single sales separating it from Enya's chart-topping 'Orinoco Flow'. In Australia it was less successful, reaching #12; even the ungrateful French couldn't place it higher than #15.

Complimenting the continental flavour of the song, the accompanying video, directed by Kylie's longtime collaborator Chris Langman (bizarrely, the same man behind *The Henderson Kids*), shows the singer being stood up in a rainy Parisian street and being warned by a local woman not to trust tardy fellas! Kylie then enjoys a romantic dance with a mystery man in a scene inspired by Robert Doisneau's famous 1949 photograph of a couple dancing on Bastille Day.

Although the song didn't climb higher than the #2 spot in the UK, Kylie still claimed a new British record for the first female artist to have four consecutive Top 3 hits plucked from one album, and a debut album to boot. The same month, Kylie was also voted 'Most Fanciable Female' and 'Best Female Singer' at the inaugural 1988 *Smash Hits Poll Winners' Party*.

'Especially for You'

Released November 1988 (UK)
Written and Produced by Stock Aitken Waterman
Highest chart position #1 (UK), #2 (Australia)

Flipside: 'All I Wanna Do is Make You Mine'
Video directed by Chris Langman

Kylie's final scenes in *Neighbours* had been screened in Australia in July 1988, when she bade Ramsay Street a final tearful goodbye. Although Charlene may have moved onto relative anonymity in suburban Brisbane, in the UK she was still very much an item with Scott Robinson, their romance playing out every teatime on BBC1. Part of the appeal of 'Kylie the pop star' was that *Neighbours* fans might be able to imagine it was actually Charlene who was singing the songs, and PWL and the BBC did little to discourage a separation of the two personae. This was never more apparent than when Kylie and Jason (or is that Charlene and Scott?) sang together for the first time on *Top of the Pops*.

In real life Kylie and Jason dated for nearly three years, but fans could never be entirely sure. 'We did what we thought was best and tried to keep our relationship under wraps,' Kylie admitted in 2002. 'This being near impossible we tried the second best thing and did our utmost not to confirm or deny our romance. This nebulous zone made us feel safer.'

1988 had been an awesome year for Kylie, four massive-selling singles, a #1 album in the UK and international success on an unprecedented scale, with millions of records sold worldwide. But still the public wanted something else from their new favourite pop star, and it was the same question on every journalist's lips: 'Kylie, when are you going to release a single with Jason Donovan?'

In the 1980s it was still something of a novelty for a soap star to become a pop star overnight. But, for a while, it seemed anybody could do it. Probably still smarting from his rejection at the hands of Molly Meldrum in *Neighbours*, Jason (or was it Scott?) began following in Kylie's dainty footsteps. Mushroom Records in Australia offered SAW the chance to work with Donovan, but Waterman's first reaction was to refuse. ('The idea seemed too tacky,' he recalled.) After some gentle persuasion from Kylie, Waterman eventually relented, and in an almost carbon-copy of her own career trajectory Jason signed with PWL in the summer of 1988.

By the end of August he had released his first solo single in Britain. 'Nothing Can Divide Us' was a cast-off from big-booming Rick Astley, but Donovon's version was only notable for the strained vocals. 'I wouldn't call myself a Frank Sinatra or whatsisname, Eddie Van Halen,' he helpfully told *Smash Hits*. Admittedly, Donovan got better the longer he spent working with SAW and his March 1989 hit 'Too Many Broken Hearts' was unquestionably good. Waterman was shy of pairing up the *Neighbours* sweethearts; as noted, he thought the concept 'sickly', as did Kylie, but incessant questioning from the media and even from fans in the street was hard to ignore. Waterman knew he could sell a hell of a lot of records, even if it meant going against his better instincts.

Kylie had topped off an unforgettable year by performing 'I Should Be So Lucky' and 'Made in Heaven' at the Royal Variety Performance in November 1988, before jetting off to Australia. Waterman rang both her and Jason and told them he'd written them a duet; demand was so high it was a surefire #1 but it needed to be recorded pronto. Kylie wasn't so convinced. 'The idea for a duet was taboo for a long time,' said Kylie in December 1988. 'We were always dead against the idea, but PWL were telling us they had thousands of pre-orders for this song no one had even spoken or heard about. So I guess we did it because of public demand.' Waterman and Aitken duly flew to Australia on 9 November and spent the next 36 hours with Kylie and Jason in Mushroom's Sydney studio recording the duet. With the finished tapes they returned immediately to London to mix the song. 'Especially for You' was released just three weeks later, on the 28th.

Smash Hits, now Kylie's spiritual British home, were keen supporters of the singing partnership, even affording the young lovebirds their first dual cover for the 30 November issue and a corresponding three-page spread. 'They've just made a slushy, drippy and utterly romantic duet,' wrote chief scribe Chris Heath, 'and it's rather brilliant as it happens.' In the interview Kylie still sounded unhappy about her latest career move. She said, 'Speaking for myself, I wouldn't have wanted to do it at the start. A rumour went round that we were going to do it before we'd heard anything about it!' It can't have escaped Kylie's attention that Jason wasn't in the same league as her vocally, as a cover of Lionel Ritchie and Diana Ross' 'Endless Love' had graphically proved; she and Jason had misguidedly performed it in a sea of dry ice during a July 1987 episode of *Young Talent Time* in Australia, following their *Neighbours* wedding. The results were excruciating.

Reassuringly, in Pete Waterman's safe hands 'Especially for You' was nothing less than a critic-silencing triumph. The single was shipped to retailers with silver sales status, meaning Kylie became the first female artist to have her first five singles all sell *at least* 200,000 copies apiece. In fact, the new duet sold 400,000 copies at Woolworths alone. In December 1988 you couldn't move for Kylie and Jason – either on radio, in the newspapers or on TV. The song, a beautifully simple ballad about young lovers reuniting after a time apart, with luscious opening backing vocals and gentle guitar, is one of the best things Stock, Aitken and Waterman ever penned. Its gorgeous, uplifting romantic sentiment – 'You were in my heart, my love never changed' – hit a chord with record buyers worldwide.

In the UK it remained lodged at #2 behind the seemingly unassailable Cliff Richard and his 'Mistletoe and Wine'. Kylie was thus denied a Christmas chart topper, but by the first week of January 1989 Cliff was dislodged and the Australian duo held firm at #1 for three weeks. It became the first of Kylie's singles to sell in excess of one million copies. It also hit #1 in Hong Kong (for six straight weeks), Ireland, Belgium and France. In Australia it made #2. In addition, Kylie's first UK video collection also debuted in the top slot over Christmas, going double platinum within three weeks and remaining the bestseller until February.

The video for 'Especially for You' shows Kylie and Jason (now having wisely cut off his infamous mullet) in their prime, believably in love. Shot in Sydney, the video was filmed during the coldest November temperatures recorded in over a century. If Kylie and Jason were freezing they certainly didn't show it; the video positively radiates warmth. 'I can laugh about it now,' Kylie said afterwards, 'but we were exhausted by the end of it. We spent the whole of the next week recovering.'

The couple's love affair was still providing tabloid journalists with more column inches than they knew what to do with. Their names were inexorably linked wherever they went. Even British trance group The KLF released a single entitled 'Kylie Said to Jason', a tongue-in-cheek homage to Britain's most talked about couple since Charles and Diana. A loved-up duet like 'Especially for You' did nothing to deter the 'are they or aren't they?' rumours and it certainly didn't harm sales either, even if Jason was at pains to deny their relationship. 'She's a good mate and a good buddy,' he told *Smash Hits*, 'and I'm sure she considers me the same. It doesn't mean to say we're having a love affair.'

Whatever it really meant, 'Especially for You' is three minutes and 36 seconds of musical brilliance and unquestionably Kylie's first perfect pop moment.

'It's No Secret'

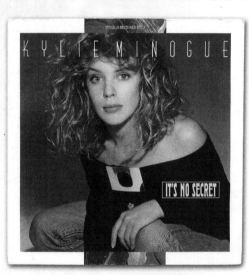

Released December 1988 (USA)
Written and Produced by Stock Aitken Waterman
Highest chart position #37 (USA)

Flipside: 'Made in Heaven'
Video directed by Chris Langman

'It's No Secret' was originally scheduled for release in Europe and Australia in February 1989, but PWL, fearing audience apathy towards a fifth single from Kylie's debut album, decided against it. Michael Jackson had famously extracted a total of nine singles from his 1987 album 'Bad' over a two-year period and the gimmick had rapidly worn thin. Sensing Kylie fans needed a fresh song, especially after the huge commercial success of her duet with Jason Donovan, plans for 'It's No Secret' were withdrawn in favour of brand-new track 'Hand On Your Heart'. However, Kylie had already shot a video for 'It's No Secret' in Port

Motherly love – Madge Mitchell (Anne Charleston) and her rebellious daughter, Charlene. *Neighbours*, 1986

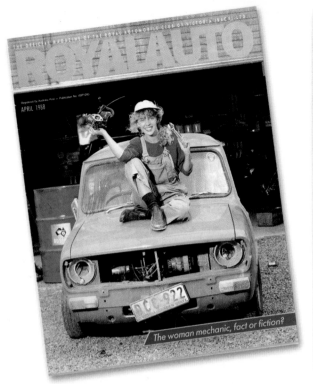

Clockwise:
Kylie makes the front of Australia's *Royal Auto* magazine, April 1988
Go to pieces over Kylie with an unofficial jigsaw (1988)
The video they tried to ban (1989)
US cover of 'Enjoy Yourself' (1990)

Limited edition Australian sleeve for 'Rhythm of Love' 1991

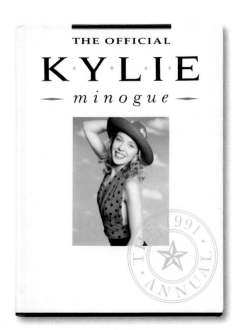

Kylie gets raunchy at the Plymouth
Pavilions, October 1991

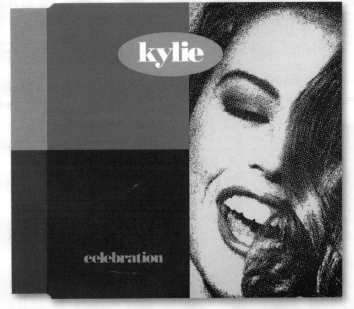

Top left:
Japanese sleeve for 'If You Were with Me Now' (1991)

Above:
1991 tour programme for *Let's Get To It*

Left:
UK cover for 'Celebration' (1992)

Kylie, 1994

Douglas, Queensland, and the song was exclusively released as a single in Canada (peaking at #22), Japan (#4) and the US, where it reached a less than awe-inspiring #37, but nevertheless according Kylie her third consecutive Top 40 American hit.

The extended version of the video is noteworthy as it features a sullen-faced Kylie (in a prologue to the song) working behind the bar in a tacky Sydney nightclub. In a cute in-joke the jukebox is playing 'The Loco-motion' in the background, but it's not enough to cheer up Kylie because her floppy-haired boyfriend is cheating on her, right under her nose. The scenario is a world away from Daphne's Coffee Shop in *Neighbours*, but for a brief moment when Kylie tells a creep at the bar to get lost she's right back in Charlene's zone.

'It's No Secret' is a forgotten gem of Kylie's early career, never given the exposure it deserved in Britain; a shame since it showcases one of her strongest vocals and most heartbreakingly melancholic moments: 'You shattered my dreams, tore me apart. What can I do?'

'Turn It Into Love'

Released December 1988 (Japan)
Written and Produced by Stock Aitken Waterman
Highest chart position #1 (Japan)

Flipside: 'Made in Heaven'
No video produced

Along with Britain and Australia, Kylie's biggest, and some might claim most fanatical, fanbase was in Japan, a country which had never been exposed to the *Neighbours* experience. Japanese youth have long been obsessed with Western pop music, especially of the 'bubblegum' variety. During the 1980s Madonna and Michael Jackson were elevated to near godlike status in Japan, alongside less obvious pop stars like Pete Burns, the androgynous lead singer of Dead or Alive and one of SAW's leading lights. Long after his group's hits had started to dry up in Europe, Burns' career was sustained by Japan. Unsurprisingly, diminutive, blonde, ever-cheerful Kylie was the latest singer to catch the public imagination of frenzied Japanese teenagers.

Kylie had made her so-called 'Asian debut' at the Canton nightclub in Hong Kong on 1 July 1988 where she sang to a backing track, using the opportunity to showcase her first three singles. The evening, costing $88 per ticket, was a sell-out and was described by one local newspaper as 'a night of magic'. In December Kylie won the coveted 'Record of the Year' gong at the Japanese Popular Disc Awards, sealing what had already been an incredible 12 months. In Tokyo there was an insatiable demand for new Kylie product and PWL made the snap decision to release a sixth track from the 'Kylie' album.

'Turn It Into Love', another Stock, Aitken and Waterman composition with a fabulous lolloping beat, was an obvious choice for exclusive Japanese release. The single shot to #1 on the Oricon Japanese international chart and remained at the summit for an unprecedented ten weeks. Simultaneously, Kylie had four other tracks in the Top 40 – 'I Should Be So Lucky', 'The Loco-motion', 'It's No Secret' and 'Especially for You'. This achievement is even more impressive when you consider that, cumulatively, Kylie spent a total of 27 weeks at #1 with various singles in the Japanese charts.

Despite her fans' unfaltering devotion it would be another nine months before Kylie played a series of live concerts in Tokyo. While 'Turn It Into Love' was still sitting at the top spot as her third consecutive Japanese #1, the country's Phonographic Record Association presented Kylie with awards for 'Best Selling New Artist' and 'Best Selling Single of the Year' for 'I Should Be So Lucky'.

Even though 'Turn It Into Love' was never released as a single outside Japan – consequently there was no video or 12" remix – the song remains to this day one of her most famous singles in Asia. The track was popular enough to be covered by domestic schoolgirl duo Sachiko and Shōko, better known as Wink, adored for their interpretations of Western pop tunes. Their version – renamed 'Ai ga Tomaranai' – also reached #1 and became the first in a series of chart-toppers for them, helping to spearhead the 'J-Pop' phenomenon.

Back in Britain the song was re-recorded by Hazell Dean, another of SAW's alumni, who had built up a strong gay following after she hit the Top 10 with two massive Hi-NRG floor fillers in 1984. Dean had recently been undergoing a brief revival with her comeback hit 'Who's Leaving Who', but her clubbier interpretation of Kylie's 'Turn It Into Love', released in September 1988, could only muster a high of #21.

'Hand on Your Heart'

Released April 1989 (UK)
Written and Produced by Stock Aitken Waterman
Highest chart position #1 (UK), #4 (Australia)

Flipside: 'Just Wanna Love You'
Video directed by Chris Langman

The start of 1989 saw Kylie barely having time to rest after the relentless promotion of 'Especially for You'. In February she was straight back in the studio with Stock Aitken Waterman; there was no time to waste when the Hit Factory assembly line was speeding along at full tilt.

The first new song which emerged from those early recording sessions was 'Hand on Your Heart', yet another introspective heartbreaker fiendishly disguised as an uplifting pop song. The lyrics, echoing the upsetting sentiments which dominated her first album, bemoan how Kylie's early optimism regarding true love was dashed when her boyfriend put an end to the relationship. 'I thought that we were just beginning. And now you say we're in the past,' she sings. For PWL it was more of the same, delivering what they were best at and wisely not tampering with the winning formula. But even with an infectious melody and superb vocal performance, 'Hand on Your Heart' was hardly a progression from Kylie's previous singles.

Although Kylie had temporarily left behind Aussie TV in favour of music she was still nominated for three Logies in March, including the Gold award for 'Most Popular Personality on Australian Television'. She also received her second Australian Variety Club Award for 'Recording Artist of the Year' and a *Daily Mirror* award for 'Best Actress'. Encouraged by her manager Terry Blamey to consider one of the dozens of film roles she had been offered since departing *Neighbours*, Kylie eventually signed to play the female lead in *The Delinquents*. Shortly afterwards she was honoured with a wax likeness at Madame Tussaud's museum in London's Baker Street. It would be the first of four effigies she would model for over the next two decades.

'Hand on your Heart' was released simultaneously in Britain and Australia in April, at the same time Kylie was starting rehearsals for *The Delinquents*. The barrel-scraping video, shot in Melbourne a month earlier and the last directed by Chris Langman, featured a 1950s-style Kylie dancing round a multi-coloured house that looks like a dizzyingly bad surrealist take on the *Cheggers Plays Pop* set. She playfully dances for the camera with an animated red heart, complimenting the one stitched to her naff dress. Kylie is on record as saying it was the least enjoyable moment of her early career. Behind the smiles she was cringing. She turned 21 on 28 May, celebrating her coming-of-age at a family party in Melbourne, and it wouldn't be long before she was taking charge of her image and consigning the horrors of the 'Hand on Your Heart' video to history.

The superior sleeve photo for the UK 7" single shows Kylie in more relaxed mood (it's a still from the 'It's No Secret' video shoot) and the song debuted at #2 in the UK charts. Within a week it peaked at #1 in both the Top 40 and the official dance chart, the latter with the cleverly named 'Great Aorta 12" Mix' by DJ Phil Harding. Rather unexpectedly, in 2005, celebrated Swedish singer-songwriter José González recorded his own version of the song – a virtually unrecognisable acoustic interpretation – which quietly reached #29.

'Wouldn't Change a Thing'

Released July 1989 (UK)
Written and Produced by Stock Aitken Waterman
Highest chart position #2 (UK), #6 (Australia)

Flipside: 'It's No Secret'
Video directed by Pete Cornish

Kylie's next single wasn't released until her filming commitments for *The Delinquents* were completed in June 1989. 'Wouldn't Change a Thing' was recorded during the same London sessions as its predecessor, but, despite signalling a return to SAW's trademark stuttering vocal tricks of 'I Should Be So Lucky', the track has a much clubbier flavour and is an obvious precursor to the more contemporary sound of Kylie's singles from her third album. As it was, Kylie hadn't even finished recording her much anticipated second album, so for the time being fans had to contend with 'Wouldn't Change a Thing'. The song's opening frenetic drumming has a fantastic hip hop flavour, akin to James Brown's 'Funky Drummer', but from thereon in it's classic

Stock Aitken Waterman with unremittingly uplifting lyrics about being head-over-heels in love with someone nobody else approves of.

The song was Kylie's third UK single in a row to debut at #2, but unlike 'Hand On Your Heart' it failed to reach the top slot and dislodge the five-week chart residency of the atrocious Jive Bunny and the Mastermixers' Butlins' holiday camp anthem 'Swing the Mood'. The song's accompanying video, directed by Pete Cornish, was her first shot exclusively in Britain, presenting a much more mature-looking Kylie shaking her ass with four male dancers. She also dressed in 'streetwise' gear, more befitting a young woman than the dreadful concoction she was made to wear for her previous promo. Unfortunately the same couldn't be said of the UK vinyl single cover, which exhibits perhaps the very worst publicity photograph of Kylie ever taken in her entire career.

By 1989 Stock Aitken Waterman were coming in for a lot of flak; other artists, from The Smiths to U2, were happy to vent their vitriol about SAW's so-called manufactured music and their almost divine ability to totally dominate the world's pop charts. Incredibly, by the end of the year SAW controlled 27 per cent of the UK record business, a statistic the bigger players like EMI were not very happy about. SAW viewed the criticism as simple jealousy. 'If Stock Aitken Waterman do anything we make music for people to buy,' said Waterman defensively. 'What a *big* crime that is! We *entertain* people. We write songs about life as we see it and as the kids see it.' The lowest point came when the trio got booed and pelted with urine at an awards ceremony, and later threatened with violence. 'We were all proud of our success,' Mike Stock said, 'but soon Pete began calling us the saviours of the music industry. We started making enemies and it was the start of the backlash.'

Disco in Dream Tour / The Hitman Roadshow

Executive Producers – Kylie Minogue and Terry Blamey / Sound Engineer – Boyoya 'Yoyo' Olugbo / Choreography by Venol John / Principal Dancers – Venol John, Ritchie Smith, Paul Smith and Kevan Allen

2-9 October 1989 (Japan)
15-27 October 1989 (UK)

Set list: The Loco-motion, Got to Be Certain, Tears on My Pillow, Je Ne Sais Pas Pourquoi, Made in Heaven, Hand on Your Heart, Wouldn't Change a Thing. **Encore:** I Should Be So Lucky.

With Kylie officially crowned Japan's favourite pop star of 1989 it seemed only proper that she embarked on her first fully fledged promotional concerts there. When Kylie had five records in the Japanese singles charts simultaneously PWL realised it would be a wise move to tap into Kylie's most excitable market. Kylie therefore flew into Tokyo with her mother Carol in September 1989, with just two weeks to put together a show curiously translated as *Disco in Dream*.

Mum and daughter holidayed at the peaceful Hakone National Park and then began rehearsals. There was to be no live band; Kylie was to perform exclusively to pre-recorded backing tracks, scrupulously engineered by PWL luminary 'Yoyo' Olugbo. Keyboardist Yoyo started working as Pete Waterman's tea boy before being promoted to sound engineer on the 'Enjoy Yourself' album and then taking responsibility for making Kylie sound perfect for her live debut. With Carol acting as wardrobe mistress, Yoyo doing the sound production, four backing dancers and her manager Terry Blamey overseeing things, Kylie opened at Nagoya's Rainbow Hall, 30kms from Tokyo, on 2 October. The 8000 fans seemed to lose some of their Japanese reserve by relentlessly chanting 'Kylie, Kylie!' before she came on. Next were two dates in Osaka, before the tour culminated at the 40,000-capacity Tokyo Dome. 'I was a little nervous before going on in Tokyo,' she admitted, 'but I said to myself "Let's do it and just forget there are so many people out there."'

Despite nearly being blown offstage by the sheer force of the stadium's wind machines, the Tokyo date, in particular, was a huge success. The Japanese press dubbed it 'The biggest disco in history', presumably because Dead or Alive and Sinitta also appeared on the bill. The tour's production was basic, to say the least. Kylie made her entrance on stage to 'Loco-motion' walking behind a plywood train supported by her dancers. It was incredibly unsophisticated stuff, but the predominantly middle-class, exceptionally smart, well-behaved audiences didn't seem to care.

Unsurprisingly, because Kylie only performed eight songs, most were presented in their extended 12" mixes with additional dance breaks. Kylie seemed totally at ease with her little brood of dancers, the same boys who had accompanied her on *Top of the Pops*, *Wogan*, the Royal Variety Performance and even *Jim'll Fix It*. Here on stage Kylie almost appears vampish at times in spangly hotpants, flirting with her boys and displaying a hitherto undisclosed sexual side to her personality, something she was acutely aware of. 'What I have achieved which I'm really glad about – and I didn't know if I could do or not – was to take a step forward with my image and my music,' she confessed. 'But at the same time I didn't want to ignore the audience I already have.'

On Kylie's return to the UK she immediately started a promotional tour featuring a virtually identical set list as her Japanese concerts. These British gigs were sponsored by Coca-Cola and formed part of Pete Waterman's ongoing *Hitman Roadshows*, which also featured dumpy Lancashire songbird Sonia Evans, the muscle-bound London Boys, Hazell Dean and gay-friendly boy band Big Fun. Heavily supported by local commercial radio stations, Kylie's short tour commenced on Sunday 15 October at the Hammersmith Palais in London. Each night Pete Waterman would proudly come out on stage and introduce his Australian protégée: 'Here's the girl you've all been waiting for – Kylie Minnogew!' (his joke).

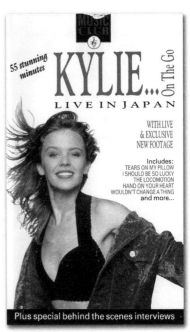

The shows were specifically aimed at 14- to 18-year-olds and tickets were given away free because, as Kylie asserted, 'This is a big thank you to the fans.' The British kids were ecstatic to see her. 'Touring in England was fantastic', Kylie later revealed. 'It was an incredible learning experience for me.' Kylie's Hammersmith debut was particularly notable for the moment when Ben Volpeliere-Pierrot, the lead singer from 1980s band Curiosity Killed the Cat, drunkenly crashed the stage while Kylie sang 'Tears on My Pillow' and started jigging excitedly beside her while she tried her level best to ignore him. He was promptly escorted off by Kylie's minders. After the London date the tour was less eventful as it snaked around Britain, calling in at Plymouth, Swansea, Manchester, Liverpool, Bristol, Newcastle, Sheffield, Birmingham and Edinburgh. In all there were ten gigs, followed by an appearance at the second annual *Smash Hits Poll Winners' Party* at the London Arena, where Kylie performed her new single 'Never Too Late' and won a gong for 'Best Female Solo Singer'.

In April 1990 the Japanese leg of the tour was released on video as *Kylie ... On the Go!* The 56-minute film was directed by Roger Yager and produced by Michael Baumohl and features Kylie both on stage and in rehearsal for her Japanese concerts, as well as feeding Koi carp and making a sushi roll! Confusingly the video is edited to show a different order of the actual tour track listing.

'Enjoy Yourself'

Released October 1989 (UK)
PWL / Mushroom Records
Produced by Stock Aitken Waterman
Highest chart position #1 (UK), #9 (Australia)

Track listing:
'Hand on Your Heart'
'Wouldn't Change a Thing'
'Never Too Late'
'Nothing to Lose'
'Telltale Signs
'My Secret Heart'
'I'm Over Dreaming (Over You)'
'Tears on My Pillow'
'Heaven and Earth'
'Enjoy Yourself'

Bonus track: 'Especially for You' (USA and Canada only)

Recorded in three blocks between February and July 1989, Kylie's 'difficult second album' actually wasn't very tricky at all, successfully doing more to consolidate the winning Stock Aitken Waterman brand than anything that had gone before. 'I'm so pleased with it because it's exactly what I hoped it would be,' said an excited Kylie prior to its launch. 'I sat down with Pete months ago and we were discussing what the album would be like and what direction we were going in and it's been exactly that!' Like its multi-million selling predecessor, 'Enjoy Yourself' again hit the #1 spot in Britain and made the Top 5 throughout the world – although surprisingly not in Australia, where the public were temporarily suffering from Kylie fatigue.

Alongside the old skool chug of 'Hand on Your Heart' and 'Nothing to Lose' emerges the more contemporary groove of 'Wouldn't Change a Thing', the surprisingly smoky maturity of wine-bar ballad 'Telltale Signs' and the smoothly uplifting Bananarama-style title track (the collection's best song, originally slated as a single release, but sadly never to be). Only the saxophone smooch of 'Tears on My Pillow' appears conspicuously out of place among the chunky SAW beats, whereas shiny fan-favourite 'I'm Over Dreaming (Over You)' sounds suspiciously like it was originally written for Rick Astley, bizarrely ending up as the B-side to the radically different 'Better the Devil You Know' the following year.

'Enjoy Yourself' went on to sell nearly 1.5 million copies in the UK alone, earning itself quadruple-platinum status in less than three months. The album was released in America on the Geffen label in 1990 in new cover artwork and with 'Especially for You' incorporated into the track listing. Failing to chart there, it would be Kylie's last official US album release until 'Fever'.

'Never Too Late'

Released October 1989 (UK)
Written and Produced by Stock Aitken Waterman
Highest chart position #4 (UK), #14 (Australia)

Flipside: 'Kylie's Smiley Mix'
Video directed by Pete Cornish

In many ways Kylie's autumn 1989 single 'Never Too Late' marked the end of an era; it is the very last 'traditional' Stock Aitken Waterman pop hit of her career. Sounding more like a companion to 'Hand on Your Heart' than 'Wouldn't Change a Thing', 'Never Too Late' reverts to the heavy bassline and all-pervasive 'unlucky in love' theme of her earlier hits. This time Kylie's desperately attempting to salvage a broken relationship with a man who's quite obviously been deceiving her. 'Why can't you see I'm still mad about you,' she pleads,' 'even though I've found out about you.' Once again, purely listening to the uproariously gleeful music you'd be forgiven for thinking 'Never Too Late' is a song brimming with positivity. But listen to the lyrical content and you want to slap some sense into Kylie. Give him up, darling. He's just not worth it!

The original plan had been to release 'Enjoy Yourself', the motivational title track from Kylie's second album, as her new single. However, PWL, fearing same-title confusion in the market, quickly replaced it with 'Never Too Late' at the eleventh hour. Because of the last-minute change the 12" remix of 'Never Too Late' wasn't ready for its 23 October release and as a result the single debuted at an unexpectedly low #17 in the charts. *NME* journalists praying for an early downturn to Kylie's career were disappointed, though, when the 12" disc was hurriedly pressed and shipped to retailers, helping the single climb to #4 in the UK Top 40. It became Kylie's eighth consecutive Top 5 chart hit.

The flipside of 'Never Too Late' features a club megamix (by DJ Tony King) of the Stock Aitken Waterman-penned singles taken from the 'Kylie' album – 'Je Ne Sais Pas Pourquoi', 'Turn It Into Love', 'I Should Be So Lucky', 'Got to Be Certain' and the 'All aboard!' sample from the re-recording of 'The Loco-motion'. The 12" extended mix also included excerpts from album track 'I'll Still Be Loving You' and US single 'It's No Secret'.

'Never Too Late', allegedly a favourite of INXS frontman Michael Hutchence, was boosted by an incredibly spirited video, shot by British director Pete Cornish in London in September 1989. In the most expensive promo of her career to date, Kylie has a blast dressing up in various costumes – a 1920s flapper girl, dripping in beads; a 1930s Ginger Rogers-style movie star, a sexy 1950s Suzie Wong; a Texan cowgirl, complete with chaps and Stetson, and a psychedelic 1970s disco dancer. Presented in the style of puppets performing in a toy theatre, the inventive vignettes showcased just how great a mover Kylie really was, displaying a confidence and enthusiastic versatility absent from her previous videos filmed in Australia.

The opportunity to work with a professional choreographer was something Kylie relished. 'If you've got it in you it comes very easily,' she said excitedly, 'and learning a routine is no problem. I mean I know a lot of people have a lot of difficulty dancing, but I find it comes quite easy and I enjoy it so much. Hopefully that comes across!'

The colourful promo for 'Never Too Late' (which won the award for 'Most Popular Video' at the 1990 Logies) also signposted the beginning of a definite change in artistic direction for Kylie. She looks happy, carefree and relaxed, quite obviously seeking more creative control over her image and music; something that would come to the fore in 1990.

The Delinquents

1989 / A Cutler-Wilcox Production / Australia / 101 minutes / cert 'M' (Australia), cert '12' (UK) / Opened December 1989 (UK)

Directed by Chris Thomson / Produced by Alex Cutler and Mike Wilcox / Cinematography by Andrew Lesnie / Written by Clayton Frohman and Mac

Gudgeon / Based on the novel by Criena Rohan / Original Music composed by Miles Goodman

Cast: Kylie Minogue (*Lola Lovell*), Charlie Schlatter (*Brownie Hansen*), Bruno Lawrence (*Bosun*), Todd Boyce (*Lyle*), Desirée Smith (*Mavis*), Angela Punch-McGregor (*Mrs Lovell*), Melissa Jaffer (*Aunt Westbury*), Lynette Curran (*Mrs Hansen*), Duncan Wass (*Bert*), Rosemary Harris (*Isobel*), Rachel Szalay (*Maxine*), Daryl Hukins (*Bodgie*), Lyn Treadgold (*prison matron*), Jonathan Hardy (*magistrate*), Yvonne Hooper (*landlady*), Errol O'Neill (*cinema manager*), Russell Krause and Ove Altman (*sailors*)

some rules were meant to be broken

kylie minogue
charlie schlatter

THE delinquents

Featuring the hits "Please Send Me Someone to Love" by Johnny Diesel and Kylie's "Tears on My Pillow"

M 15+ RECOMMENDED FOR MATURE AUDIENCES 15 YEARS AND OVER
SEXUAL REFERENCES, ADULT THEMES

Making the transition from soap star to movie star isn't easy. Making the transition from pop star to movie goddess is even more fraught, but in 1989 this was the task that befell Kylie. '*The Delinquents*, to me, is my debut movie, which is fantastic because obviously you can only do it once,' said Kylie at the time. 'It's very dear to me because I want it to be something special. It really is a new experience from TV.'

Having only departed British screens as Charlene in *Neighbours* six months earlier, and already with eight hit singles and two #1 albums under her belt, Kylie had a lot to prove with her debut movie. The pressure on her was intolerable as the press reported that fans would see Kylie in a more 'grown-up' role, a million miles from Ramsay Street and the bubblegum antics of the 'I Should Be So Lucky' video. In fact, they claimed, she was also preparing to go topless in a bid to dispense with her soap alter-ego for good. The British tabloids were already frothing at the collective mouth at the thought of that. 'If people hate it and it's a flop, well, that's all there is to it,' she admitted. 'But I have to believe in myself and not listen to what other people say.'

Since filming her final scene for *Neighbours* several movie projects had been offered to Kylie's manager Terry Blamey, but it wasn't until May 1989 that she finally had a break in her hectic schedule to fit in a movie. The project chosen for Kylie's big screen debut was an adaptation of Deirdre Cash's post-war Australian novel about forbidden love between two streetwise teenagers.

Cash, a Melbourne-born author and aunt of tennis star Pat, struggled to get her work recognised in Australia, so adopted the Irish nom de plume 'Criena Rohan' to get her first novel published in London. Released in 1962 to great acclaim, the *Times Literary Supplement* called *The Delinquents* 'a triumph'. Buoyed by the book's success, Cash started work on her second novel, *Down by the Dockside*, but tragically died of cancer shortly after it was completed, aged just 38. Since her untimely death *The Delinquents* has become a cult novel, especially in Australia where its depiction of alienated, working class youngsters fighting against their parents and authority figures resonated for each subsequent generation of kids that read it.

Deirdre Cash's novel was adapted for the screen by TV writers Clayton Frohman and Mac Gudgeon, and with David Bowie, himself a much-quoted casualty of the transition from pop to film, mooted as executive producer. Originally journalists assumed the film would be an old-fashioned musical, because Kylie was a singer now and must have forgotten how to act. Jason Donovan was also tipped to be Kylie's love interest in the film. None of the rumours came true. Bowie backed out of the project, Kylie doesn't sing on screen and Donovan was replaced by an actor better known to the Americans.

With the film budgeted at Aus $8.5 million, and with an eye on the US market, Kylie's co-star was announced as Charlie Schlatter, fresh from playing opposite 92-year-old George Burns in *18 Again!* the year before. Schlatter – now better known for being Dick Van Dyke's sidekick in trashy detective series *Diagnosis Murder* (1993-2001) – was perfect casting for the role of her teenage boyfriend. Kylie was required to act as a 15-year-old at the start of the movie and Schlatter 16. Both performers were considerably older than their roles, but diminutive Kylie pulls it off effortlessly and baby-faced, 5'6" Schlatter is every inch the naïve young kid. The actor celebrated his 23rd birthday on the very first day of filming, which took place between 1 May and 23 June 1989.

Kylie plays Lola Lovell, the rebellious daughter of an alcoholic bar pianist in 1950s Brisbane, who catches the eye of young Brownie Hansen (Schlatter), the local telegram delivery boy. After a chance encounter outside a local cinema, the teenagers find themselves instantly attracted to one another and discover a mutual love of all things anti-authoritarian – from Marlon Brando's *The Wild One* to wild dancing, underage drinking and especially rock 'n' roll music. Lola can't wait to trade in her prim cardigan for a leather jacket, her mousy hair for a bottle of peroxide and her Tchaikovsky-led piano lessons for something a little more boogie-woogie.

After Brownie endures a gruesome beating at the hands of his violent stepfather, Lola visits him and they have sex for the first time. Their clumsy, fumbling attempt at lovemaking is poignant and touching, but sets the pattern for their uncontrollable desire for each other. Freed from the constraints of a daytime soap opera Kylie is finally able to display genuine passion as a girl who desires sex just as much as her boyfriend. Lola gets pregnant and the young lovers run away together, but her mother snatches her back and forces her to have an abortion.

The Delinquents charts Lola and Brownie's three-year uphill struggle to be with one another, their fight against the police and social workers and their dream of being together once and for all. Briefly reunited at a greasy spoon café in downtown Melbourne, where a careworn Lola has been working, the runaway lovers are caught by the cops and she is sent to a home for girls – a chintzy, suburban nightmare run by a vinegar-faced bitch called Auntie Westbury (a grandstanding performance by award-winning actress Melissa Jaffer). 'I decided to devote my life to unwanted girls,' says the purse-lipped matron. 'I have been auntie to two generations of poor unfortunates and I always tell them how much happier one can be in one's own home, instead of chasing cheap thrills.'

'Auntie' does her best to teach her surly young charge about cake-baking, good manners and flowery dresses, but by now Lola is boiling over with anger at being separated from her boyfriend. She taunts her guardian with shocking sex talk and, in *The Delinquents'* most memorable sequence, erupts with fury when she discovers Brownie's love letters have been systematically thrown away in the trash month after month. Kylie was always quite handy with a right hook in *Neighbours* and here she displays it again by punching the old lady hard in the face, smashing crockery and ripping off her drab, square clothes. 'You had such fun running this up on your nice little electric machine that goes frontwards and backwards and sideways and all around the town and buttonholes and god knows what other shit!' she screams. 'Well you can stick your stupid little frock!'

Kylie fans had never seen anything like this before; it is an amazingly powerful, and funny, scene, designed for cinema audiences everywhere to cheer loudly in support of their heroine. Unsurprisingly, things go from bad to worse for poor Lola when she is shipped off to a Corrective School for Girls – a sort of mini-*Prisoner Cell Block H* – run by tough-talking lesbians. However, after an oestrogen-fuelled riot which would puts St Trinian's to shame, Lola finally gets her release aged 18 years and two weeks.

Chris Thomson's direction is crisp and unfussy, preferring to let his talented leading actors dominate the screen, through good times and bad. He doesn't flinch either from showing the dirt and the grime of 1950s Melbourne and the brutality of the correctional service. *The Delinquents* also prides itself on great period detail reminiscent of classic Aussie soap *The Sullivans* and the clever use of lighting gives the film some particularly evocative moments, notably the tentative first moonlit encounter between Lola and Brownie.

Unfortunately the movie flags a little towards the end, when the story shifts temporarily to the plight of Lola's friends, English Lyle and his Australian wife Mavis. American actor Todd Boyce's excruciating attempt at a weird hybrid Mancunian/Liverpudlian accent is maybe the worst ever committed to celluloid and spoils whatever scenes Kylie shares with him, but the movie still ends on a high note when Lola and Brownie finally marry. 'Kylie is an extraordinary actress,' said Thomson, heaping praise on his star. 'I knew she was going to be good when we first started rehearsing, but I honestly didn't think she was going to be this good. The only time she was ever irritable was with herself, whenever she didn't get something right on the first take.'

Kylie and Schlatter are well matched as the defiant lovers, and the attraction between their characters sizzles from the start. This is even more impressive given that the two performers had little prior knowledge of each other. Prior to filming Schlatter only knew about his Australian co-star from watching a few of her music videos on MTV in the States, whereas Kylie had never heard of him at all. 'I guess I'm the envy of every guy in the world playing her lover,' joked Schlatter. The media made much of the actors' love scenes, particularly one where the briefest of glimpses of Kyle's bare breasts are visible. The more prolonged sight of Schlatter's bare arse created barely a ripple in the tabloids, but a blouse-less Kylie became the main talking point of the movie's pre-publicity.

Initially, the frank sexual content of the film worried Kylie too. 'Whenever I saw people being interviewed after they'd done a movie they would say, "Oh, doing a love scene is just like another day at work," I'd be sitting at home thinking "Oh yeah! Sure!"' admitted the actress. 'It's very difficult and I was embarrassed, but I would hope that Charlie was embarrassed too. Since we did it a few times it was OK in the end.' Thomson was also quick to protect Kylie's modesty. 'It is part of the story,' he explained to slavering British journalists during shooting. 'One of the most important things about the relationship between these two teenagers is that they develop, almost by accident, a physical relationship very early on. They're not frightened by their physical attraction for each other. They're not embarrassed by it, not inhibited by it. They enjoy it.'

The initial trailers advertising *The Delinquents* were rejected by British TV and heavily cut in Australia because they were deemed too 'raunchy', something Kylie was furious about. 'You catch a glimpse of virtually nothing,' she retorted. 'I wouldn't have let it through if it wasn't [like that].'

The Delinquents was released in Australia on 21 December 1989 and in Britain on Boxing Day. Some bitchy film critics were already busily sharpening their pencils, predicting a flop bigger than *Howard the Duck*, but audiences turned out in their millions, making it the #1 box office movie of the Christmas period on both sides of the globe. Derek Malcolm, writing in the *Guardian*, commented that 'Kylie produces an unstudied and effective portrait of a young, underage provincial girl.' Not everybody was as generous as Malcolm, though. The obviously sex-starved *Independent* complained the movie was 'curiously unerotic throughout', while the snooty *Times* claimed its 'maudlin sentimentality is enough to make one run back to Ramsay Street in search of genuine art.'

In the great British tradition of 'build 'em up and then knock 'em down', the hostile reviews of Kylie in *The Delinquents* are a regrettable legacy that has haunted her throughout her subsequent acting career. The film's commercial success notwithstanding, it did little to boost her confidence in the face of criticism. Perhaps as a result it is the only leading role Kylie has ever enjoyed on the big screen.

With hindsight some of the crueller reviewers may want to re-watch her film debut and eat their words. Kylie is never anything less than adorable, authentic and ballsy on screen, showing a versatility she had only ever touched on in her earlier incarnation as a soap actress. Kylie appeared defiant at the film's Australian premiere, with new boyfriend Michael Hutchence in tow. Asked by the paparazzi what she thought of her debut movie,

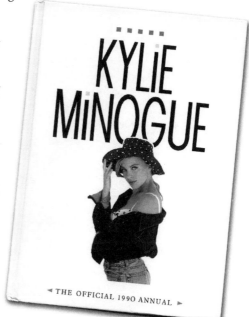

KYLIE MINOGUE

◄ THE OFFICIAL 1990 ANNUAL ►

a smiling Kylie was succinct and polite, as always: 'It was a fantastic experience. I'm extremely proud of it.'

Two years later she appeared on Australian TV and was probed about how she had felt about *The Delinquents* and her future plans for acting. 'I was expecting to get a lot of criticism as usual because, of course, I'm an easy target,' she said, 'but I think it was good for my first movie, and for an Australian movie. In England it beat *Back to the Future II*, so that was something! I hope to do another film but it's just a case of finding time and, of course, the right script and right director.' Kylie also had other thespian ambitions. 'I would love to do a comedy,' she confessed in 1990. 'It would be just great. I don't think I'm funny at all. I'd need to have a very experienced director to guide me, but I'm really keen to do it sometime in the future.'

'Tears on My Pillow'

Released January 1990 (UK)
Written by Sylvester Bradford and Al Lewis
Produced by Stock Aitken Waterman
Highest chart position #1 (UK), #20 (Australia)

Flipside: 'We Know the Meaning of Love'
Video directed by Pete Cornish

Such was Pete Waterman's encyclopaedic musical knowledge that he had no difficulty in authentically replicating the sound of his youth. In December 1987 he helped give Rick Astley his third Top 3 UK hit with an astonishingly accurate pastiche of Nat King Cole's 'When I Fall In Love', full of lush violins and harps. Two years later he was set to do it all over again with Kylie's retro cover version of 'Tears on My Pillow', originally a million-selling hit for American 'doo-wop' band Little Anthony and the Imperials in 1958.

The song was a favourite of Waterman's but was unknown to Kylie. When she heard it for the first time, she suggested to her producer it would be an excellent track for inclusion on *The Delinquents* soundtrack album. Waterman agreed and the song was recorded in July 1989.

Kylie's version retains the 1950s *Happy Days* quality of the original with smooth saxophone and some 'doo-wops' courtesy of Mike Stock. In accordance with the brevity of the original, Kylie's cover version is also the shortest hit of her career, clocking in at just two minutes 19 seconds. 'I wanted to keep the film as an acting piece,' explained Kylie. 'I like the fact that my song is not distracting during the movie, it just runs over the credits.'

The Delinquents premiered in London's West End in December, a few weeks after Kylie had been invited to switch on the festive lights in Regent Street. Rather than release the single for the Christmas market, however, it was put back until January 1990. The main reason for this was to prevent the song clashing with Band Aid II's much-derided remake of 'Do They Know It's Christmas', which coincidentally was also produced by Stock Aitken Waterman and featured vocal performances from Bananarama, Bros, Jason Donovan and Kylie herself. This song remained at #1 for three weeks over the holiday period.

By this time, the last completely SAW-free chart had been published as long ago as 28 February 1987. Waterman, still smarting from constant criticism in the music press, articulated his motivation with a football analogy. 'Everybody's got a hit single in them, but that's not the point,' he told the *Guardian* in 1990. 'You've got to win the League Cup one season, then come back and do it all over again. You've got to be like Liverpool.'

The hitmaking trio had accumulated an armoury of silver, gold, platinum discs and their flashy accolades bore witness to their epoch-making success. When Kylie's 'Tears on My Pillow' eventually climbed to #1 it became their 95th hit single; 49 others reached the Top 40, 12 others made it to the top. It was also announced that 'Especially For You' had been the biggest selling single in the record industry for the last two years. As a 'thank you', readers of *NME* voted Messrs Stock, Aitken and Waterman the second 'Biggest Bastards in Britain', just behind Margaret Thatcher. Waterman bravely laughed it off. 'Kylie could just burp into a microphone and it would be a hit,' he famously retorted.

Mercifully, 'Tears on My Pillow' didn't feature any belches, but the song was backed by a brand-new ballad, 'We Know the Meaning of Love', which itself hit the Top 10 in Sweden, where it was listed as the A-side in preference to Kylie's latest British #1. At the same time Kylie was atop the singles chart, *The Delinquents* was Britain's top box-office draw at the cinema. And by spring 1990 Kylie was preparing for her *Enjoy Yourself* tour of Britain, Europe and the Far East.

Enjoy Yourself Tour

Devised and Produced by Kylie Minogue / Musical Director – Adrian Scott / Tour Manager – Nick Pitts / Production Manager – Alan Hornall / Choreography by Venol John

Musicians: Adrian Scott and Mal Stainton (keyboards), James Freud (bass), James Jardine (guitar), John Creech (drums), Nicki Nichols, Jamie O'Neill, Lisa Edwards (backing vocals), Pat Powell & Mike Scott ('Ten Wedge' vocalists)

3-9 February 1990 (Australia)
17 April-18 May 1990 (Europe)
24-26 May 1990 (Asia)

Set list:
Act One: The Loco-motion, Got to Be Certain, Hand on Your Heart, Look My Way/Chick on the Side, Love at First Sight, Made in Heaven.
Act Two: My Girl (performed by male backing singers), Tears on My Pillow, I Should Be So Lucky, I Miss You, Nothing to Lose/Blame It on the Boogie/ABC (medley), Telltale Signs.
Act Three: Je Ne Sais Pourquoi, Never Too Late, Wouldn't Change a Thing, Dance to the Music.
Encore: Better the Devil You Know (UK and Asia dates only), Enjoy Yourself.

Enjoy Yourself was Kylie's first all-live (or at least *nearly* all-live) world tour, encompassing 22 dates over three continents – her first serious attempt at showing the media that she was growing into a more mature, and credible, artist.

The tour opened on 3 February 1990 at the Brisbane Entertainment Centre, the very first time Kylie had played in front of a big Australian audience with a live band. She gained positive notices in the local press and two further dates followed in Sydney and Melbourne. However, it was back in England, nearly two month later, where real Kylie mania was getting ready to explode. And explode it did, with 12,500 screaming kids ripping off the roof at the NEC on 17 April. An impressed *Music Week* commented, 'It's a triumph ... The hits came flooding thick and fast, guaranteeing an ecstatic response from the audience!'

From Birmingham to London, from Belfast to Dublin – and even a bizarre stop-off at Whitley Bay ice rink on 2 May – Kylie wowed the crowds with her vigorous performances. A few sniffy tabloid reporters claimed that, at times, Kylie was singing over a pre-recorded tape of her voice, while obviously appearing microphone-less. Yet the slow numbers like 'Tears on My Pillow' and 'I Miss You' proved she really was hitting those high notes totally unaccompanied by any technical wizardry. An unexpected vocal highlight was Kylie and her backing singers creating musical mayhem with Sly and the Family Stone's 'Dance to the Music', regularly causing the young audience to surge forward, anticipating the electrifying encore.

The audience during her British dates were overwhelmingly composed of girls under 14 and many British tabloids took the time to smirk that Kylie was doing an admirable job of 'babysitting duty'. 'It's hard to imagine that Miss Minogue feels inspired by the thought of performing before an exclusively child audience,' pondered the *Guardian* after attending her first London Arena gig. 'The squeals between songs are so high pitched that you practically need canine ears to pick them up,' added the *Times*.

However, *Enjoy Yourself* would be the final time children would turn out en masse to see their idol. Slowly but surely, Kylie was getting sexy; her younger audience (and their attendant parents) might have found some elements of the 90-minute stage show slightly uncomfortable to watch. The late John Peel, who took his daughters to one of the concerts, noted that 'The fathers I observed seemed sheepish rather than lustful as they herded their charges.'

The younger fans who had expected to see anodyne versions of 'The Loco-motion' might well have been a bit surprised, especially when with each costume change Kylie displayed more and more bare flesh, until she was down to a white halter-neck top and lamé hotpants with the Aussie flag printed on her backside. Certainly there was plenty for the kids to enjoy (particularly the joyful cover versions of The Jackson Five's Motown hits), but alongside the usual suspects of 'Got to Be Certain' and 'I Should Be So Lucky' the European leg of *Enjoy Yourself* also gave fans the first opportunity to hear the more sophisticated sound of 'Better the Devil You Know' – prophetically presented as the encore, surely signposting the sound, and shape, of things to come.

Word of mouth among fans, and hype from excitable journalists, created a huge buzz about 'that new Kylie song'. Somehow the intuitive fans knew the lyrics even better than the woman performing it, even in Paris and Brussels. By the time Kylie returned to Britain on 14 May (at the Scottish Exhibition Centre in Glasgow), 'Better the Devil You Know' was already comfortably nestled in the Top 5 and was the #1 dance track in clubs across Europe. *Enjoy Yourself* concluded with two far-flung dates in Kowloon and Bangkok, a far more confident, and passionate, Kylie now in attendance. The miraculous 'Better the Devil' had suddenly turned Kylie's career around.

*   *   *

After three years of clandestine romance, during which they continually played cat-and-mouse with tabloid reporters, Kylie finally split with Jason Donovan in 1989. With the pair promoting their own records in different cities in different countries, it became almost impossible for them to maintain a close relationship. They broke up via an emotional long-distance telephone conversation, Kylie secretly determined that her next love affair would not be conducted amid rumour and innuendo.

The man who revolutionised her life was Michael Hutchence, the bad boy of Australian rock and unpredictable lead singer with INXS. The couple had first met in a Sydney bar in 1988 while Kylie was still dating Jason. Hutchence was drunk and allegedly told her, 'I don't know what we should do first, have lunch or have sex.' They did neither, at least for another year, anyway.

Twelve months later the couple met up again in Osaka, Japan, where Kylie was performing her *Disco in Dream* show. 'I'm amazed at her,' Hutchence told a British journalist. 'I really didn't know what to expect but what I saw was just unbelievable. She has so much energy.' An impressed Hutchence pursued Kylie intently and their love affair progressed quickly and passionately, pushing Jason completely out of the picture. 'Our break-up was like a blow to the stomach,' said a heartbroken Donovan. 'How could I possibly complete with Michael? It was a battle I could never win.'

The first public outing for the new superstar couple was at the Sydney premiere of *The Delinquents* and reporters were shocked at how mature Kylie looked – hair tucked up in a short 1960s-style blonde wig and dressed in a stunning 'noughts and crosses' dress – confident and sexy. It almost felt as if, at the stroke of midnight, Kylie had transformed from sweet, demure Australian schoolgirl into strong and self-assured woman. 1990 was going to be the milestone year where everything changed for Kylie. 'Michael has given me a lot of confidence,' Kylie told an interviewer. 'Before we met I was very reserved, but now I'm not. He encourages me to be outrageous and just go for it!'

Growing in confidence and stature, this was the period during which Kylie started taking far more control over her pop career. Boosted by two #1 albums, international hit singles and a new movie, Kylie was ready to stamp more of her personality on her songs, videos and image.

Feeling like she was just another part of Pete Waterman's conveyor belt of manufactured hits, Kylie politely asked her musical mentor whether she could have more input in the songwriting process. He refused; Stock Aitken Waterman was an impenetrable team. They did not write with anybody else, not even their most profitable star. As a compromise Kylie did collaborate with other writers and producers on her next album, 'Rhythm of Love', but SAW were not wholly comfortable with this situation. It was almost like they had created pop star Kylie and nobody else was going to tamper with their winning formula.

'Better the Devil You Know'

Released April 1990 (UK)
Written and Produced by Stock Aitken Waterman
Highest chart position #2 (UK), #4 (Australia)

Flipside: 'I'm Over Dreaming (Over You)'
Video directed by Paul Goldman

With Kylie rapidly growing up, so did SAW – and their next single with her proved to be their most dramatic change in direction yet. From the cheeky, bubblegum pop of just 12 months earlier, SAW's sound suddenly shifted up a gear to a clubbier, more polished, contemporary dance sound. This is where Kylie put the brakes on being a cute teenage pop star and became a fully fledged dance diva; where her loyal audience of prepubescent girls, who'd never even stepped into a club, gave way to an army of gay men who virtually lived in one.

'Better the Devil You Know' – the title of which archly exemplified how SAW had been browbeaten into changing their distinctive sound – is one of the most hugely significant songs Kylie ever recorded. The song boasts a spiky electro keyboard intro, hard, chunky bassline, intoxicating vocal hooks and a huge killer chorus. It is light years away from the safe, cheesy naffness of 'Hand on Your Heart'. Yes, there's a throwback to the stuttering vocal tricks of the past, but the unrelenting thumping beat was designed to induce goose pimples wherever it played. The song is, quite simply, a stroke pf SAW genius. Music journalists were left scratching their heads: who knew Pete Waterman was capable of this? *Number One* magazine wrote, '*Raunchy* appears to be the current Kylie buzz-word – and have you seen that new vid yet? – Wow!'

Naturally, along with her new, more sophisticated sound, Kylie also demanded more hands-on control over her pop videos. 'Better the Devil You Know' was the first time she had the final say on how she presented herself on film. Never again would she submit to the kind of celluloid atrocity that was the 'Hand on Your Heart' promo. 'In the early days, I would sit there, and it would be like, "Kylie, would you like to see your record sleeve?" Just being able to choose my own dress was a victory,' recalled Kylie many years later. 'The changes really started to happen when I went and made the video for 'Better The Devil' on my own and presented it to them. They were uneasy at first, but they eventually came around.'

Unlike the British-made promos for her last few singles, Kylie filmed the video in Australia away from PWL's prying eyes. Looking more passionate and fiery than she ever had previously, Kylie is seen being pursued down an alley in a see-thru mackintosh, gyrating in a little black dress with the straps *hanging loose* and, most shockingly of all, relaxing in a naked (post-coital?) embrace with a big, muscular black man. 'I was longing for choice,' Kylie admitted in 2002, 'and there wasn't really a part in the Hit Factory's machinery or ethos for this. Out of the studio and confines of PWL I started to experiment where I could with image. I wanted to develop, to experience different things and express myself beyond primary colours and a shallow set of TV answers.'

The main influence on Kylie during this period was undoubtedly Hutchence. 'I was 21 and metaphorically he took the blinkers off and opened my eyes to a bigger world,' said Kylie. Her new boyfriend was considered somewhat dangerous by those around her, but for Kylie the relationship was revelatory; in every way Hutchence 'corrupted' the image PWL had tried so hard to maintain. Initially Hutchence was overwhelmed by Kylie's child-like innocence, but soon Kylie was basking in her own sexual revolution. Tabloid whispers of drug taking in hotel rooms and handcuffs poking out of airport suitcases began to emerge, but Kylie stood defiantly by her man. In the 'Better You Devil You Know' promo she sports a chunky ring with the letter 'M' on it, a defiant reference to Michael's all-encompassing influence on her changing career. 'I was 21, so I was blossoming in front of his eyes,' she told the *Observer* several years later. 'I was changing every day. It was almost frightening to him, but he loved it.'

Within weeks Kylie's momentous new song, particularly the extended 'Mad March Hare' remix, was tearing up dancefloors in clubs across Europe. 'Better the Devil' became the first Kylie song to earn itself club respect and was the first gay anthem of her career. Stock Aitken Waterman were well used to marketing their early Hi-NRG successes to a gay market, but they'd experienced nothing like this before. 'Better the Devil' gave Kylie her tenth Top 5 single in the UK, hitting #2. In Australia it peaked at #4, but throughout the world it was a #1 club chart track.

Forget the embarrassing cover version by boy-girl group Steps in 1999 – a re-recording which extracted every hint of sexual energy from the original version – and fondly remember Kylie's breakout hit, a record that still stands up today as well as it did back in 1990. The song marked the beginning of the next phase in Kylie's career, yet also signified the beginning of the end for SAW. 1990 was to be the year Pete Waterman finally watched his worldwide domination of the charts trickle through his fingers.

'Step Back in Time'

Released October 1990 (UK)
Written and Produced by Stock Aitken Waterman
Highest chart position #4 (UK), #5 (Australia)

Flipside: 'Step Back in Time' (instrumental)
Video directed by Nick Egan

Kylie's new grown-up image was, in Britain at least, helped by the fact that she was no longer appearing as a poodle-permed garage mechanic in *Neighbours*. Her final scenes were screened in the UK in November 1989 and finally she was freed from the tabloid shackles of soap star-turned-pop star. There's no denying that *Neighbours'* daily screenings had had the biggest impact on the success of Kylie's early releases in the UK. In many ways it was the best promotion any new singer could have – a single in the charts, a song playing on the radio and your face on BBC1 five days a week. Conversely, Kylie's static, suburban *Neighbours* image also worked against her pop persona. Now she had finally escaped from all that.

After losing her musical virginity with 'Better the Devil', Kylie's follow-up wisely plugged into the same socket as its memorable predecessor. 'Step Back in Time' is a super-funky homage to 1970s disco floor fillers, inspired by Pete Waterman's time as a DJ for Mecca 20 years previously. The inventive lyrics hark back to the past and cleverly name-check one of the biggest Philadelphia Soul bands of the day. 'Remember the old days,' sings Kylie. 'Remember The O'Jays.' She also slips in subtle – or not so subtle, depending on your knowledge of disco – references to hits by Van McCoy, The Jacksons, Wild Cherry, Eddie Kendricks, The Floaters, The Blackbyrds and The Temptations.

The song's awe-inspiring production, enhanced by an incredible mix by Phil Harding and Ian Curnow, plays on a cleverly constructed rhythm section, Barry White-esque strings and frantic keyboard work. All this is topped off by the chanting 'I wanna funk, I wanna F.F.U.F.U.N.K!' mantra which opens the song, sounding like a 1970s disco sample but counting instead as a perfect pastiche).

Kylie enjoyed her very first American video shoot for 'Step Back in Time'. Filmed on location in Los Angeles in September 1990 by director Nick Egan, the promo is a Technicolor parade of platform shoes, flares, afros and ostrich feathers. Kylie, displaying acres of bare flesh, models a series of outrageous 1970s fashions against a shimmering background, and then rides around LA in a huge red open-top Cadillac, grinning wildly. The funky dance moves are reminiscent of the 'Never Too Late' video, but Kylie appears to be even more liberated here.

The single entered the UK charts at #9 and climbed to #4, where it peaked, a week later. In Israel it hit #1, her second consecutive chart topper, yet in other markets the song curiously underperformed: #21 in New Zealand, #36 in Germany. Elsewhere Kylie was posing for lascivious photo shoots with style magazines like *The Face*; in one shoot she dressed in bra and knickers and dragged on a cigarette. PWL were not happy and it was apparent some of Kylie's younger fans were finding it hard to adapt to her new more 'adult' image, too. This was never more apparent than when, in the 1990 *Smash Hits Poll Winners' Party*, Kylie won several 'worst' gongs including 'Worst Dressed' for the 'Step Back in Time' video, the irony of which went totally over the heads of fickle teenagers. Quite obviously, Kylie had now transcended her traditional kiddie audience. She was making giant steps forward in time.

'Rhythm of Love'

Released November 1990 (UK)
PWL / Mushroom Records
Produced by Stock Aitken Waterman (tracks 1-5,
7 and 9), Keith 'KC' Cohen (track 8), Keith 'KC'
Cohen and Stephen Bray (tracks 10 and 11), and
Michael Jay (track 6)
Highest chart position #9 (UK), #10 (Australia)

Track listing:
'Better the Devil You Know'
'Step Back in Time'
'What Do I Have to Do'
'Secrets'
'Always Find the Time'
'The World Still Turns'
'Shocked'
'One Boy Girl'
'Things Can Only Get Better'
'Count the Days'
'Rhythm of Love'

The more ripened, assertive Kylie is all too evident on 1990's
'Rhythm of Love'. Here she was on her third studio album, co-
writing four of the 11 tracks and working with producers other than
SAW. This was definitely *not* how Pete Waterman usually liked to run
the show. Grappling for more artistic control over her musical output,
Kylie had backed the Hit Factory into a corner: 'Do things more my way
or not at all'. Part-recorded in Los Angeles, Kylie sought a more hands-
on approach to her new album and she certainly got it. 'This time I was
much more involved with everything, even the SAW songs,' said Kylie at
the time. 'When I was in America they would send over mixes and ask
whether I liked them or not! Now I know Pete is interested in hearing
my ideas whereas a while ago I'm sure he wouldn't have been.'

Alongside the surprisingly contemporary European dance beats
of 'Better the Devil' and 'What Do I Have to Do' sit very American-
sounding tracks like 'One Boy Girl' (produced by 'KC' Cohen, a much
in-demand remixer of tunes by Paula Abdul, Seal and Prince's Paisley
Park label). In addition, 'Count the Days' and the album's percussion-
heavy title track were engineered by Stephen Bray, a US producer best
known for his work with Madonna, notably her classic singles 'Into the
Groove' and 'Express Yourself', both favourites of Kylie's. In particular,

the bouncing 'Count the Days' owes far more to Madonna's early 1980s New York sound than anything coming out of London and is about as alien to SAW as you can get.

'It was such an enjoyable experience working with Stephen,' enthused Kylie. 'It was the very first time I'd worked on a song from nothing and been totally involved with the end product. I want to break new ground and be seen as an individual artist in my own right. The Stock Aitken Waterman team are very formulated. When they have a success with somebody they tend to stick to the same formula. It's not very easy to break away from that.'

But credit where credit's due, SAW take some big chances here, none greater than the epic production on 'Shocked', which boasts a gloriously gratuitous 90-second instrumental intro, gradually building to a disco crescendo burnished with galloping keyboards and fuzzy electric guitar, all mixed to perfection by PWL's Pete Hammond. SAW's 'Things Can Only Get Better' continues in a similar vein, gleefully tearing meaty strips off the Kylie sound of yesteryear, and only the cute tinkle of 'Secrets' lets down the home team.

The British and American elements may clash at times, making this definitely an album of two halves, but at the same time the mix-and-match approach finally allowed Kylie to lay the ghost of her cheesier 'Loco-motion' sound and also signposted future rhythms. While Kylie's new album sold only a fraction of the amount of her previous two releases it was still a milestone release for her, eventually shifting in excess of three million copies worldwide. Undoubtedly, somewhere deep among the record's 11 tracks the twin seeds of 'Light Years' and 'Fever' had already been planted.

In Australia the album was reissued twice, once as the 'Australian Tour Edition' to coincide with her February 1991 concerts, featuring a bonus disc of three 'Shocked' remixes, and again in May as the 'Gold Edition', with additional remixes of 'Step Back in Time', 'What Do I Have to Do' and 'Shocked'.

* * *

In December 1990 Stock Aitken Waterman gave *Smash Hits* the most candid interview of their career. SAW had always been detested by the trendy music press but suddenly they were under attack from their biggest supporter. Britain's number one teen pop bible had the temerity to ask: 'Are Stock Aitken Waterman down the dumper?'

For the past 12 months there had been rumblings that SAW had hit their peak and critics were already circling like ravenous sharks. Despite the fact they had won the Ivor Novello songwriting award for 1987, 1988 and 1989 it now seemed like the hitmaking trio were gradually losing their golden touch. The world's bestselling girl group Bananarama had moved on to pastures new, Rick Astley had gone, so had Sonia and Donna Summer, and several of their newer acts such as Big Fun and Lonnie Gordon had seen their latest singles stall well outside the Top 40. Even a deluded Jason Donovan suddenly wanted to abandon pop and become a dirty rock 'n' roll star. He further alienated his loyal gay audience by suing *The Face* magazine over slurs regarding his sexuality. He then opted for a long stint in the stage musical of *Joseph and the Amazing Technicolor Dreamcoat*. His pop career was finished. To cap it all, the second week of October 1990 was the very first time since March 1986 that a Pete Waterman track was absent from the UK Top 100.

Pete Waterman and Mike Stock, both in defensive mood, told *Smash Hits* they were unhappy with the increased creative control Kylie was demanding over her musical output. 'The thing is,' said Stock, 'having had such a massive success Kylie is hardly likely to want to retain just one aspect of the recording process – just coming in and singing – so it's probable that she'll want to do it all very soon and we won't be involved any more.' Waterman also had a sly pop at Michael Hutchence. 'She's got a boyfriend in the industry who's probably spurring her on, so I think it's something we expect to happen. I don't know what the future is for Kylie,' he added bleakly. 'She's doing her own thing.' Stock added, rather prophetically: 'It's fair to say, though, that this isn't the sort of direction in which we'd want to take her.'

Undoubtedly, 1990-91 was a transitional time for Kylie and her fans. Some of her audience left her, some stayed, and she gained new admirers too. It's fair to say that SAW were uncomfortable with her new 'adult' direction though, sensing it would erode her record sales. They weren't proved wrong.

'What Do I Have to Do'

Released January 1991 (UK)
Written and Produced by Stock Aitken Waterman
Highest chart position #6 (UK), #11 (Australia)

Flipside: 'What Do I Have to Do' (instrumental)
Video directed by Dave Hogan

In January 1991 'What Do I Have to Do', originally planned as the autumn follow-up to 'Better the Devil', was remixed for 7" release by Phil Harding and Ian Curnow with added 'what's that sound?' samples at the beginning. It became the first Kylie single to miss out on a Top 5 placing. In Australia it missed the Top 10 completely and in Germany it peaked at an outrageously low #48. Ironically, 'What Do I Have to Do'

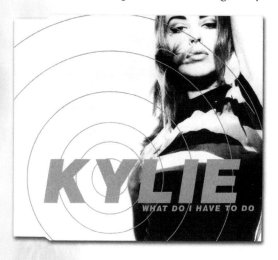

and its follow-up 'Shocked' are two of the coolest pop singles Kylie ever released; smooth, sexy, innovative, and just as snappy, if not more so, than her hits from two years previously.

Part of the problem for Kylie's younger fans was their idol's more seductive image; they felt alienated by it. But for Kylie herself she was stuck between a rock and a hard place. She couldn't keep everybody happy all of the time. The question 'What do I have to do?' was never more apt. She was growing up and her fans needed to grow up with her; Kylie couldn't remain an Erinsborough High School pupil forever. 'Everyone wanted to be Kylie Minogue except Kylie Minogue, who wanted to be Madonna,' said Pete Waterman in his autobiography. 'On top of that I think Kylie was getting embarrassed by her past because it was part of her growing up. She had to reject her past so that she could find her own identity.'

Part of that rejection was fuelled by Kylie's relationship with Michael Hutchence, which was probably the one thing paternal Pete Waterman feared most. Hutchence encouraged her to actively promote her sexuality wherever possible and as a consequence the video for 'What Do I Have to Do' became Kylie's most controversial yet. It certainly did nothing to allay the fears of Waterman or Kylie's younger fans. 'When I spoke to director David Hogan on the phone, he asked me what style I was into,' recalled Kylie. 'That was easy: Italian *Vogue*. There was a particular issue I had in mind that was bulging with black and white photographs of impossibly beautiful and glamorous women!'

The final promo sees Kylie paying homage to cinema sex sirens like Brigitte Bardot, Elizabeth Taylor and Joan Collins, and modelling the sexiest outfits – some courtesy of Thierry Mugler – she'd ever worn. 'How many movie stars can you look like in three and a half minutes?'

Kylie joked amid images of dazzling flashbulbs and pouting lips. The partly monochrome video, filmed over two gruelling 18-hour days in a freezing London, features a plethora of stunning visuals – Kylie sporting a tattoo of a panther on her left shoulder ('It will wash off thank goodness!'), emerging from a steaming swimming pool and, in its most notorious scene, doing the ironing in a saucy French maid's outfit. The nightclub sequence showing Kylie doing some lesbian canoodling with another beautiful model also features a tiny, but energetic, cameo from her sister Dannii, hidden behind a blonde wig.

*   *   *

Since graduating from TV's *Young Talent Time* in 1988, Dannii had followed her sister into soap land with a stint in *Home and Away* as stroppy teenager Emma Jackson, for which she won a Silver Logie award. As Kylie's pop career went global there were persistent rumours that Dannii was jealous of Kylie's success – after all it was she who had started off as a singer first. Kylie invited her sister to appear in the 'What Do I Have to Do' video to prove that 'We don't hate each other,' but the newspapers were still having none of it, preferring to write endlessly about the sisters' intense rivalry.

In Australia Danni eventually signed to Mushroom and recorded her debut album, released as 'Love and Kisses' in the UK in 1991. Two months after her cameo in Kylie's video she released the album's title track, which reached #8 on the UK chart, although her subsequent music career has been unpredictable to say the least. However, her 1997 top five hit 'All I Wanna Do' is arguably one of the most wonderfully hypnotic dance tracks of the decade. Interestingly, on Kylie's advice, Pete Waterman had passed on signing Dannii to his own label. With her older sister's career going through a difficult transitory phase he may well have come to regret his decision.

Rhythm of Love Tour

Devised by Kylie Minogue / Musical Director – Adrian Scott / Tour Manager – Nick Pitts / Production Manager – Henry Crallam / Choreography by Venol John

Musicians: Adrian Scott and Tania Smith (keyboards), Craig Newman (bass), Jamie Jardine (guitar), John Creech (drums), James Uluave, Jamie O'Neill and Susie Ahearn (backing vocals)

10-23 February 1991 (Australia)

4-10 March 1991 (Asia)

Set list:
Act One: Step Back in Time, Wouldn't Change a Thing, Got to Be Certain, Always Find the Time, Enjoy Yourself, Tears on My Pillow, Secrets, Help.
Act Two: I Should Be So Lucky, What Do I Have to Do, Je Ne Sais Pas Pourquoi.
Act Three: One Boy Girl, Love Train, Rhythm of Love, Shocked.
Act Four: Hand on Your Heart, Count the Days, The Loco-motion, Better the Devil You Know

Disgruntled Australian and Asian fans who may have considered they'd been short-changed by just a handful of live dates on the *Enjoy Yourself* tour were richly rewarded for their loyalty in the spring of 1991 when Kylie embarked on the first part of her second world tour. Sponsored by Coca-Cola, *Rhythm of Love* opened at the Canberra Stadium on 10 February before zig-zagging between Perth, Adelaide, Melbourne and Brisbane for a further five dates. With the exception of 'Better the Devil' and a handful of cover versions, her previous concerts had dipped heavily into Kylie's first two albums. Now she had the clubbier, more diverse 'Rhythm of Love' collection to showcase and a new gospel choir arrangement of 'Hand on Your Heart'.

Suddenly the new, more energised and raunchy Kylie was apparent to everybody. The daring costume changes kept coming: mini-PVC dress, a fluorescent green taffeta skirt slashed to the waist, hot pink harem pants and a skin-tight purple body suit, plus a bout of frantic pumping and rubbing with one of her male dancers during 'Always Find the Time'. Some bitchy commentators were quick to say Kylie's stage show was merely aping what Madonna had done before. The criticism stung Kylie when reporters repeatedly asked her if she was trying to 'steal Madonna's crown,' an accusation she angrily denied. 'She has been a great inspiration not only with my work but because she is also a great businesswoman,' Kylie responded. 'But I don't want to be a new Madonna and I have tried not to model myself on her. I want to develop my own style. But I do like the way she changes her image. If she can do it, so can I.'

Dodging the brickbats, in March 1991 *Rhythm of Love* jumped to Japan for four dates before touring Singapore, Bangkok and Kuala Lumpur, the latter being Kylie's first visit to Malaysia. By the time the tour resumed in England in October under the revised title *Let's Get to It*, Kylie suddenly had yet another new album to promote and she wasn't going to tone down her act for anybody.

'Shocked'

Released May 1991 (UK)
Written and Produced by Stock Aitken Waterman
Remixed by DNA
Highest chart position #6 (UK), #7 (Australia)

Flipside: 'Shocked' (Harding/Curnow 7" mix)
Video directed by Dave Hogan

If there was one single that demonstrated just how far Kylie had come in the past four years 'Shocked' is it. One of the standout cuts from 'Rhythm of Love', the original album version has one of the dreamiest and most innovative mixes ever to grace a SAW production, but for the single release the song was radically reinvented as a deliriously catchy companion piece to 'What Do I Have to Do'.

Doing the honours were production duo Nick Bett and Neal Slateford, better known as DNA; this was the first time PWL had allowed external remixers to tamper with any of the Hit Factory's hallowed product. The previous summer DNA had ripped up the Top 40 and the dance charts with their sublime reworking of American singer-songwriter Suzanne Vega's acoustic track 'Tom's Diner', adding layer upon layer of decadent dance grooves under the melancholy vocals and scoring a #2 hit in the process.

DNA approached PWL and, because Kylie loved their work, the dynamic duo were allowed to get their hands on 'Shocked', ruthlessly editing it, speeding it up and adding a rap. Even Waterman loved it, despite initially not wanting to release a fourth single off the 'Rhythm of Love' album. 'We had a lot of fun with it,' Waterman told *Vox* magazine in July 1991, 'one of the multi-tracks got up to 11 and a half minutes long and DNA's remix is amazing!' The rap is courtesy of Jazzi P (aka the more suburban-sounding Pauline Bennett), who had guested on several other British dance records and whose biggest success to date had been 'Get Loose', a #25 hit in July 1989. Within a decade, having a rapper do a cameo on a pop record would be commonplace; back in 1991 it was positively radical, especially for a single out of Pete Waterman's studios.

Rapper Jazzi also features in the super saucy 'Shocked' video, shot at Pinewood ('It's quite exciting being at the 007 studios,' Kylie said) on the next sound stage along from *Alien3*. The voyeuristic promo features a chauffeur-driven Kylie arriving at a creepy old mansion and then dressing up in a variety of sexy guises – a pink ostrich feather skirt; leather S and M hot pants and bra, and a girly gingham bikini with her hair in adolescent bunches. She's continually spied on through a keyhole, the intimation being that perhaps she's a working girl, hired to pander to a rich man's kinky fantasies.

'There are some shocking scenes in it,' said Pete Waterman of the video, obviously having grown accustomed to Kylie's desire for more autonomy. 'She'll say, "Look, I want to do this in the video" and you sit there and think, "Either Kylie's on acid or I am." Then you see the video and think "Wow, that's amazing..." We still think of Kylie as the little girl who came from Australia, but you see her on screen and think, "Jeez, was she actually sitting on my desk an hour ago?" If it has that effect on me, and I've known her for five years, it's got to have the same effect on someone who only sees her on video or television.'

And it's not just Dave Hogan's video which is sexually suggestive. The song's theme of utter amazement at finding true love ('Cos it struck me like lightning; like a bolt out of the blue') also led to a persistent urban myth that Kylie swears in the chorus. It has been suggested that she actually sings 'I was fucked to my very foundations' rather than 'rocked to my very foundations'. The claim was always vehemently denied by PWL, but it makes for a great story.

Annoyingly, 'Shocked' continued Kylie's downward sales trend, bizarrely at odds with a huge improvement in her musical style. The single, like its predecessor, peaked at #6 in the UK, and with only seven weeks on the chart was Kylie's weakest seller to date. 'I'd be lying if I wasn't concerned about it,' Kylie told *Smash Hits*, 'but Top 10 ain't bad and I have to keep my sense of proportion. I think I've reached a stage where I have to be true to myself. I'm not the Kylie I was a few years ago, so for me to be making the same kind of videos as before would be holding myself back and I'd go crazy!'

Despite missing the top of the charts Kylie still became the first artist in UK chart history to have all her first 13 single releases make the Top 10. 'Shocked' also became the very first PWL production to be released on a picture disc, a format Waterman detested because his adage was 'the songs sell themselves.' Along with Kylie's previous three singles 'Shocked' also became a colossal hit in gay clubs. 'I was more or less adopted by my gay audience,' Kylie admitted. 'In fact, I was possibly the last to know. I don't like to analyse our relationship too much as it is what it is and it's wonderful, but I think they related to my initial struggle to be accepted as myself. Not to mention my penchant for all things pink and showgirl.'

* * *

As with 'What Do I Have to Do', Kylie's male co-star in the 'Shocked' video was South African model Zane O'Donnell, who was prolific during this time on magazine covers for *The Face*, *Arena*, *GQ* and *Vogue*, as well being the early 1990s face of Armani's European advertising campaigns. Known for his distinctive boxer's nose and huge height (he was previously a champion surfer), O'Donnell dated Kylie for a while after her break-up with Michael Hutchence in February 1991.

The Hutchence liaison had ended, as had the Jason one, during an emotional phone call. 'I spent a good part of my time crying into my pillow case,' Kylie confessed many years later. The high-profile rock relationship may have faltered due to Hutchence's constant need for new thrills, but for Kylie her transformation from girl-next-door to sex bomb was complete. 'I'd have burned out if I'd lived his rock 'n' roll lifestyle for too long,' she told the *Daily Mail*. 'But he was a wonderful teacher and lover. It was as if I'd been living with blinkers on before I met him. He encouraged me to travel, taught me about books and how to enjoy the high life. We'd all be very lucky if we could experience a man as charismatic, wise, sexy and funny as Michael.'

It would also have been inconceivable, even 18 months earlier, that Kylie would have contemplated shooting a video as libidinous as 'Shocked'.

'Word is Out'

Released August 1991 (UK)
Written and Produced by Mike Stock and Pete Waterman
Highest chart position #16 (UK), #10 (Australia)

Flipside: 'Say the Word, I'll be There'
Video directed by James Le Bon

By May 1991 the once invincible, all-conquering Stock Aitken Waterman was no more. Plagued by vicious press articles questioning their

musical integrity and media speculation about their crumbling empire, and with all but Kylie left on the PWL roster, the three-way partnership finally split. After the company was re-structured, Matt Aitken, who had found a new and time-consuming hobby in motor-racing (much to the chagrin of Pete Waterman), left the Hit Factory and the legend that was SAW effectively dissolved overnight. Stock and Waterman continued as a duo for the next few months, but as Waterman himself said, 'It was never really the same.'

The benefit for Kylie, working with a slightly weakened Hit Factory, was that it gave her greater freedom to experiment with new musical styles. Despite the huge critical success Kylie had enjoyed with the clubbier, more contemporary sound of her last four singles, she was keen to take her music in a totally different direction; less pop, more sexy R'n'B. But would her fans like it? 'It was obvious that she wasn't primarily interested in making pop records for her public, but for herself instead,' claimed a disgruntled Waterman many years later.

The first taste of her new output was 'Word is Out', a jazz-flavoured Chicago dance track heavily influenced by 'New Jack Swing', a very commercial hybrid of R'n'B and hip hop popularised in the US by performers like Color Me Badd, Keith Sweat and Bobby Brown, as well as producers Jimmy Jam and Terry Lewis.

In accordance with what Kylie wanted to achieve, 'Word is Out' is a huge departure from her previous singles – featuring tinny drum machine beats, promiscuous keyboard work and some soulful backing vocals courtesy of Leroy Osbourne and Lance Ellington. The song's sexy saxophone is courtesy of session musician Gary Barnacle, who had previously guested on SAW's downright appalling 1990 charity record 'You've Got a Friend', sung by Sonia and Big Fun. At least Barnacle's talents are used to better effect here.

'Word is Out' became 'Single of the Fortnight' in a slightly surprised *Smash Hits* but the fans weren't convinced. Peaking at #16 it became Kylie's least successful song to date, breaking her stunning run of consecutive UK Top 10 successes. For PWL, having a brand-new Kylie single charting so low was nothing short of disastrous. Some critics ascribed the song's failure to Kylie's lack of TV promotion and her over-reliance on the controversial video. In the promo Kylie plays a sassy, streetwise temptress, wearing an outrageous see-thru, all-in-one Galliano black lace outfit and dancing in the 'ghetto' (in actual fact, London's Camden Lock) with some very sharp-suited black guys.

Whereas Kylie looked sultry in her 'Shocked' video, here she just looks downright slutty. Pete Waterman was particularly unhappy about her new image. 'Dressing up as a prostitute wouldn't have been my choice and the public seemed to understand that as well, because once they saw it her popularity just fell away,' he said bitterly in 2000. 'I've found throughout my career that acts do what the public wants and then there comes a point when they decide to do what they want and the public doesn't like them any more.' Today the video is less memorable for Kylie's stockings and suspenders than for a fleeting appearance by a later-to-be-famous Davina McCall as Kylie's beret-wearing best mate.

*   *   *

Throughout this period Kylie became increasingly irritated by the British, and to a lesser extent Australian, press's obsession with her changing image and their inability to let go of her cute *Neighbours* persona. The hooker image in the 'Word is Out' video seemed to provoke tabloid journalists, who then became outraged at her equally revealing stage outfits in her autumn 1991 'Let's Get to It' tour.

In a lazy *TV-am* interview with Martin Frizzell that October, Kylie was forced to defend her 'raunchy' new image. 'I'm confused,' she said wearily. 'They keep saying 'the new Kylie'. I mean, is there another one? I'm getting confused as to which change they're talking about at the moment because I've been constantly changing for the last two years.' When Frizzell seemed to side with the tabloids, Kylie rapidly retorted, 'The point of the press is to sell as many papers as they can and to do that they need to be sensational. In the past few months I've actually had great press, but they love you, they hate you, they feel sorry for you. They can't seem to be saying the same thing all the time and they love to contradict themselves. I am disappointed at the moment that I have to keep going on about this 'bad press'. I've had it before and I will have it again. Well, I think if I hadn't changed at all they probably wouldn't be interested in me today anyway. If I was still doing exactly what I was doing four years ago I would certainly be bored to tears.'

'Let's Get to It'

Released October 1991 (UK)
PWL / Mushroom Records
Highest chart position #15 (UK), #13 (Australia)

Produced by Stock and Waterman

Track listing:
'Word is Out'
'Give Me Just a Little More Time'
'Too Much of a Good Thing'
'Finer Feelings'
'If You Were with Me Now'
'Let's Get to It'
'Right Here, Right Now'
'Live and Learn'
'No World Without You'
'I Guess I Like It Like That'
Bonus tracks: 'Word is Out', 'Step Back In Time' and 'What Do I Have to Do' (all instrumentals) (Japan only)

'We're gonna do it! Let's get to it!' Absolutely, but with a #16 single – a flop by Kylie standards – as the new album's lead-in it was always going to be an uphill struggle. 'Let's Get to It' may be the most easy-to-forget album of Kylie's career, but there is still much to enjoy.

It's a solid collection of predominantly R'n'B dance tunes with bouncy percussion, big brass horns and pulsating hip hop rhythms, ranging from the dirty breathlessness of 'Too Much of a Good Thing' to the appealingly acoustic 'No World Without You', the hypnotic voodoo of 'Right Here, Right Now' and the sheer insanity of 'I Guess I Like It Like That', the latter exploding in every direction with tight vocal loops and wicked Euro techno beats. There are whispers of Madonna's 'Erotica' album to be heard here, plus a fist-full of Brooklyn's Full Force and some soft and gentle Chicago house vibes. In many ways the singles, 'Word is Out', 'If You Were with Me Now' and 'Give Me Just a Little More Time', are almost incidental to the plot, for it's the lush and emotional ballad 'Finer Feelings' which helps set this slickly sophisticated album apart from Kylie's earlier PWL productions.

The recording of the album had not been an especially happy time for Kylie. After her experience working with American producers for part of the 'Rhythm of Love' album, Waterman had now regained complete control on this project, though conceding that Kylie could have a shot at songwriting with him and Mike Stock. As a result, six of the ten tracks are co-written by Kylie, but with the Aitken 'jam' now absent from the SAW sandwich the doomsayers were already predicting a swift end to Kylie and Waterman's pop careers. Certainly Kylie's last full album for the Hit Factory was her most commercially unsuccessful to date, peaking well outside the Top 10 and remaining on the UK chart for barely three months. Despite this track record, however, 'Let's Get to It' is an underrated gem. 'Her strongest album to date... quite a revelation,' wrote an impressed *Music Week*. 'An album of greater subtlety and depth than could ever have been imagined.'

If You Were with Me Now

Released October 1991
Written by Stock and Waterman, Kylie Minogue and Keith Washington
Produced by Stock and Waterman
Highest chart position #4 (UK), #23 (Australia)

Flipside: 'I Guess I Like It Like That'
Video directed by Greg Masuak

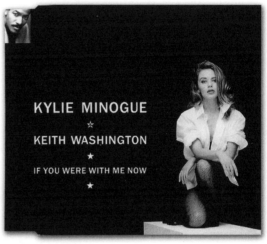

After the comparative failure of 'Word is Out', PWL decided that Kylie needed to return with something a little bit more conservative. 'Finer Feelings', a beautiful track she had recorded for her upcoming album, had been pencilled in as the follow-up but was pulled at the last moment in favour of the slushy ballad 'If You Were with Me Now'.

With the once-impenetrable hitmaking trio of SAW finally broken, 'If You Were with Me Now' marks the first time Kylie was credited with co-writing one of her singles – a four-way collaboration between pop star, producers and black soul singer Keith Washington. Virtually unknown outside of the US, Detroit-born Washington had a massive stateside R'n'B hit with 'Kissing You' in 1991 after signing to the legendary Quincy Jones' own label. Washington's debut album 'Make Time for Love' earned admirers in the UK too and brought him to the attention of northern soul-loving Pete Waterman. Washington – a romantic balladeer with a mellifluous Luther Vandross-like voice – wasn't the obvious choice as the new Jason Donovan but the partnership is surprisingly rewarding. Kylie and Washington recorded their vocals separately at the Hit Factory but the song was mixed by Phil Harding so it appeared as though the performers were singing to each other.

The song echoes Patti Labelle and Michael McDonald's stunning duet 'On My Own', a US #1 in 1986, which also had the singers recording their vocals miles apart. And just like the 'On My Own' video, neither Kylie nor Washington actually shared any scenes in their promo either. Because the couple didn't actually meet up they never performed the single together on *Top of the Pops* or Australian TV, so Washington remained somewhat of an enigma to Kylie's core audience. And on the thrown-together 7" single sleeve poor Washington makes only a bizarre 'cameo' appearance in the top left-hand corner, looking like a design afterthought.

The duet was intended to relaunch Kylie on the American market, but notoriously hard-line R'n'B radio stations in the US took exception to Washington singing with a white pop star, especially one best known over there for the bubblegum sound of 'The Loco-motion'. As a result the song was never released in America. Over in Britain 'If You Were with Me Now' safely returned Kylie to the Top 5, despite the relative invisibility of her mysterious singing partner.

Let's Get to It Tour

Devised by Kylie Minogue and John Galliano / Musical Director – Adrian Scott / Tour Manager – Nick Pitts / Production Manager – Henry Crallan / Choreography by Venol John / Wardrobe by John Galliano

Musicians: Adrian Scott and Tania Smith (keyboards), Craig Newman (bass), Jamie Jardine (guitar), John Creech (drums), James Uluave, Jamie O'Neill and Susie Ahearn (backing vocals), Jazzi P (rapper)

25 October-8 November 1991 (UK)

Set list:
Act One: Step Back in Time, Wouldn't Change a Thing, Got to Be Certain, Always Find the Time, Enjoy Yourself, Tears on My Pillow, Secrets.
Act Two: Let's Get to It, Word is Out, Finer Feelings.
Act Three: I Should Be So Lucky, Love Train, Je Ne Sais Pas Pourquoi, Hand on Your Heart, If You Were with Me Now, Too Much of a Good Thing, What Do I Have to Do.
Act Four: I Guess I Like it Like That/Keep On Pumpin' It, The Loco-motion, Shocked, Better the Devil You Know.

What the *Rhythm of Love* tour had started on the other side of the globe Kylie completed with *Let's Get to It* in Great Britain and Ireland. This is the tour derided by the tabloid press for being

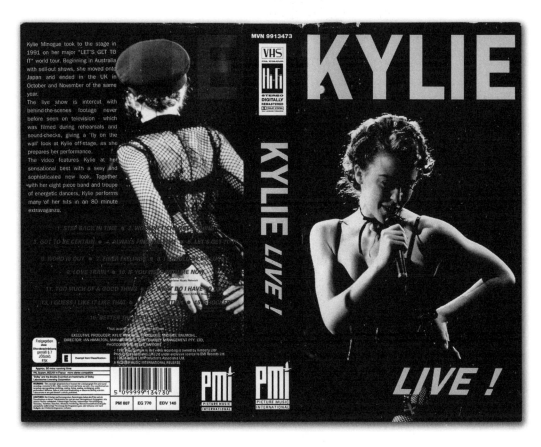

'pornographic' but universally adored by her fans. The British press' obsession with 'Whatever happened to Baby Kylie?' was well borne out when her latest tour opened at the Plymouth Pavilions on 25 October 1991. Where once had stood a cute, wholesome teenager now strode a tiny figure draped in revealing fashions courtesy of British designer John Galliano. There were black garters, fishnet stockings, suspenders, frilly knickers and pointy bras on show and suddenly the media was accusing Kylie once again of imitating Madonna.

'I love Madonna,' Kylie was pressed into saying. 'She's a heroine of mine, but I honestly don't want to be her. I'm me!' Certainly some of the costumes and the choreography in Kylie's new tour were reminiscent of Madonna, but they owed just as much to Janet Jackson. Kylie was growing up, after all. Why shouldn't she get sexy on stage like her contemporaries? 'I'm reacting against the old days,' she admitted.

'When all the suits told me, "This would look nice, Kylie, why don't you put in on?" Telling me to smile, smile, smile...'

Tellingly, the *Let's Get to It* tour was the first occasion when Kylie's adult fans finally outnumbered the kids. The *Independent* noted that the audience at her Wembley arena gigs were 'late teenagers with ravers' hairdos and smart couples in their twenties.' This crowd definitely wasn't going to be shocked by a cheeky glimpse of stocking top or a plunging neckline. The staging of *Let's Get to It* was simple but impressive – big grey blocks for the band to sit on, a ramp and a long staircase. Everything was draped in black, but the relatively basic lighting was surprisingly effective.

The show began with Kylie emerging robotically through a door beneath the drum podium as a back-lit silhouette. She was wearing a see-through plastic jacket ('inspired,' said Galliano, 'by Lolita!'), saucy black underwear clearly visible underneath. The familiar rumble of 'Step Back in Time' started and everything suddenly exploded into life. The tour was probably the most athletic of Kylie's career – full of leaping, high kicks and back flips, even, for Kylie, an amazing cartwheel midway through the terrific techno workout of 'I Guess I Like It Like That'.

Other moves were far more sexually suggestive. There was more than enough gyrating and Hot Gossip-style spreading of legs to keep even the most jaded music reporter happy. For 'Always Find the Time' Kylie performed a daring dance duel with choreographer-in-chief Venol John. Leaping around like randy frogs, Venol (dressed in a PVC vest and tight black trousers) launched himself to bite Kylie's bum, but she pinned his chest to the floor with one of her high heels. Their playful skirmishes continued with Kylie riding him on all fours and then thrusting her cleavage into his face. By today's standards it's all quite tame stuff, but back in 1991 journalists still obsessing over the legacy of sweet Charlene Ramsay were supposedly 'disgusted'. Instead of khaki overalls Kylie was now dressing in bondage gear and a peaked cap, more *Night Porter* than *Neighbours*.

Energising high points included a long, and fast-moving, version of 'I Should Be So Lucky', a stirring cover of The O'Jays' 'Love Train' (first premiered on the *Rhythm of Love* tour) and a brilliant mix of the under-exposed 'Too Much of a Good Thing', characterised here by lots of mad hopping around from foot to foot. The best thing in the entire tour was a barnstorming rendition of 'Shocked' with extended rapping duty from Jazzi P, who regularly got some of the biggest whoops of the night. 'Say Jazzi! Say Kylie! Gonna get sexy y'all!' she yells. The howls of pleasure from the audience, the broad smiles from the topless male dancers, the growling guitar solo and the eruption of sheer joy from Kylie when she started to sing was something to behold. It's still one of her signature performances; downright dirty, but never crude. 'My parents have faith in me,' Kylie told a journalist. 'I wouldn't do anything to, you know, blacken the family name!'

A film of the 8 November gig (the tour's final date), at The Point in Dublin, was released on video in April 1992 as *Kylie Live!* The 80-minute production featured most of the songs performed on the tour, interspersed with brief snippets of Kylie rehearsing and messing about with her dancers. It was directed by Ian Hamilton and produced by Michael Baumohl.

'Keep on Pumpin' It'

Released November 1991
Written by Kylie Minogue, Stock and Waterman
Produced by Stock and Waterman
Highest chart position #49 (UK)

Flipside: 'Keep on Pumpin' It (Astral Flight Mix Edit)'
No video produced

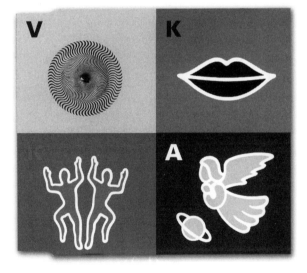

The flipside to 'If You Were with Me Now' couldn't have been more radically different to the radio-friendly main attraction. 'I Guess I Like It Like That' might be considered Stock and Waterman's first flirtation with the burgeoning UK techno 'rave' scene. Ostensibly a six-minute instrumental with Kylie repeating the song title and backing vocalist Carol Kenyon insisting 'You gotta keep on pumpin' it up, cos I like it!', the number was a throwback to SAW's more experimental 1987 hit 'Roadblock', which had silenced critics who claimed the hitmakers could only pen throwaway pop.

The heavy, abrasive keyboard hook of 'I Guess I Like It Like That' was undoubtedly inspired by the trademark sound of minimalist Euro dance act 2 Unlimited, a Dutch boy-girl duo who had taken the continent by storm with their infectious 'Get Ready for This', itself a #2 UK hit in the autumn of 1991. The group was dubbed '2 Untalented' by the British media, but one man just sat back and counted the money. Canny Pete Waterman had signed the act for the British market with his newly created PWL Continental label. Within four years they'd notched up 11 consecutive UK Top 20 hits, the biggest of which was the annoyingly hypnotic 'No Limit', a worldwide #1 smash loved and loathed by the public in equal measure.

The 2 Unlimited-style 'I Guess I Like It like That' was released to clubs on white label prior to the 'Let's Get to It' album and was credited to the mysterious 'Angel K', with few suspecting it was actually Kylie. The song proved to be so successful that when the artist's true identity was revealed fans were astounded. On its official release as the B-side to 'If You Were With Me Now', DJs completely ignored the slushy Minogue/Washington ballad on the reverse and flipped it over to set the dancefloors ablaze. In Australia the track was massively popular in the gay clubs and the Aussie 12" even had 'I Guess I Like It Like That' listed as the A-side.

To further complicate things the track was then unconditionally remixed by club DJs the Vision Masters (Paul Taylor and Danny Hibrid), and Tony King. Taylor, a good friend of Waterman and one of the hottest DJs in the north of England, was, at the time, the resident hero at the legendary Angels nightclub in Burnley. Waterman was so impressed with Taylor's remake of Kylie's album track that he agreed to release the song on the PWL label as 'Keep On Pumpin' It', credited to the tongue-twisting trio 'Vision Masters and Tony King featuring Kylie Minogue'. The resulting dance-trance remix, with sweeping dreamlike synths straight off Rozalla's massive 1991 club hit 'Everybody's Free', some Italio-House keyboards and punchy extraterrestrial laser noises akin to an episode of *Battlestar Galactica*, made 'Keep On Pumpin' It' one of the biggest club hits of the year. A decade later the song could still be relied upon to fill the dancefloor during Taylor's unforgettable retro nights at Manchester's Ascension club.

Released with little fanfare, no accompanying video and with Kylie's name strangely absent from the front of the record sleeve, 'Keep On Pumpin' It' quietly crept into the UK singles charts at #49 then promptly disappeared back into the clubs again, where it rightfully belonged. However, it paved the way for two further Kylie dance experiments, 'Do You Dare' and 'Closer', the fabulous rave-influenced B-sides to her next two single releases.

'Give Me Just a Little More Time'

Released January 1992 (UK)
Written by Brian Holland, Lamont Dozier and
Eddie Holland
Produced by Stock and Waterman
Highest chart position #2 (UK), #9 (Australia)

Flipside: 'Do You Dare'
Video directed by Greg Masuak

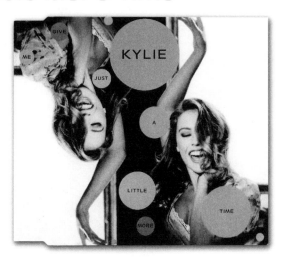

For the third cover version of Kylie's career – following her #1 hits 'The Loco-motion' and 'Tears on My Pillow' – the singer opted for a far mellower and more soulful Detroit sound. 'Give Me Just a Little More Time' was composed by the legendary songwriting trio of Brian Holland, Lamont Dozier and Eddie Holland, very much the Stock Aitken Waterman of their era. Their classic hits for Martha and the Vandellas, The Supremes, The Four Tops and Marvin Gaye dominated American pop music during the 1960s and established the much imitated 'Motown sound'.

Eventually leaving Motown after a very public and messy row over songwriting royalties, Holland Dozier Holland started their own record label, Invictus, but had only a fraction of the success they had enjoyed previously. Legal wrangling meant that most of their subsequent songs had to be credited to the mythical 'Ron Dunbar and Edyth Wayne'. However, before they broke up in 1974, the trio still managed to write several more pop-soul classics, including Freda Payne's worldwide smash 'Band of Gold' and the painfully heartfelt 'Give Me Just a Little More Time', the debut single and biggest commercial success of Chairman of the Board, a soul group fronted by ex-gospel singer General Norman Johnson. The track hit #3 on both sides of the Atlantic in 1970.

Kylie's version doesn't tamper with the distinctively earthy American sound – carefully ignoring 1982's appallingly diluted disco cover by American vocalist Angela Clemmons – and sticking faithfully to the original single's spontaneous feel, even replicating the distinctive tongue-rolling, lip-vibrating 'brrrr' hook, which proved so memorable back in 1970. Kylie manages to lift the song (which, in truth, is nothing more than the musical equivalent of a desperate begging letter) into something cheekier and almost irascible.

The track's sun-bleached video saw Kylie in playful mood, dancing around a packed Detroit diner (actually a London studio one chilly November day in 1991), and provided the template for the virtually identical 'Everything Changes' promo by Take That, shot three years later by a director obviously lacking in inspiration.

'Finer Feelings'

Released April 1992 (UK)
Written and Produced by Stock and Waterman
Additional Production by Brothers In Rhythm
Highest chart position #11 (UK), #60 (Australia)

Flipside: 'Closer'
Video directed by Dave Hogan

The final single released from 'Let's Get to It' is unquestionably the best track on the album. A lush, profoundly moving ballad, 'Finer Feelings' shows Kylie at her most emotional and vulnerable, reassessing her life after being hurt by a selfish lover. 'Finer Feelings' is also perhaps the finest ballad Stock and Waterman ever touched and it's no coincidence that the song name-checks Marvin Gaye's 1982 hit 'Sexual Healing', Kylie's all-time favourite record from her youth. 'I love it and every time I hear it I just feel I have to dance,' admitted Kylie in *Smash Hits* in 1988. 'It's a bit raunchy, a bit bluesy ... it just attracts me, I suppose.' In her song a wistful Kylie laments her ex-boyfriend's failure at meaningful intimacy: 'But what is love without the finer feelings? It's just sex without the sexual healing.'

For single release the track was skilfully remixed by Brothers In Rhythm, at that time the most in-demand of all British production teams, who added layers of slinky Soul II Soul-accented percussion and subtly tinkling piano. What had been a stand-out album track anyway suddenly became a stunning piece of bittersweet pop perfection, more reflective and beautiful than anything Kylie had released before.

The haunting Edouard Boubat-flavoured video (which reunited Kylie with her favourite director, Dave Hogan) transported the singer back to the monochrome world of 1940s Paris. Unlike the stage-bound promo for 'Je Ne Sais Pas Pourquoi', this time Kylie was allowed the luxury of actually shooting on location in the French capital and she's never looked more photogenic when mournfully strolling in the shadow of the Eiffel Tower. Frustratingly, the song narrowly missed out on a Top 10 placing in the UK, probably due to its late post-album release, yet had 'Finer Feelings' been the album's opening gambit it could well have hit the #1 spot.

In 2002 the song was remixed by Manchester's awesome Project K, radically updating the 1992 single version into an outstanding trance-dance track and making it one of the most in-demand bootleg remixes of Kylie's career.

'What Kind of Fool
(Heard All That Before)'

Released August 1992 (UK)
Written by Kylie Minogue, Stock and Waterman
Produced by Stock and Waterman
Highest chart position #14 (UK), #17 (Australia)

Flipside: 'Things Can Only Get Better'
Video directed by Greg Masuak

So who thought this was a move in the right direction? Supposedly a tongue-in-cheek response to her critics, 'What Kind of Fool' still sounds like it could have been recorded any time during the summer of 1989 and is an oddly derivative and peculiarly dated return to SAW's old 'unlucky-in-love' style of 1980s pop. An absurd step backwards for Kylie, it's almost like 'Better the Devil' and 'Shocked' never happened. Co-written by Kylie and Messrs Stock and Waterman, and recorded as a new track for inclusion on Kylie's forthcoming 'Greatest Hits' album, the song's subtly ironic streak was lost on her fans and music journalists alike. Regressive, over-produced and peppered with stuttering vocal tricks, the track is only really enlivened by the neat middle keyboard section and some sampled brass.

The song fell between two stools – not clubby or contemporary enough for the trendier gay clubs and recorded too late in the day to reignite the interest of Kylie's teen fanbase. Sadly, the PWL magic had gone. Even Kylie admitted to not being enamoured of the track. 'I particularly didn't like 'What Kind of Fool', though I don't know if it was the song or my relationship with PWL at the time,' she told the *Guardian* in 1994. More impressive than the song is Greg Masuak's video clip featuring a Lolita-like Kylie (hidden behind heart-shaped sunglasses), in homage to the 1956 movie *Et Dieu créa la femme* (And God Created Woman), which starred original French sex kitten Brigitte Bardot.

'Greatest Hits'

Released August 1992 (UK)
PWL / Mushroom Records
Produced by Stock Aitken Waterman (tracks 1-15), Stock and Waterman (16-21)
and Phil Harding and Ian Curnow (track 22)
Highest chart position #1 (UK), #3 (Australia)

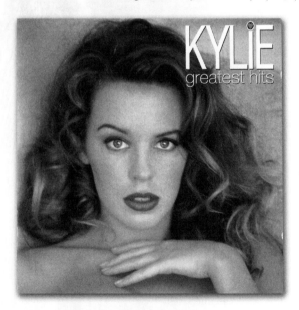

Track listing:
'I Should Be So Lucky'
'Got to Be Certain'
'The Loco-motion'
'Je Ne Sais Pas Pourquoi'
'Especially for You'
'Turn It Into Love'
'It's No Secret'
'Hand on Your Heart'
'Wouldn't Change a Thing'
'Never Too Late'
'Tears on My Pillow'
'Better the Devil You Know'
'Step Back in Time'
'What Do I Have to Do'
'Shocked' (DNA radio edit)
'Word is Out'
'If You Were with Me Now'
'Give Me Just a Little More Time'
'Finer Feelings'
'What Kind of Fool (Heard All That Before)'
'Where in the World?'
'Celebration'

Kylie's first 'Greatest Hits' collection and the last album she was contracted to do for PWL is a full retrospective of her time at the Hit Factory. Alongside the worldwide number ones there are also her Japanese and American hits, 'Turn It Into Love' and 'It's No Secret', plus 'Especially for You', not previously available on a European Kylie album (though it had appeared as the eleventh track on Jason Donovan's bestselling 'Ten Good Reasons' in 1989). Early tracks like 'The Loco-motion' sit rather awkwardly beside the more sophisticated 'What Do I Have to Do' and 'Shocked', illustrating the huge leap in musical maturity and credibility Kylie achieved in just a few years.

The album also boasted three new tracks – the recent single 'What Kind of Fool', a cover version of 'Celebration' and the oddly under-produced ballad 'Where in the World?', which seemed to take Kylie's story at PWL full-circle. 'Greatest Hits' debuted at #1 in the UK, eventually selling over 300,000 copies and being certified platinum. In Australia, where the album was released in superior, sexier artwork and in digipak format, the collection peaked at #3.

'Celebration'

Released November 1992 (UK)
Written by Robert Bell and James 'JT' Taylor
Produced by Phil Harding and Ian Curnow
Additional Production by Stock and Waterman
Highest chart position #20 (UK), #21 (Australia)

Flipside: 'Let's Get to It'
Video directed by Greg Masuak

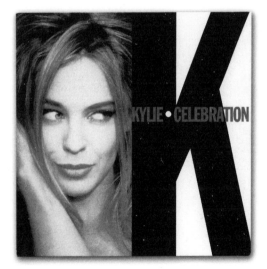

'Celebration' marked the end of Kylie's professional association with Pete Waterman. The final single she released with PWL is, in every respect, a true end-of-term gala of her five hugely successful years with the Hit Factory and a poignant farewell to the first era of Kylie's musical career. Kylie herself chose the song, a cover version of Kool and the Gang's #1 US single which was taken from their inspirational 1980 album *Celebrate!* Like Marvin Gaye's 'Sexual Healing' this was another track which proved to be irresistible to Kylie.

It was a childhood favourite of hers and a song which she loved dancing to as she leapt around the Minogue family lounge. 'You can't hold me down when it's on,' she confessed to *Smash Hits* way back in 1988.

The PWL version of the perennially popular party tune adds very little to the version Kylie so adored as a child. It's certainly infectious, but its energy cannot surpass the 1980s disco original. *Music Week* called Kylie's cover an 'insipid hits-by-numbers recording', but the contagious 'whah hoo' chanting and palpable joy in Kylie's vocal performance still makes 'Celebration' one of her most cherishable singles. Originally recorded in 1991 for possible inclusion in the 'Let's Get to It' album, it was held back by PWL specifically for release as her final single.

The song was issued, with impeccable timing, just before the festive party season was in full flow but unfortunately was a chart casualty, probably since the original version was a standard party anthem anyway, and also because Kylie's remake had already been available on the mega-popular #1 'Greatest Hits' album, released some three months earlier. Much beefier was Harding and Curnow's 12" 'Have a Party Remix' or the more hard-edged, but misleadingly titled, 'Techno Rave Mix' of the song, which eventually emerged as a bonus track on Kylie's 1993 compilation album 'Non-Stop History 50+1'.

The 7" edit of the song works far better with the accompanying video, shot on location in Rio de Janeiro and showing Kylie whooping it up with fans during a street carnival and on the beach. None of the beaming extras in the promo were professional dancers, just enthusiastic locals whom director Greg Masuak had commandeered.

Although 'Celebration' charted at a disappointing #20 in the UK it still was a perfect choice for Kylie's final fling with PWL and it remains one of her all-time favourite songs. Undoubtedly, Kylie had helped PWL become a massive money-making business, but the company never really recovered from her departure, especially since UK sales of her singles alone had reached nearly three million copies. 'Kylie was the best artist I ever had in my studio from day one,' Pete Waterman confessed in a nostalgic interview with the *Daily Express* in 1996. 'She was absolutely brilliant.'

✻   ✻   ✻

'The Hit Factory was aptly named,' said Kylie many years after her departure from PWL. 'Their system is one truly to be admired and I now understand why they weren't so keen to indulge some of my fancies. It was where I cut my musical teeth and I'm thankful for the lessons I learned there. My first steps into the world of songwriting were tentative ones, but now I love the creative process. The fact that you start a session with nothing and end up with a kind of friend in a new song is so exciting and inspiring.'

Kylie's desire to be more creative and more in charge of her musical destiny became stronger the longer she remained with Pete Waterman. But after her contracted five-album deal (including the 'Greatest Hits' package) came to an end she felt she had to move on, try new styles of music and work with a different group of songwriters and producers. Kylie admits to initially panicking after she broke with PWL, although she knew she'd made the right decision. 'It was like finishing a marathon,' she joked.

Media interest in which label she would sign with was rife. Rumours abounded that Warner Bros and Sony were chasing her, so it came as a huge surprise in February 1993 when she announced a deal with deConstruction Records, a contemporary dance label owned by Keith Blackhurst and Keith Hadfield and home to M People, Black Box and K-Klass. 'We regard Kylie as a potential radical dance diva,' Hadfield helpfully told the press. 'She's not a trashy disco singer.' Whatever the view in London, over in Australia Kylie negotiated her future with Mushroom Records.

'Confide in Me'

Released August 1994 (UK)
Written by Steve Anderson and Dave Seaman
Produced by Brothers In Rhythm
Highest chart position #2 (UK), #1 (Australia)

Additional tracks: 'Nothing Can Stop Us' and 'If You Don't Love Me'
Video directed by Paul Boyd

KYLIE MINOGUE

Almost immediately after signing her new deals Kylie went into the recording studio and stayed there for the best part of a year, but something strange happened when Kylie moved to deConstruction. With a lower public profile and the extra kudos attached to signing to a trendy new independent label, Kylie suddenly became hip. In August that year she was even voted 'Coolest Woman in Music' by London's *Select* magazine, and this was before anybody had even heard what her new post-PWL material would sound like. In January 1994, after Kylie was introduced to celebrated American photographer Bert Stern by filmmaker Baz Luhrmann, she appeared in an unprecedented 21 pages of Australian *Vogue*, and by the summer she was gracing the front covers of *The Face* and *I-D*, both for the second time around.

Music industry insiders presumed that since Kylie had signed to a predominantly dance-orientated label, and had enjoyed her biggest critical successes with her quad of uptempo tunes from the 'Rhythm of Love' album, that she would return with a huge club sound. Her grandstanding appearance in front of nearly 20,000 hysterical fans at the Sydney Gay Mardi Gras in February 1994 had further indicated that uplifting house might be her new direction. 'I felt I owed it to them because they supported me years before anybody else did,' she said gratefully.

One of Kylie's favourite remixes from her PWL era was the Brothers In Rhythm revamp of 'Finer Feelings', not her biggest hit by any measure but a beautiful swirling piece of pop, nonetheless. Brothers In Rhythm had worked wonders for other artists including Pet Shop Boys and New Order, although they probably reached their pinnacle of perfection with a lush re-imagining of Heaven 17's classic 'Imagination', a hit second time around in November 1992. When Kylie had the opportunity to work with Steve Anderson and Dave Seaman, the real names behind the production duo, she jumped at the chance. 'When she first came into the studio her voice was the sound of PWL,' recalled Anderson. 'Throughout the course of recording the album she gained confidence in her vocals and she surprised herself with what she was able to do.'

Their first public collaboration was 'Confide in Me', released in late summer 1994 to a spellbound Kylie fanbase. Instead of a rapid-fire club monster, the song was a slow-burner full of sublimated strings, melancholic beats and manipulative vocals, ultimately revealing a darker, more eerie side to Kylie's pop persona. It is no exaggeration to say it is a truly epic production and, at nearly six minutes, easily Kylie's most dramatic performance to date. The song, coupled with Scottish director Paul Boyd's brilliantly innovative 'pop art' video, presents Kylie as more sinister than cuddly; at times she seems downright dangerous. It's clear that director and singer both pushed each other to their limits and when Kylie sings, 'Stick or twist, the choice is yours', it's obvious, too, that only Kylie is calling the shots. Persuasive to the point of creepiness, 'Confide in Me' is a brand of eccentric pop straight out of the Pet Shop Boys' theatre: moody, magnificent and absolutely unapologetic.

Even if die-hard Kylie fans weren't immediately won over by her intelligent new sound they still couldn't help but be blown away by the sheer lavishness of her single. In Australia, where Kylie's profile had been waning for some time during her latter PWL days, the public took to 'Confide in Me' en masse. The song shot to #1, remaining there for five solid weeks, eventually winning ARIA awards for 'Best Single' and 'Best Video'. Not only was it Australia's bestselling song of the year, it also became Kylie's biggest commercial single release of the entire 1990s – a fabulous achievement, but it was still only 1994. The next few years were going to be eventful to say the least.

'Kylie'
(promo book)

Published August 1994
Produced by deConstruction

One of the rarest pieces of Kylie memorabilia escaped almost by accident from the deConstruction publicity offices. *Kylie* is a strictly limited edition text-less publication made up of 32 A3-size pages slung together with ribbon-binding and presented in a matt black box. The book was initially printed for promotional use only, to be given away to record stations and journalists to stimulate the release of 'Confide in Me', but inevitably copies escaped into fans' hands. The racy photos by Katerina Jebb and Ellen von Unwerth are both colour and black-and-white, the front 'cover' showing a surprisingly elongated Kylie reclining on her double bed in just knickers and skimpy t-shirt, with a collage of vintage images on the wall behind her, including a still from the 'What Do I Have to Do' video. Other photos show Kylie in hotpants and laddered tights, and a bikini bottom and transparent top.

The obvious analogy was Madonna's controversial 1992 book *Sex*, a comparison she was quick to refute. 'It would be incredibly foolish of me to try and copy Madonna,' Kylie angrily told the press. 'I'm just trying to find out who I am; that was the idea of putting the book together. I saw a recent picture of Janet Jackson and there's a man holding her breasts on the cover of one of her records, for heaven's sake. She's discovering her sexuality, and so am I.'

THE KYLIE BIBLE

'The Kylie Bible' (promo book)

Published September 1994
Another Publishers Ltd for deConstruction

The now-famed, and extremely collectable, *Kylie Bible* is a 16-page, A4 size, staple-bound collection of alluring photographs taken by John Rankin. The publication was given away as a freebie with the September 1994 issue of legendary British style magazine *Dazed and Confused*. In its one full page of handwritten text Kylie likens her new musical journey to a treacherous drive up a hill. From the summit Kylie can see whatever is coming: 'What lays before me is beautiful, dangerous, breathtaking, seductive, challenging and inspiring...' *The Kylie Bible* was produced as a way of promoting the forthcoming UK release of her debut deConstruction album, in shops from 19 September 1994. Such was the mini-magazine's reputation that 12 years later the belated *Kylie Bible II* was released as an added extra in the tour programmes for *Showgirl Homecoming*.

'Kylie Minogue'

Released September 1994 (UK)
deConstruction / Mushroom Records
Produced by Brothers In Rhythm (tracks 1, 4, 6 and 7), Gerry Deveux (track 2),

Jimmy Harry (tracks 3 and 5), Pete Heller and Terry Farley (tracks 8 and 9) and M People (track 10)
Highest chart position #4 (UK), #2 (Australia)

Track listing:
'Confide in Me'
'Surrender'
'If I Was Your Lover'
'Where is the Feeling?'
'Put Yourself in My Place'
'Dangerous Game'
'Automatic Love'
'Where Has the Love Gone?'
'Falling'
'Time Will Pass You By'
Bonus tracks: 'Love is Waiting' and 'Nothing Can Stop Us' (Japan), 'Confide in Me' (Franglais version) (Canada)

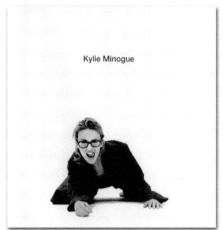

Kylie Minogue

You can almost hear the tingle of excitement in Kylie's voice on her first deConstruction album; her eagerness to please, surprise, and to blow away the PWL cobwebs. Quickly out of sparkly hotpants into something a little more serious, the cover image even transforms Kylie into a bespectacled, power-suited executive, albeit one with a cheeky tongue. In a bid to relaunch herself the album dispenses with any clever names, preferring to keep it simple. 'Kylie Minogue' is the collection, the new sound and the re-energised artist.

Not that the recording of the album always ran so smoothly. Kylie began work in 1993, initially laying down a couple of songs with English indie band Saint Etienne ('Nothing Can Stop Us' became the B-side to 'Confide in Me') and several more with remix whizzkids, the Rapino Brothers. But these were put to one side in favour of a new set of sessions with Brothers In Rhythm, and a few other notables, in the driving seat.

The result is a cool, sophisticated collection with Kylie's voice given the opportunity to shine among a sweet assortment of lightweight funk grooves ('Surrender' and 'If I Was Your Lover') and smoochy ballads. Among the latter, 'Dangerous Game' is a painfully beautiful diary entry written by a broken heart ('I'm so alone, I feel so lonely...') and elegantly produced by Brothers In Rhythm, arguably the masterminds behind the album's finest moments, including 'Confide in Me'. The sheer scale of that first single's dramatic sweep tends to overshadow proceedings and there's nothing else on the album which comes close to its epic quality, although Jimmy Harry's comely 'Put Yourself in My Place' matches it for chic refinement.

Elsewhere the uplifting 'Where is the Feeling?' is full of funky beats, tinkly piano and soulful strings, making it a natural successor to 1992's 'Too Much of a Good Thing'. Unfortunately, the Pet Shop Boys-penned 'Falling' is surprisingly minimal; Neil Tennant subsequently complained that he was very disappointed with Heller and Farley's overbearing deep house production, which was at odds with their vision of the song as 'old Stock Aitken Waterman Kylie'. Understandably, however, this was something Kylie was trying to escape from.

The album concludes with the predictable clap-happy soul of the M People-produced 'Time Will Pass You By', but overall Kylie's self-titled album is perhaps the most congruoent collection of her career thus far and an impressive debut on deConstruction. As David Sinclair summed up in the *Times*, 'It is an album which successfully scrapes the pop fluff off her shoes and heralds a new maturity in her work.'

In 2003 'Kylie Minogue' was reissued with a bonus disc of 14 additional tracks, mainly remixes, but also including an acoustic version of Kylie's cover of Prefab Sprout's classic 'If You Don't Love Me' and the sought-after 'Franglais Version' of 'Confide in Me'.

The Vicar of Dibley

Season 1, Episode 3 'Community Spirit'

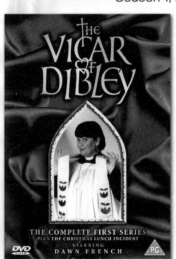

BBC TV / A Tiger Aspect Production / 30 minutes / Episode broadcast (UK) 24 November 1994

Created by Richard Curtis / Written by Richard Curtis and Paul Mayhew-Archer / Directed by Dewi Humphreys / Produced by Jon Plowman / Theme Tune composed by Howard Goodall

Starring: Dawn French (*Revd Geraldine Grainger*), Gary Waldhorn (*David Horton*), James Fleet (*Hugo Horton*), Emma Chambers (*Alice Tinker*), Roger Lloyd Pack (*Owen Newitt*), Trevor Peacock (*Jim Trott*), John Bluthal (*Frank Pickle*), Liz Smith (*Letitia Cropley*), Philip Whitchurch (*Reg Dwight*) with Kylie as *herself*

The last time Kylie was this close to a vicar on TV it was her wedding day to Jason Donovan in 1987, but this time she's in church for a completely different reason. While Jennifer Saunders was enjoying huge critical

success with her BBC1 sitcom *Absolutely Fabulous*, her TV comedy
partner Dawn French was on the lookout for a new starring vehicle of
her own. When Richard Curtis (the co-creator of *Blackadder* and *Mr
Bean*) offered her the lead role in his new sitcom *The Vicar of Dibley*
Dawn saw a new opportunity for laughs. The show proved a huge hit for
primetime BBC1, with up to 12 million viewers per episode.

Episode #3 of the first season has the locals organising their annual
village fayre and the Revd Geraldine (French) suggesting they secure
the services of a celebrity to open the event. When the Beverley Sisters
turn down the gig Geraldine turns to her faithful verger's second cousin
Reg Dwight (aka Elton John). But when a lanky, bald Brummie turns up
they realise it's the wrong Reg Dwight. Cue Kylie to save the day.

Playing a close approximation of herself, Kylie shows up
unexpectedly at the vicarage, dressed casually in blouse and jeans,
looking for Elton. 'I'm sorry to interrupt,' she says sweetly. 'Has Elton
arrived? I'd heard he was opening the fayre, so I thought I'd drop
by and surprise him!' Embracing Dibley's favourite Antipodean pop
star to her voluptuous breast, Geraldine promises her the best seat in
Heaven if she can fill Elton's glittery shoes, which naturally, she does.
Embarrassingly though, Kylie is introduced to the spellbound villagers
beneath a banner proclaiming 'Dibley Welcomes Elton John'. 'We are
so lucky, lucky, lucky, lucky to have with us the genuinely perfect ... the
one and only ... Kylie Minogue!' says the vicar.

The fayre eventually raises £3,456 and gauche Hugo (James Fleet)
gets a kiss from Kylie herself when he wins top prize for 'Most
Misshapen Vegetable'. This may well be the only time Kylie appeared in
a storyline with phallic cucumbers and marrows, but it wasn't to be her
only brush with saucy situation comedy.

✻ ✻ ✻

By the time Kylie had released her first material with deConstruction
the label had already been gobbled up by the multinational BMG, home
to Whitney Houston, Celine Dion and Rod Stewart, but the new-look
Kylie certainly wasn't going to fall into line with her middle-of-the-
road stablemates. During her 1993-94 sabbatical, the tabloids, both
in the UK and Australia, had predicted Kylie might collaborate with
unpredictable Grammy Award-winning American singer Prince.

Kylie had admired him since she'd been a teenager, first seeing him
on his *Lovesexy* tour in London in 1989. 'I'm a die-hard Prince fan,' she
beamed. Many years later the two singers had met quite accidentally

when they discovered they shared the same security people. After Kylie went backstage at one of his mid-1990s gigs they struck up a friendship and Kylie was invited to Prince's Paisley Park studios in Minneapolis. Previously Kylie had joked to journalists that she thought Prince was 'Sex on a stick!' So the cheeky newspapers immediately supposed that the two pop stars would become 'instant lovers'.

Kylie was having none of it. 'He is famous for being fresh,' she told *The Face*, 'but who wants to be on that list?' Responding to rumours that they got *very* close Kylie later cheekily said, 'Maybe it was the slow dance which caused a bit of a stir. I said, "Look, I'm meant to be the one with the flashy moves on the dancefloor, OK?" It was a good night out!' The artists did jam together on a half-finished song Kylie had written called 'Baby Doll' but it never saw the light of day. On her return to London Kylie was happy to scotch any further romantic rumours. 'He's a very *nice* guy,' she told DJ Steve Wright, choosing her words carefully. 'He's suitably odd. If he wasn't a little bit odd I'd have been very disappointed.'

'Put Yourself in My Place'

Released November 1994 (UK)
Written and Produced by Jimmy Harry
Highest chart position #11 (UK), #11 (Australia)

Flipside: 'Put Yourself in My Place' (Dan's Quite Storm Mix)
Video directed by Keir McFarlane

With 'Confide in Me' still riding high in the charts and raising eyebrows in the music press, Kylie's next single release came out barely eight weeks later. Arguably a more soothing song than its predecessor, 'Put Yourself in My Place' was skilfully written and produced by American Jimmy Harry, up to that point most famous for co-penning RuPaul's outrageous 1993 single 'Supermodel (You Better Work)'. The beautiful song Harry created for Kylie couldn't have been more different from the camp frivolities of his previous international success. The grieving lyrics tell the story of how Kylie's lover walked out of her life and immediately found another girlfriend. All Kylie can do is look on and remind her ex-partner that he might be broken-hearted himself one day. It could almost be the story of Michael Hutchence deserting Kylie for his affair with Danish supermodel Helena Christensen.

The song was recorded in New York and is one of the most deliciously dreamy cuts to emerge from Kylie's entire deConstruction period. The aural equivalent of melted white chocolate, the song oozes opulence, its luxuriant lazy beat cleverly disguised by smooth ambient strings, throbbing vocals and a hint of Spanish guitar.

The infamous video, directed by Kier McFarlane, has Kylie recreating the opening sequence of the cult 1968 Jane Fonda movie *Barbarella*, in which she slowly strips off her clothes in a state of weightlessness. The promo was Kylie's most expensive to date, featuring an elaborate space-age set, a specially designed costume and exterior shots of a phallic, twirling spaceship being propelled through a pulsating red solar system. The sight of Kylie peeling off her space suit proved to be too saucy for some kids' TV shows and the video was either heavily edited or banned from several daytime broadcasts. However, it became a favourite of MTV and went on to win an ARIA for 'Best Video' in Australia in 1995.

The flawless mix of superlative song and divine video has made 'Put Yourself in My Place' an all-time Kylie classic. The favourite down-tempo moment of Kylie's career, it is, quite simply, faultless.

Street Fighter

1994 / A Capcom Entertainment Production / USA / 102 minutes / cert 'M' (Australia) cert '12' (UK) / Opened December 1994 (USA)

Directed and Written by Steven de Souza / Produced by Edward R Pressman and Kenzo Tsujimoto / Cinematography by William A Fraker / Original Music composed by Graeme Revell

Cast: Jean-Claude Van Damme (*Colonel William Guile*), Raul Julia (*General Bison*), Kylie Minogue (*Lieutenant Cammy*), Ming-Na Wen (*Chun-Li Zang*), Wes Studi (*Victor Sagat*), Simon Callow (*A N Official*), Roshan Seth (*Doctor Dhalsim*), Damian Chapa (*Ken Masters*), Byron Mann (*Ryu Hoshi*), Grand Bush (*Balrog*), Jay Tavare (*Vega*), Andrew Bryniarski (*Zangrief*), Peter Navy Tuiansosopo (*E. Honda*), Gregg Rainwater (*T Hawk*), Miguel Nunez Jnr (*Dee Jay*), Robert Mammone (*Carlos Blanka*), Joe Bugner (*torturer*)

Four years after the mixed reception given *The Delinquents*, and following a virtually unbroken run of international hit singles and albums, it was a peculiar choice that

The world's most unlikely secret agent

persuaded Kylie back to the big screen.

In 1994 Kylie was asked which movie she most admired. Without hesitation she cited *Women on the Verge of a Nervous Breakdown*, the 1988 cult classic by Spanish director Pedro Almodóvar. 'As far as directors are concerned I love Pedro,' she told the interviewer. 'I like the way his women are so lunatic. We all are at times!' She then made a direct plea to camera: 'Pedro, where are you? Give me some freaked-out role!' Unfortunately for Kylie, Pedro obviously wasn't watching. Instead Kylie signed a contract for *Street Fighter*, playing a super-charged ass-kicking British Intelligence Officer, Lt Cammy, assigned to help remove a megalomaniac dictator from an obscure East Asian country.

Offbeat European arthouse this ain't! Making no bones about it, *Street Fighter* really isn't very good. The alarm bells should have started ringing for Kylie when she was told the film was based on a kids' video game. Had she never watched the movie spin-off of *Super Mario Bros*?

The original Street Fighter was invented in Japan in 1987 by Capcom, one of the world's first companies specialising in arcade entertainment, and was followed in 1991 by Street Fighter II; it is this updated version on which the movie is based (hence the film sometimes being erroneously credited as *Street Fighter II*). Street Fighter obsessives nattered endlessly over the origins of their favourite characters but the game's female characters were not too well-rounded; Cammy, for example, was said merely to be expert in 'assassination techniques' and was fond of green leotards. That, sadly, must have been enough back-story for Kylie to accept the part, although Cammy's trademark green was eventually replaced with blue.

Street Fighter was turned into an animated Japanese movie in 1994, quickly followed by the live-action version, shot entirely on location in Thailand, Vancouver and the Gold Coast of Australia. Trying to turn an arcade game into a successful big screen movie is no simple task. The movie took elements from all the versions of the Street Fighter games, and attempted to weave them into some sort of coherent plot. 'I especially love films like *The Longest Day*, *The Great Escape* and *The Guns of Navarone*,' explained director Steven de Souza. 'What made those films great wasn't the random violence. It was the clear-cut struggle between forces of good and evil, leading to an ultimate showdown.' Certainly the film's violence is more childish than sadistic, but as to whether *Street Fighter* is up there with *The Guns of Navarone* is highly debatable.

The movie was designed as a vehicle for Belgian-born actor and martial artist Jean-Claude Van Damme, whose impressive physique had earned him the tabloid nickname 'The muscles from Brussels'. In *Street Fighter* the brawn from Benelux takes the lead role of Colonel Guile, but his blonde spikes are replaced by a sensible short back-and-sides obscured by a blue beret. Van Damme leads his troop of crack commandos from the 'Allied Nations' to the Asian port of Shadaloo (located somewhere in Burma, to judge from the map), where 63 terrified aid workers are being held hostage by psychotic bug-eyed dictator General Bison, played with undisguised glee by Puerto Rican actor Raul Julia. Bison is demanding $20 billion for their safe release or he'll shoot them all and, most probably, take over the entire globe, as all self-respecting megalomaniacs want to do. 'Peace will reign in the world,' he roars, 'and all humanity will bow to me in humble gratitude!'

Julia has all the best lines in the film ('Take them to the interrogation room. They will talk or they will die. Preferably both'), but he looks gaunt and ill throughout; tragically he was suffering from stomach cancer and died before *Street Fighter* was released. Even in poor health Julia still manages to have more fun than the rest of the cast put together, swishing his big leather cape around his subterranean base, barking orders to his storm troopers and devising a plan to kidnap the Queen of England. Thankfully, even 50 per cent of Raul Julia goes a long, long way and you can't help but cheer his baddie in preference to Van Damme's anodyne hero.

Aside from Simon Callow, most of the international, multi-cultural cast have some difficultly twisting their tongues around English vowels. Van Damme plays an English-American (he sports a stars and stripes tattoo on his shoulder to prove it), but much of his dialogue is unintelligible – 'You sun uf a betch' – so he's far better when his fists do the talking, notably in the movie's climax where he enjoys a colossal dust-up with General Bison, who then dies and promptly comes back to life with lightning-firing gloves and levitating boots. Presumably some of *Street Fighter* was played for laughs, but unfortunately it's not very funny. There are plenty of unintentional chuckles throughout, particularly the scene where Van Damme drives his crappy, plastic Thunderbirds boat up the river while listening to Euro-pop on the stereo and Kylie makes cow-eyes at him.

Poor Kylie is saddled with one of the biggest dud roles of her career as Lieutenant Cammy, who in between her karate chops and high-kicks is secretly in love with her muscle-bound commander-in-chief. From Kylie's very first scene, where she thrusts a colossal Sumo wrestler out of the back of a van, it's quite obvious that her character is no gentle wallflower. In fact, Kylie spent weeks training to get into shape for the role and worked closely with the film's stunt crew to make her physical. Naturally, it's hysterical seeing petite, pretty Kylie battering hoards of marauding thugs, but when she lets down her silly pigtails and dons her leotard it seems nobody can stop this 5ft ¼" dynamo.

Fans may have been surprised to see their pop heroine handling pistols and rocket launchers, but it was her acting which generated most criticism from the press. *Street Fighter* was released in the US in December 1994, generating almost universal scorn from the critics, much of it aimed rather unfairly at Kylie. Bitchy Richard Harrington, film critic of the *Washington Post*, dubbed Kylie 'the worst actress in the English-speaking world', which was a little extreme.

It can't have been easy for Kylie delivering excruciating dialogue like 'Stealth mode compromised, sir. We're busted!' But she can hardly be held responsible for the complete commercial failure of *Street Fighter*. The movie, envisaged as the first in a series, bombed in all territories. When it was released in Europe in the spring of 1995 continental audiences had been forewarned about how horrible it was and as a result they stayed away in droves. British reviewers were, rightly, more scathing about Van Damme ('His dismal comic timing makes Frank Bruno look like Jack Benny,' wrote the *Daily Mail*). But it was the *Guardian*'s Derek Malcolm who had the last word: 'Kylie Minogue fortunately does not sing. She doesn't act much either. Steven de Souza, the director, has fashioned a totally predictable piece of slam-bang dross.'

After the mixed commercial fortunes of her most recent album on deConstruction, *Street Fighter* also failed to provide the high-profile comeback Kylie had hoped for. Years later she voiced her disappointment with the movie. 'I should have learned my lesson by now,' she said. 'I tried combining music and acting a while ago and was lured to Hollywood to make an action film and was left totally uninspired by that ... It seemed like a good idea at the time,' she added. 'Don't ask me why. Now it just makes me cringe when I think about it.'

'Where is the Feeling?'

Released July 1995 (UK)
Written by Wilf Smarties and Jayn Hanna
Produced and Remixed by Brothers In Rhythm
Highest chart position #16 (UK), #31 (Australia)

Flipside: 'Where is the Feeling?' (Bish Bosh Mix)
Video directed by Keir McFarlane

Kylie's third single on the deConstruction label arrived nearly eight months after her last offering and suffered as a result. Busy filming the unfortunate *Bio-Dome* in America, Kylie had temporarily put her music to one side and by the time she returned to the UK to promote a re-recorded 'Where is the Feeling?' it seriously seemed like fans had lost interest.

The soulful album track – a cover version of a minor underground club hit for the group Within a Dream in early 1993 – was reworked beyond recognition into a downbeat dance tune with breathily talkative vocals (similar in style to Madonna's 'Justify My Love') layered over deep ambient beats and Brothers In Rhythm's trademark laid-back piano. Brave, yes, but hardly commercial and almost avant-garde by Kylie's standards, the single had few admirers on British or Australian radio, underperforming on both sides of the world. The sensual lyrics echo the sentiment of her 1991 single 'Finer Feelings' when Kylie sings, 'There's nobody better; better than you ... but where is the feeling?' But whereas the happy-go-lucky seven-minute album version made you want to get up and dance, the single remix just made you want to lock yourself away in a darkened room and burst into tears.

Much better was New York DJ David Morales' stomping radio-friendly remix and Brothers In Rhythm's very own 'Bish Bosh Mix';

obviously sensing a misfire on their hands, deConstruction promoted the song in this latter version. On BBC1's short-lived Saturday teatime *Steve Wright People Show* and Channel 4's *Don't Forget Your Toothbrush* it is the poppier mix of 'Where is the Feeling?' which Kylie performs to live audiences. It is perhaps interesting to note that the single had originally been scheduled for a spring 1995 release and the music press had already been sent promos of Felix da Housecat's even less accessible, minimalist remixes by April that year. 'Where is the Feeling?' certainly has its supporters who appreciate Kylie needed to take risks with her music, but for many the single is one of the weakest moments of her career.

Hayride to Hell

1995 / A Flat Rock Pictures Production / Australia / 11 minutes

Directed by Kimble Rendell / Written by Kimble Rendell and Phil Roope / Produced by Victoria Treole / Cinematography by Peter Menzies Jnr / Original Music composed by Dave Faulkner

Cast: Kylie Minogue (*The Girl*), Richard Roxburgh (*George Weygate*), Victoria Langley (*Hilary Weygate*), Chloe Angel and Ellie MacCarthy (*Weygate children*), Patsy Flanagan (*Buelgie woman*), Daphne King (*neighbour*), Iris Shand (*old woman*), Ross Sharp and Scott Love (*detectives*)

Hayride to Hell was the brainchild of Kimble Rendell, a former director of TV commercials and pop promos, notably for Australian rock group The Hoodoo Gurus, of whom he was a founder member. Admired for his distinctive directing style and fearless editing, Rendell asked Kylie whether she would accept the leading role in his first foray into movie-making, albeit a short film. After the critical pasting she had received over *Street Fighter*, Kylie was more than pleased to be involved in a lower-profile production, particularly one being shot on home ground.

Without the constraints and pressure of a multi-million dollar Hollywood picture hanging over her, Kylie gives a more self-assured (and surprisingly scary) performance than anything she had done previously. Definitely her most adult-orientated role to date, she even raised eyebrows by swearing for the first time on film.

In a nutshell: kindly family man George Weygate (brilliantly played by handsome Oz actor Richard Roxburgh) is driving home from work one evening when a crazy-looking girl (Kylie), in neat black dress and high heels, suddenly materialises in front of his car, claiming she is suffering from a serious diabetic seizure. She demands that he immediately take her to a block of flats in the Darlinghurst district of Sydney. The driver complies, while his new companion slumps into the passenger seat dribbling saliva down her face. When they reach their destination the girl flees the vehicle, but Weygate realises she has left her handbag behind. Pursuing her on foot, he finds her gloomy, dilapidated apartment, but is mysteriously locked inside with no obvious way to escape. Terrified he stands on the balcony and screams for help, but to no avail. 'What is going on?' he pleads. 'What the hell is going on?'

In desperation he is forced to escape by climbing down the side of the building, losing a shoe in the process. Swinging into the comparative safety of another flat he unexpectedly suffers an unprovoked attacked by a group of cackling, geriatric residents brandishing golf clubs and a yappy Jack Russell dog. Weygate eventually discovers the girl slumped on the floor of the block's elevator but, refusing his help, she screams back at him: 'What the fuck have you done with my things? Where are my things, you shit?' Arms and legs frantically spinning round like a windmill's sails, the girl launches a ferocious attack on her good Samaritan. Somehow, bewildered Weygate manages to escape from her clutches ('You're fucking crazy!'), but is his terrifying experience really all that it seems?

The film's final twist asks more questions than answers. As Weygate reports the attack to the police over the telephone, Kylie, flanked by two detectives, turns up on his doorstep and upsets his blissful suburban life. Who really assaulted who? Is Weygate a kerb-crawler and the girl a drug-addled prostitute? Is the accuser really the accused?

Rendell's film is a beguilingly creepy little arthouse gem, set to Dave Faulkner's disconcerting fairground-style music and featuring a demented central performance from a liberated Kylie who has really been allowed free rein to go totally bonkers. Kylie is genuinely mesmerising throughout, helped no doubt by the fact that the actress claimed to have 'adopted' her character's psychotic behaviour for the week of filming so she could be as convincing as possible!

Hayride to Hell – inspired by The Hoodoo Gurus' 1985 song of the same name – garnered superb notices when it was screened at film festivals throughout Australia, before appearing on Channel 4 television in the UK in 1996, its late-night slot precluding those viewers easily offended by excessive swearing and saliva.

NICK CAVE AND THE BAD SEEDS + KYLIE MINOGUE Where The Wild Roses Grow

'Where the Wild Roses Grow'

Released October 1995 (UK)
Written by Nick Cave
Produced by Nick Cave and the Bad Seeds with
Tony Cohen and Victor Van Vugt
Highest chart position #11 (UK), #2 (Australia)

Additional tracks: (performed by Nick Cave)
'Ballad of Robert Moore and Betty Coltrane' and
'The Willow Garden'
Video directed by Rocky Schenck

A song in which Australia's Prince of Darkness bashes the world's favourite pop princess over the head with a rock and then sings to her corpse while it's floating in water might not be everybody's cup of tea, but 'Where the Wild Roses Grow' nevertheless became one of the most unpredictable successes of Kylie's career.

Nick Cave is a writer and musician, originally from Victoria, who established a fanatical cult following throughout the 1980s and 90s. With his most famous band, The Bad Seeds, Cave perfected his own peculiar brand of mausoleum rock packed with finely detailed, and often disturbing, lyrics. The group's eerily poetic sound coupled with Cave's undertaker voice (not dissimilar to that of Joy Division's late frontman Ian Curtis) and his uncompromisingly scary Herman Munster looks, made them Gothic superstars. During the mid-1990s Cave based himself in London and enjoyed his biggest international success with the 1994 album 'Let Love In'. His next project was even more magnificently morbid – a collection of chilling songs entitled 'Murder Ballads'. 'I've always enjoyed writing songs about dead women,' he quipped.

Kylie was invited to duet with Cave on 'Where the Wild Roses Grow', the album's debut single, released worldwide in October 1995. 'If I Was Your Lover' and the M People-produced 'Time Will Pass You By' had previously been earmarked as further singles from Kylie's eponymous deConstruction album, but were waived in favour of her fruitful collaboration with the Bad Seeds. The song recounts how Cave's character falls dangerously in love with a girl named Elisa Day (Kylie). She is quite receptive to his romantic attentions and he visits her home

Kylie arriving for the première of *Muriel's Wedding*, March 1995

Nick Cave duets with
Kylie at London's Brixton
Academy, 1996

Kylie faces a barrage of photographers at the London launch of her second deConstruction album. Tower Records, March 1998

Limited edition lenticular artwork for 'Impossible Princess'

Australian DVD sleeve for *Intimate and Live*

VOGUE

JUNE
£3.20

ROMANCE
AND
REVOLUTION
THE TWO LOOKS
OF SUMMER

WHO
MAKES
LONDON
GLAMOROUS?

THE NEW
CHIC GYMS

KYLIE
MINOGUE
POP VENUS

FROZEN
EMBRYOS
MIRACLE OR
MADNESS?

THE PERFECT MINISKIRT

GQ

July 2000 £3.00

David Beckham
Scott Walker
Boris Johnson
Jason Barlow

Charlize Theron
She's the new Cameron Diaz!

Tom Ford
is Gucci-fabulous

Kylie
At your service!

Kylie Minogue
photographed for GQ
by Terry Richardson

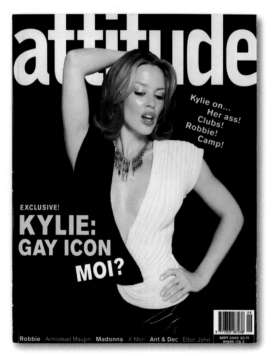

attitude

Kylie on...
Her ass!
Clubs!
Robbie!
Camp!

EXCLUSIVE!
KYLIE:
GAY ICON
MOI?

Robbie Armistead Maupin Madonna X Men Ant & Dec Elton John

SEPT 2000 £2.75
WHERE IT'S

TimeOut

London's living guide
October 3-10 2001
WIN A snowboarding holiday

Carry on
Kylie!

'I feel most
free when
I'm camping'

PROPERTY
SPECIAL
Five areas where you
can still afford to live
Six househunters
tell their tales
The gen on part rent,
part buy schemes
How to sweet talk
your estate agent

Music
Stockhausen, the
godfather of electronica

Film
Reporting from the San
Sebastian Film Festival

Theatre
Ian Holm's 'Homecoming'

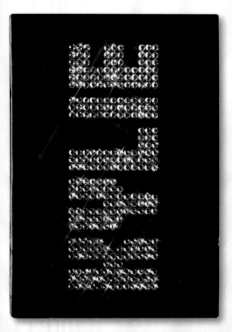

Programme for the *On a Night Like This* tour, 2001

'Spinning Around' heralds Kylie's comeback, 2000

Flirting with Kermit in *An Audience with Kylie Minogue*

Kylie performing at the Smash Hits Poll Winners' Party, March 2002

Making a spectacular entrance
at the 2002 BRIT Awards

KYLIE
GREATEST HITS

CONTAINING THE VIDEOS TO KYLIE'S 20 TOP 20 HITS INCLUDING 4 #1's
ALL TOGETHER FOR THE FIRST TIME. ALSO CONTAINS EXCLUSIVE BONUS FOOTAGE

2002's 'Greatest Hits' – with somebody else's body!

KYLIE
la la la

Kylie La La La paperback

Singing at the Monte Carlo Music Awards, 2002

three times. On his second visit he brings her a single red rose, but since all 'beauty must die' he then takes her to the river and horrifically caves in her head with a sharp rock.

Hearing Kylie singing her vocals from the point of view of a dead woman is a startling concept, although not entirely palatable. She reveals the most fragile vocal performance of her career, her voice almost cracking with tender emotion, but the ghoulish theme of the song was not to everyone's taste. Even so, the song won over the harshest of Kylie's critics in the alternative music press. One journalist called the track a 'perfect love song', which is perhaps slightly overstating things considering Cave's lyrics celebrate the obsessions of a psychotic necrophile. Cave has been vaunted as the Leonard Cohen of his generation, but at times his poetic aspirations have been called into question. Kylie's opening verse in 'Where the Wild Roses Grow' is a case in point. 'They call me the Wild Rose. But my name was Elisa Day,' she sings. 'Why they call me it I do not know.' For those 'I Should Be So Lucky'-bashers out there it could be argued that Cave's flat childish lyrics were no more banal than the best Pete Waterman had to offer a decade earlier.

The video has Kylie portrayed as a cold clammy corpse lying on a riverbank, like Hamlet's drowned Ophelia as painted by Millais – glassy-eyed, singing to herself as a snake slithers over her pale, lifeless body. A lethargic Kylie, being groped by a creepy Cave, seemed to appeal to an audience not usually won over by the singer's poppier charms. 'Where the Wild Roses Grow' became a mainstay of MTV and a huge international chart hit, peaking at #2 in Australia and crashing into the Top 20 throughout Europe. The biggest commercial success of Cave's career, the song was named 'Single of the Year' at the 1996 Australian ARIA Awards.

*   *   *

On the 'Murder Ballads' album Kylie also contributed vocals to Nick Cave's cover version of Bob Dylan's 'Death is Not the End' alongside P J Harvey, Anita Lane and Shane McGowan. Thankfully she was not asked to sing on Cave's later album 'Abattoir Blues', but he did persuade her to perform a reading of the 'I Should Be So Lucky' lyrics at the 1996 Poetry Olympics at London's Albert Hall, as if it were serious verse. 'I wasn't going to do it,' she admitted. 'I turned up in my tracksuit with no make-up on, so I was stripped of all the securities of a performer. Being on stage was a cathartic experience. It was like meeting the girl

I'd been ten years before. I had to confront her and say: "Yes, you've embarrassed me a bit, but without you, I wouldn't be here today."'

Kylie's impromptu performance shocked everybody and SAW's simple words, delivered with a wry smile, became a watershed in Kylie's career. For the first time since leaving PWL she was able to look back on her past and actually enjoy it. 'The crowd response was amazing; they laughed with me, not at me,' she recalled later. 'It was a real relief. I came to embrace and be proud of the past and the history that I'd been trying so hard to run away from, and stopped trying to be something I'm not.'

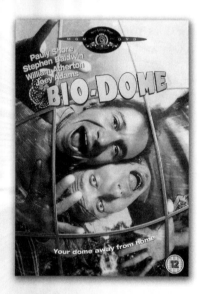

Bio-Dome

1996 / A Three Arts Production / USA / 88 minutes / cert 'M' (Australia) cert '12' (UK) / Opened January 1996 (USA)

Directed by Jason Bloom / Written by Kip Koenig and Scott Marcano / Produced by Bradley Jenkel, Brad Krevoy and Steven Stabler / Cinematography by Phedon Papamichael / Original Music composed by Andrew Gross and Steven Poltz

Cast: Pauly Shore (Bud Macintosh), Stephen Baldwin (Doyle Johnson), William Atherton (Dr Noah Faulkner), Joey Adams (Monique), Teresa Hill (Jenny), Kylie Minogue (Dr Petra von Kant), Dara Tomanovich (Mimi Simkins), Denise Dowse (Olivia Biggs), Kevin West (T C Romulus), Henry Gibson (William Leakey), Patricia Hearst (Doyle's mother), Roger Clinton (Professor Bloom)

Everybody is permitted to make a few mistakes occasionally. Reflecting on an all-time low in her professional life, Kylie has subsequently had the good humour to call *Bio-Dome* her 'very worst career move.' It is a film without a single redeeming feature, a picture so horrible that Kylie admitted in 2002 that 'I can't bring myself to watch it. I hope I never see it.' Universally derided by critics and shunned by the public, the film was even loathed by Kylie's usually extremely supportive family. 'With parents, when you do something not so great they usually say they loved it,' explained Kylie. 'Well, my dad said, "I can't believe you did that film. It was diabolical."'

You have to agree with his paternal feelings. The film is a stinker of the foulest kind. It's easy to argue that Kylie obviously wasn't well-advised in her latest foray into movies, but in a film characterised by such an appalling script, pedestrian direction and heart-stoppingly bad central performances, even an actress as good as Meryl Streep wouldn't have got out of this one alive.

The blame for *Bio-Dome*'s now legendary cataclysmic failure lies squarely at the door of its main 'star'. The film was built as a showcase for American comedian, and former MTV presenter, Pauly Shore, a performer so talentless and loathsome that even his comedy series *Pauly* was cancelled by the Fox Network after just one episode, having scored the lowest ratings of any US programme at that time. Nicknamed 'the weasel' for reasons too obvious to explain, Shore became something of a cult figure in the early 1990s after the critically panned but commercially successful *Encino Man* (UK title: *California Man*, 1992), about two grungy college kids who discover a caveman frozen in a block of ice in their backyard. Hated by the critics and loathed by anybody over 15, Shore continued to trot out under-performing movies before mercifully committing professional suicide in *Bio-Dome*, one of the biggest wastes of celluloid ever to come out of Hollywood.

Shore plays Bud Mcintosh, yet another of his deadbeat characterisations, a camp, giggling social outcast who lives in a disgusting apartment with his lifelong best buddy Doyle Johnson (Stephen Baldwin), a dreadlocked, gonad-scratching fool who is Butthead to Shore's Beavis, gurning and twitching through a virtually unwatchable series of pathetic, crude charades where everything is 'really cool'. Somehow our two anti-heroes end up trapped in the 'first space station on Earth' – a supposedly huge glasshouse in the middle of the Arizona desert where 'unique' environmental experiments take place. The Bio-Dome itself looks more like a B & Q garden centre than a multi-million dollar eco-research facility, not surprisingly since the film was shot on location at a water purification plant in Van Nuys, California.

Unable to escape, the two idiots face 364 days under glass with only the company of five bright botanists led by the neurotic Dr Noah Faulkner (a scary William Atherton). Kylie gets lost among the foliage in an instantly forgettable role as English scientist Petra Von Kant, whose speciality is cultivating root vegetables. Amazingly, Von Kant and her glamorous colleague Mimi (Tara Tomanovich) fall for the boys' hackneyed chat-up lines ('Did it hurt when you fell from Heaven?') and start flirting with them. Seeing Kylie sucking on a root vegetable and purring 'A carrot is a miracle' and then passionately snogging Shore while he paws at her hot pants are images no die-hard Minogue fan expects, or wants, to see. No wonder her father wanted to walk out of the cinema after watching this crap.

Looking at *Bio-Dome* you might care to imagine that you can actually see the regret written all over Kylie's face, but in an unpalatable twist the off-screen story was even worse. Several years later, in an American interview, ferret-faced Shore revealed that he had a 'steamy, six-month fling' with Kylie after finishing the movie. 'I fell in love with her big time,' he explained. 'I didn't know who she was and she didn't know who I was, but we just had a great time together'. One can just hope this is a figment of Shore's fervid imagination. Surely, please, Kylie had better taste than this?

A single highlight among the witless dross of *Bio-Dome* is a brief turn by a young Jack Black as one-half of the then-unknown Tenacious D, singing eco-tune 'We Just Wanna Save the Trees'. Unsurprisingly, throughout the US and Europe *Bio-Dome* bombed big time at the box-office. In Britain the *Mirror* advised it was a 'film to avoid like the plague' while the *Observer* was more succinct, calling it 'unbelievably awful'. Shore famously won the 'Worst Actor' gong at the 1996 Golden Raspberry Awards (he also walked away with it the year before) and it quite rightly finished his career as a leading man.

Vilified in the press at the time, *Bio-Dome* has since provided a bench-mark for appalling movies. In the film's nauseating script Shore's character is described as 'a symbol of everything that is wrong with this world'. More accurately *Bio-Dome* is a symbol of everything that is wrong with Hollywood; it is a complete and utter waste of time and squanders every last cent of its $15,000,000 budget. Even for a Kylie obsessive this is one performance to be avoided at all costs.

Men Behaving Badly

'Comic Relief Special
– Men Behaving Very Badly Indeed'

BBC TV / A Hartswood Film Production / 10 minutes / Episode first broadcast (UK) 14 March 1997

Created and Written by Simon Nye / Directed by Martin Dennis / Produced by Beryl Vertue

Starring: Martin Clunes (*Gary Strang*), Neil Morrissey (*Tony Smart*), Caroline Quentin (*Dorothy*), Leslie Ash (*Debs*) with Kylie as *herself*

Kylie at London Fashion Week, February 1996

In the midst of recording her next album for deConstruction, and having obviously not learnt her lesson from hanging around with overgrown schoolboys in *Bio-Dome*, Kylie was tempted to shack up with a better class of idiot, English this time – and at least it was strictly for charity. Starting out on ITV but moving later to BBC1, *Men Behaving Badly* was the shambolic story of two boorish 30-something 'lads' whose main preoccupations were shagging and getting pissed, preferably at the same time. The sub-Neanderthal 'New Lad' humour of the series struck a chord with male viewers who, like the protagonists, had been happily rearranging their testicles and scratching their arses in front of the telly for years. Female viewers relished the opportunity to see how stupid men really were and delighted in the withering put-downs provided by the two female characters.

Nye's incisive scripts, full of colourful language and absurd sexual fantasies, coupled with the perfect playing of the four central characters (Neil Morrissey, Martin Clunes, Leslie Ash, Caroline Quentin), won *Men Behaving Badly* critical plaudits and huge ratings for BBC1. Among the plethora of breaking wind, bragging and burping, Gary and Tony share one passion in particular: their undying lust for Kylie Minogue. Their drooling obsession for the world's greatest living Australian became a running joke throughout the series' run and then, finally, in 1997, the boys finally reached their nirvana. The BBC's regular bi-annual Comic Relief telethons liked to mix stand-up comedians with specially filmed episodes of popular TV sitcoms and *Men Behaving Badly* was summarily awarded the privilege.

The *Men Behaving Very Badly Indeed* special, screened for the seventh official Comic Relief night, finds Gary and Tony reminiscing about their everlasting admiration for Kylie, using clips from previous episodes. However, when Tony's dilapidated old van has a nasty prang with another car, the naughty boys fail to notice one *very important* thing. The other vehicle's driver – Kylie, naturally – turns up at the flat, hoping to swap addresses so Gary can claim on her insurance. Amazingly, neither Gary nor Tony recognise their idol. Stupidly assuming her accent is Dutch, Gary goads her to say something in Australian to prove her credentials. 'OK,' says Kylie. 'I'll strangle the pommie bastard if he mentions his van again!'

Unconvinced that she really is an internationally famous pop star ('You're in the entertainment business?' Tony asks incredulously), the louche lads prefer to ask her to unblock the sink's foul plughole with her 'tiny hands' and then judge their bizarre artwork made of empty lager cans. Kylie is unable to make a choice between Tony's five-feet-high metal chicken and Gary's repulsive self-portrait, complete with characteristic rubber lips and jug ears. She nervously scribbles down her details on a pad and makes a quick exit. 'Huh, Dutch birds eh?' chides Gary, looking at her details. 'What's her name then? Helga van Hinderblurgen?' 'It's Kylie Minogue,' replies Tony, colour draining from his face, 'c/o Deconstruction Records, London and New York!'

As the boys realise their blunder and charge off after her – demolishing their lounge wall in the process – you could almost forgive them for not recognising Kylie. After all, by 1997 she was a brunette. If Clunes had his way Kylie wouldn't only have shown the hair on her head, either. Promoting the special in the *Daily Mirror* the actor hinted that as their sketch was going out late at night it might involve some nudity. 'She drops 'em,' said Clunes, cheekily. 'There's an almighty clank behind us, we look round and her pants are on the deck! If we were to imply that Kylie is to appear naked we'd get peak viewing figures!'

'Some Kind of Bliss'

Released September 1997 (UK)
Written by Kylie Minogue, James Dean Bradfield and Sean Moore
Produced by James Dean Bradfield and Dave Eringa
Highest chart position #22 (UK), #27 (Australia)

Flipside: 'Limbo'
Video directed by David Mould

In 1996, hugely influenced by Nick Cave's esoteric approach to songwriting, Kylie began work on what was to be her sixth studio album. Kylie had started dating eccentric French photographer-director Stéphane Sednaoui, who had encouraged her to travel to southern China and across America on a 'baby rollercoaster ride full of ups and downs,' as Kylie later recounted. The couple sought inspiration wherever they went, taking endless photographs and devouring underground music. When Kylie returned to the UK she immediately began writing, recording and, on Sednaoui's recommendation, taking singing lessons, something she had never done previously.

The new album was originally envisaged wholly as a Brothers In Rhythm production but Kylie was persuaded to work with various other musicians, some of whom were fairly unlikely choices. With deConstruction taking a back seat, Kylie had the opportunity to experiment; this was the first time she had unilateral creative control over her music, co-writing all the tracks. It seemed that what Hutchence had started Cave and Sednaoui had continued. 'It was the coolest thing to work with Nick Cave. He opened my eyes to so many other ways of being. If there's one person in this world that would teach me about integrity it's Nick Cave,' Kylie said in 1997. 'And then to have the opportunity to work with James Dean Bradfield is just magical. I'm a lucky girl!'

Bradfield was the lead singer with hugely influential Welsh rockers Manic Street Preachers, who despite forming in the mid-1980s had enjoyed their biggest success in 1996 with their superb synth and string-led 'Everything Must Go' album. By then Kylie was heavily influenced by the nineties' Britpop sound and admitted that the Manics, as they were commonly known, were one of her favourite bands. 'I think I'm very influenced by living in London,' she said at the time, 'listening to the Verve, Finlay Quaye, Ocean Colour Scene, Supergrass, Chemical Brothers, Underworld and all kinds of Britpop if you want to call it that.'

Kylie first met the charismatic Bradfield at his home and they played around with some lyrics she had written while he strummed along on his guitar. 'It was quite unusual having the mixture of him and me,' she admitted afterwards, 'especially as he was in an anarchist band for years and I'm a super-sudsy pop girl!' The first result of Kylie's collaboration with Bradfield and the Manics' drummer Sean Moore, was 'Some Kind of Bliss', a blistering rock track with soaring strings straight out of the 'Everything Must Go' LP.

Nobody in the music press had seen this coming, perhaps not even Kylie herself, who seemed to be struggling with her new musical identity. She told *Q* magazine: 'I'm quite envious of people who have their own style. You hear a Manics song or a Nick Cave song and you know exactly who it is.' It was obvious Kylie was also worried by the public reaction to her new musical venture. 'Because the album was done over a two-year period and with four different producers there's obviously different sounds,' she admitted, 'and I even sound different from one track to the next just because it's the first time I've written for myself.'

It was always going to be a struggle for Kylie to be accepted as a 'credible' musician and songwriter, especially as only a few years previously London's Virgin Radio had the gall to run a humiliating ad campaign saying, 'We've done something to improve Kylie's records. We've banned them.' Ironically, 'Some Kind of Bliss' was far more Virgin Radio fare than BBC Radio One and the tabloid press were saying their favourite pop star had turned her back on pop in favour of 'difficult' indie music. Part of the problem was that on 'Some Kind of Bliss' Kylie was unrecognisable as Kylie. Her personality was notably absent from the track and things weren't helped by a record sleeve that portrayed her as a heroin-addicted waif. The singer was swiftly labelled 'Indie Kylie' by a less-than-impressed *Sun* newspaper.

As it was, 'Some Kind of Bliss' turned out to be an extremely expensive experiment for Kylie and a commercial disaster for deConstruction. In the UK the single entered the Top 40 at #22 and by the following week had plummeted to #43, making it Kylie's biggest flop of her solo career. Things hadn't been helped by the unlucky coincidence of Elton John releasing 'Candle in the Wind 1997', in tribute to the just deceased Diana Princess of Wales, the same week. 'I think the statistic was that Elton had 75 per cent of the singles bought that week, so mine didn't get off to a good start,' Kylie commented.

Pete Hadfield, one of the founders of Kylie's new record label, was devastated. Regardless of timing, journalists were still asking how deConstruction had allowed Kylie to record an edgy rock track for a label famed for its club music. This was not the work of the 'radical dance diva' Hadfield had once promised. Part of the inherent problem was not that 'Some Kind of Bliss' was rubbish, because unequivocally it was an intelligent, classy rock tune which wouldn't have seemed out of place on a Manics album. But for Kylie it was just all wrong. It felt like her fans were willing Kylie to succeed but were reluctant to invest in her new sound, yet at the same time remaining fascinated by the possibility of what might still be around the corner.

Misfit

1997 / A Euphoria Film Production for BBC / UK / 4 minutes / unrated
Directed and Written by Sam Taylor-Wood / Camera by Kate Stark / Produced by Keith Alexander and Rodney Wilson

Kylie Minogue (*The Misfit*), Alessandro Moreschi (*singing voice*) ertainly the biggest curiosity among all Kylie's films, *Misfit* is best described as her first excursion into 'arthouse' territory. Conceived and directed by the British artist Sam Taylor-Wood and lasting less than four minutes in length, *Misfit* was shot in 1997, the year that Taylor-Wood won the Illy Café Prize for 'Most Promising New Artist' at the prestigious Venice Biennale and a year before she was shortlisted for the Turner Prize in London.

The mini-movie presents a topless Kylie ('straight out of a Caravaggio painting', said the director), filmed from the side with her right arm covering her breasts, lip-syncing in Latin to 'Incipit Lamentatio', the only surviving recording by Alessandro Moreschi (1858-1922). The singer was the most famous castrato of all time, a male soprano cruelly created by castrating a boy before he reached puberty so that he retained his high voice. The practice was common until the 19th century in parts of Europe, particularly in Italy where artificially preserved child voices were in great demand for operas. At its peak it is estimated that around 4000 Italian boys a year were castrated for the services of 'art'. Alessandro Moreschi was the last Italian castrato, singing regularly in the Sistine Chapel until his retirement in 1913.

Luckily for Kylie there was no body mutilation required for Sam Taylor-Wood's beautiful film. All she had to do was look sexy and mime to another language, but that's no easy feat. *Misfit*'s music is melancholy, yet Kylie manages to toss a few seductive looks to the camera and, in a curiously affecting way, she is able to challenge, and confuse, ideas of male and female identity – a stunning contemporary female pop star miming to the voice of her asexual male equivalent from a century before.

Misfit was one of several films commissioned by the BBC and the Arts Council of England in which up-and-coming performance artists and young directors were given the opportunity to present their work to a larger audience. All the productions were broadcast on BBC2 in November 1997 as part of a late-night strand called *Expanding Pictures*. The British tabloids predictably concentrated on the 'nude Kylie' element of the film, completely missing the emotional point of the exercise.

Writing to Kylie about the film in 1999, Taylor-Wood said, 'The combination of your beautiful androgyny and the voice of a man who paid a high price for his talent made for the most curious of misfits.'

'Did It Again'

Released November 1997 (UK)
Written by Kylie Minogue, Dave Seaman and
Steve Anderson
Produced by Dave Ball and Ingo Vauk
Highest chart position #14 (UK), #14 (Australia)

Flipside: 'Tears'
Video directed by Pedro Romanyi

Kylie Minogue
Did it again

The unexpected death of Diana
Princess of Wales had greater
repercussions for Kylie than just the
commercial failure of 'Some Kind of Bliss'.
There was also the little matter of her
new album, still waiting to be released. Called 'Impossible Princess'
(named after Billy Childish's book of poetry *Poems to Break the Hearts
of Impossible Princesses*), it was felt that the title was, in light of recent
events, rather insensitive. The album was held back from its planned
autumn 1997 release, creating headaches for deConstruction and anxiety
for Kylie. 'I've told myself not to get frustrated,' she told the *Times* in
November, 'but actually I *am* frustrated because the album should be
out. The point of doing it is to get it out, and maybe people will like it,
maybe they'll hate it, but then at least it'll be out of my hands. I could
be quite upset about it,' she continued, 'but then you look at the bigger
picture and I have no right to be annoyed. It's been delayed because a
tragedy occurred. It was a reality check. Shit happens.'

After long discussions it was decided that, in Europe at least, the
'Impossible Princess' album title would be dropped in favour of plain
old 'Kylie Minogue', the third album to bear her name. Surely a better
compromise would have been to call it 'Impossible', but the die was
already cast. 'I have lived with the original title for two years,' said Kylie.
'We've taken the name off for now, but I'd like to keep the option for
putting it back in the future. That's what the album is called; it just
won't be on the cover.'

The album was slated for a new release date of early 1998 but
deConstruction, sitting on an expensively produced LP nobody could yet
buy, were losing money as each week went by; they desperately needed
a new hit to patch over the delay. Despite the perceived indie guitar
gloominess of 'Some Kind of Bliss', Kylie quickly returned to the charts

with an uptempo, far eastern-tinged pop track. 'Did It Again', one of the most immediate cuts from the forthcoming album, showed Kylie in mischievous mood. She's cruelly patronising a vacuous airhead (the so-called 'clever girl' in the song's verses) who just can't comprehend that the empty life she's leading is going nowhere fast.

A pretty vicious song, certainly by Kylie's standards anyway, it was co-written by Brothers In Rhythm and co-produced by Dave Ball, previously one half of the lionised Soft Cell and more recently dance outfit The Grid (who scored a massive international club hit with 'Swamp Thing' in the summer of 1994). Here the masterful Ball lets Kylie's vocals entwine with the gorgeous sound of a sitar seriously at odds with aggressive electric guitar work, yet the mix works superbly.

The acclaimed, tongue-in-cheek video for 'Did It Again' shows that despite the public's cool reception to Kylie's new musical direction she hadn't lost her sense of humour. Against a *Usual Suspects* police line-up Kylie is presented in four exaggerated guises – the snarling 'Sex Kylie', the ever-cheerful 'Cute Kylie', super-cool 'Indie Kylie' and frivolous 'Dance Kylie'. All four facets of Kylie's musical career are in violent conflict with each other, trading punches and high kicks, fighting for supremacy. With Kylie's current incarnation mediating the cat fighting (in rather a smug manner it must be noted) the video ends with 'Cute Kylie' wielding a rather menacing-looking baseball bat. With promo and song presented side-by-side it becomes more apparent that the lyrics are probably autobiographical, as Kylie struggles to come to terms with her new identity and attempts to discard her previous personae. 'Little Miss Genius,' she sings ironically, 'you make it hard on yourself.'

By the time 'Did It Again' was attempting to undo some of the commercial damage her previous single had inflicted, Kylie had learnt that Michael Hutchence, one of the greatest influences on her personal life and career, had died suddenly and mysteriously in a Sydney hotel bedroom. 'I was dumbstruck,' Kylie recalled in an interview later. 'There was always a lot of talk of Michael and his wicked ways, the bad boy of rock and all that. He was very Byronesque and I remember smiling at his funeral because as the coffin came out the thunder and lighning started right on cue. You couldn't have scripted it better. In truth I'm not sure that he corrupted me ... but let's just say he certainly opened my eyes. I would not have missed our relationship for anything and I miss him.'

Diana & Me

1997 / A Matt Carroll Film Production / Australia-UK /
98 minutes / cert 'M' (Australia) unrated (UK) / Opened
December 1997 (Australia)

Directed by David Parker / Written by Elizabeth
Coleman and Matt Ford / Produced by Matt Carroll /
Cinematography by Keith Wagstaff / Original Music
composed by Brett Rosenberg

Cast: Toni Collette (*Diana Spencer*), Dominic West (*Rob
Naylor*), Malcolm Kennard (*Mark Fraser*), Victoria Eagger
(*Carol*), John Simm (*Neil*), Serena Gordon (*Lady Sarah
Myers-Booth*), Roger Barclay (*Richard*), Tom Hillier
(*Neville*), Victoria Longley (*Pauline*), Nigel Planer (*taxi
driver*), Christina Hance (*Princess Diana*), Marshall Napier
(*bank manager*), Jim Holt (*detective*) and Kylie Minogue,
Jason Donovan, Bob Geldof, Susan George, Jerry Hall,
Marie Helvin, Eric Richardson, Oliver Tobias, Susannah
York and Jonno Coleman as *themselves*

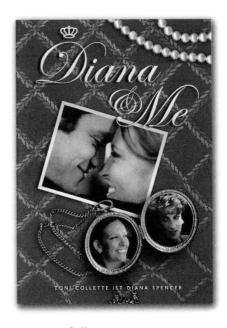

Could *Diana & Me* quite possibly be the unluckiest movie of all
time? How about filming a romantic comedy about a young
woman's romance with a British paparazzo who will do absolutely
anything to get a photo of Princess Diana, but during production the
real Diana is tragically killed after fleeing a posse of real photographers?
Obviously, back in 1997, nobody could have foreseen those awful events
in a Parisian underpass, but the circumstances of Diana's death quietly
killed any chance of success for *Diana & Me*. A film intended to be
funny and fluffy ended up macabre and prophetic, boasting some of the
most tasteless jokes imaginable. In one jaw-dropping scene a group of
tabloid photographers are told by a café owner that a celebrity drama is
rapidly unfolding in a busy London street. 'George Michael's just had a
car accident!' he says. 'Fantastic!' chorus the photographers in unison,
scrambling for their zoom lenses.

On paper, in 1996, the story of *Diana & Me* could be forgiven for
looking rather innocuous, charming even. Toni Collette – Australia's
hottest actress since her international breakthrough in 1994's *Muriel's
Wedding* – plays the 'other' Diana Spencer, a kooky 20-something,
teased throughout her youth for sharing her name and birthday with the
world's most photographed woman. In the quiet Australian backwater
of Wollongong, Diana has entered a competition to win a holiday

to England and the chance to meet the royal princess. Her slogan, 'Princess Diana is Jesus Christ', clinches it and Diana soon finds herself winging her way across the world with her unsophisticated fiancé Mark (Malcolm Kennard) and nymphomaniac chaperone Carol (Victoria Eaggar). The idealised London that Australian director David Parker rewards them with is a cliché-ridden hotchpotch of red double-deckers, gentlemen tramps, cheeky cabbies and colourful punk rockers. But it isn't pink Mohicans Diana has come to see; it's her royal namesake.

Invited to a palace garden party, Diana finally meets 'Diana' (a surreal mix of archive footage of the real Princess and a lookalike actress). The women make eye contact and the connection is instantaneous, or so it seems. The princess is greeted by hoards of foul-mouthed paparazzi desperate for the best photo and it is here that Diana Spencer meets her nemesis: dashing, daring hotshot photographer Rob Naylor, played by Dominic West, here presented as a poor man's High Grant.

The movie's bland script does its best to present the British paparazzi as unflatteringly as possible – a baying group of yelling, shoving animals prepared to do anything for *that special photo*. But *Diana & Me* is otherwise an undemanding romcom with very few interesting things to say about the uneasy relationship between the public, the press and their famous quarries. However, because of the royal subject matter the movie sometimes makes for very uncomfortable viewing, particularly a sequence where Diana and Rob chase after the Princess' car through the streets of Belgravia.

The film manages to ensnare a few real-life celebrities for cameos, but what a disparate bunch they are: Susan George, Susannah York, Bob Geldof, DJ Jonno Coleman, Jerry Hall and, most bizarrely of all, actor Eric Richardson, best known for playing Concorde-nosed Sergeant Bob Cryer in *The Bill*. Jason Donovan pops up in a big, fluffy white coat and yellow sunglasses as he 'attends' Elton John's party, although Elton declined a cameo himself, which is probably what the rest of the stars wished they'd done too.

The movie's most disquieting scene, considering the real-life pursuit and death of Princess Diana, concerns Kylie – playing herself – besieged by a screaming, venomous pack of photographers as she leaves a West End restaurant with an unlikely lunch date, Oliver *The Stud* Tobias. Doorstepped, then stalked, Kylie looks distressed and pissed off by the paparazzi, as they keep pace with her and force flashbulbs in her face. Shielding her eyes, Kylie nervously bites the back of her hand and rabid snapper Neil (a pre-*Human Traffic* John Simm) senses her discomfort.

Trying to attract her attention he shouts at her 'Kylie, suck my fucking winkle!' and gets his elusive snap. Kylie rewards him with a sharp thump, before striding off. Obviously Kylie is acting here, but you're left wondering just how true to life the situation is.

After the untimely death of Britain's most beloved royal, the producers of *Diana & Me* were left with a film that nobody had the stomach to watch. Forced to cut huge chunks out of the final movie and shoot extra scenes many months later, the film was partially salvaged with two new sequences which bookend the movie. Toni Collette is shown placing flowers at the gates of Kensington Palace, saying, 'I really miss her. She changed my life. I wonder if she knows that.' This grim tone sat uneasily with the rest of the film and *Diana & Me*'s distributor, Buena Vista UK, decided not to release the film in Britain.

Several newspapers immediately pounced on the story, with the *Mail on Sunday* reporting that 'Tacky Diana Movie Outrages Royals'. Film producer, and friend of Diana, David Puttnam leapt to the film's defence, claiming the re-edited version would be 'a moving and eloquent tribute,' but the public were not so easily convinced and the film disappeared, finally resurfacing, without fanfare, 18 months later on SKY Movies. Released theatrically in Australia just four months after Diana's death, the film also bombed Down Under. Little seen ever since, *Diana & Me* was simply an instance where bad timing suddenly became bad taste.

'Breathe'

Released March 1998 (UK)
Written by Kylie Minogue, Dave Ball and Ingo Vauk
Produced by Dave Ball and Ingo Vauk
Highest chart position #14 (UK), #23 (Australia)

Flipside: 'Breathe' (Tee's Radio Mix)
Video directed by Keiron Evans

Kylie's new album was finally released in Australia on 12 January 1998 to universally sympathetic press, but in the UK it still gathered dust in the deConstruction vault for a further two months. Hoping for one final push to promote its upcoming 23 March release, Kylie's record company snuck out a third single to precede it. 'Breathe', again a collaboration with Dave Ball and Ingo Vauk (who also co-wrote the song), evokes the sultry ambient feel of Kylie's 1994 single 'Put Yourself in My Place', with a beautiful shimmering melody and introspective lyrics. The song's tranquilising video presents Kylie floating through a psychedelic *2001: A Space Odyssey* dream in a surreal trancelike state. 'Don't blame me because I am bored,' Kylie purrs. 'I am needy; I need to taste it all.'

Kylie wasn't the only one suffering from boredom; deConstruction also seemed to be getting disillusioned with their most high-profile, and expensive, act. At the behest of her worried record label, alarmed by the mediocre sales of her previous two singles, Kylie heavily promoted her latest release in the UK. The singer trolled round *This Morning with Richard and Judy*, *The Ben Elton Show* and even the interminable *National Lottery Live*. For Ben Elton's late-night show she also performed a cover version of The Clash's seminal punk hit 'Should I Stay or Should I Go?' (later included in the set-list for the *Intimate and Live* tour).

Like Kylie's previous British single release, 'Breathe' debuted, and immediately peaked, at #14 and then went into freefall, staying on the charts for only four short weeks; a great shame since the track was head and shoulders above most of the rest of the Top 40 combined. However, it was still Kylie's 26th Top 30 UK hit, a remarkable achievement for a solo female singer. In Australia the song stalled at #23, although in Israel it hit the #1 spot, proving that at least the Middle East had great musical taste. Sadly, it seems that Kylie was sensing her own musical mortality around this period. In April 1998 she gave a melancholic interview to British *Cosmopolitan* in which she questioned her creative longevity: 'I've tried to imagine what it will be like when no one cares who I am any more and it's quite scary.'

'Impossible Princess'

Released March 1998 (UK)
deConstruction / Mushroom Records
Produced by Brothers In Rhythm (tracks 1, 2, 4, 6, 7 and 12), Dave Erigna and James Dean Bradfield (tracks 3 and 8), Dave Ball and Ingo Vauk (5, 10 and 11), and Rob Dougan (track 9)
Highest chart position #10 (UK), #4 (Australia)

Track listing:
'Too Far'
'Cowboy Style'
'Some Kind of Bliss'
'Did It Again'
'Breathe'
'Say Hey'
'Drunk'
'I Don't Need Anyone'
'Jump'
'Limbo'
'Through the Years'
'Dreams'
Bonus track: 'Tears' (Japan only)

The interminable wait for Kylie's new album was finally over, but the reaction in Europe was not always kind. ('She is a total fraud,' wrote *NME*.) The most debated and controversial of Kylie's musical output, 'Impossible Princess' still has the ability to confound, confuse and split her fanbase clean down the middle. Undoubtedly the album's six-month delay did much to reduce its impact, and its eventual release in the shadow of Madonna's landmark album 'Ray of Light' dramatically damaged its chances.

But it's easy to say that 'Impossible Princess' was just a victim of circumstance when really there is more to the story. For the very first time Kylie co-wrote all the tracks here – providing an illuminating and sometimes scary insight into late-1990s Minogue-dom. Expressing her new-found freedom, Kylie is angry, emotional, pent-up and moody, trading insults with her music, bending melodies and forcing her voice to do her bidding. In the album's darker moments there are elements of Patti Smith, Alanis Morissette and Shirley Manson. Chaotic opener 'Too Far' seems almost agoraphobic and the violent, jazzy bang and trip-hop crash of 'Through the Years' is beautifully tortuous, whereas the dark emptiness of the schizophrenic 'Drunk' is downright terrifying. 'Say Hey' finds Kylie getting sexy and holding hands with Björk ('The water's warm; it's making me in the mood to play'), the Saint Etienne-flavoured 'I Don't Need Anyone' (smoothly co-produced by James Dean Bradfield) is a breezy highpoint, and Kylie's dissatisfaction with her previous frothy pop incarnations is evident in the beautifully dramatic 'Jump'

('I run to the future and ... jump'). The ethereal 'Breathe', however, provides a soothing respite from the angst.

While Kylie's lyrics are often revelatory, and occasionally contradictory, it is the collective of disparate musicians that is responsible for landscaping most of the album. Ingo Vauk and the 'Daves' Eringa and Ball take some chances with Kylie's vocals, looping the psychedelic beats beneath, but it is undoubtedly the Brothers In Rhythm who really know what makes Kylie tick best. Their finest songs bookend the whole production. Frenetic opener 'Too Far', accented with Steve Anderson's eerie horror movie piano and Martin Loveday's serious cello, is unquestionably a magnificent piece of grand pop. Immediately after comes the electric fiddle mayhem of 'Cowboy Style', which just makes you want to leap to your feet. Jumping ten songs to the Phil Spector-style production on climactic track 'Dreams', we encounter scary strings seemingly plucked right off the *Get Carter* soundtrack, mixed with some butch drumming and huffy bass to create a powerful, swirling cinematic fairytale, displaying Kylie at her most outspoken and seemingly untouchable. 'Believe in the sacred and break every rule,' she sings.

Driven by pure emotion, 'Impossible Princess' was never destined for a charmed life. The critics were undecided and the public oddly indifferent. Its commercial failure was largely responsible for the break-up of deConstruction and the eventual re-focusing of Kylie's career. However, the often-strained period of creating, and then releasing, the album was a hugely important learning experience for Kylie. 'I think that the 'Impossible Princess' album with its few ups and many downs was an absolute blessing in disguise,' she admitted years later. 'But I never thought I'd fucked it up completely.'

In 2003, 'Impossible Princess' was reissued with a bonus disc featuring 12 extra tracks, including remixes (no fewer than three of 'Too Far'), B-sides and previously unreleased demos. By then music journalists were hailing it a 'forgotten classic'.

Intimate and Live Tour

Devised and Created by William Baker and Kylie Minogue / Music Producer – Steve Anderson / Musical Director – Chong Lim / Choreography by William Forsythe / Tour Manager – Nick Pitts / Principal Dancers – David Scotchford and Ashley Wallen / Wardrobe by William Baker

Musicians: Chong Lim (keyboards), Joe Creighton (bass), Stuart Fraser and Carl

Mann (guitars), Angus Burchall (drums), James
Mack (percussion), Lisa Edwards and Natalie Miller
(backing vocals)

2 June-4 July 1998 (Australia)
29 July-31 July 1998 (UK)

Set list: Too Far, What Do I Have to Do, Some Kind
of Bliss, Put Yourself in My Place, Breathe, Take Me
with You, I Should Be So Lucky, Dancing Queen,
Dangerous Game, Cowboy Style, Step Back in Time,
Say Hey, Free, Drunk, Did It Again, Limbo, Shocked.
First Encore: Confide in Me, The Loco-motion, Should
I Stay or Should I Go?
Second Encore: Better the Devil You Know.

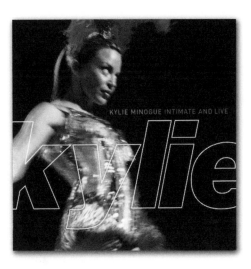

KYLIE MINOGUE INTIMATE AND LIVE

Kylie had spent most of the 1990s absent
from the stage. Her first deConstruction
album had not been performed live in its entirety and for some time
Kylie felt no strong desire to promote her music. She had enjoyed one-off
performances for various festivals, a Stonewall '95 benefit gig (where she
famously duetted with Elton John on Irving Berlin's 'Sisters') and MTV's
Most Wanted. But there was little more substantial, much to the chagrin
of her fans.

After the release of 'Impossible Princess', demand for Kylie to hit
the road again continued to grow, particularly in Australia, where
the album had received positive press coverage. Feeling like she had
nothing to lose, an out-of-practice Kylie agreed to a short Australian
tour. Little did she guess how popular it would turn out to be. The 18
dates were a complete sell-out – beginning and ending at Melbourne's
historic Palais Theatre and visiting venues in Sydney, Adelaide and
Canberra in between. By deliberately choosing smaller, more personal
venues (usually 2000 capacity), *Intimate and Live* was an apt title for the
tour. This was Kylie's tentative step back into the cosiness of the live
lounge, far away from the massive arenas of old, but the concerts were
responsible for revitalising her love of performing in front of a crowd.

The tour was basic to say the least, but that was its huge strength.
Conceived quickly and produced on a tiny budget ('We barely had two
pennies to rub together,' joked Kylie), *Intimate and Live* almost became
the tour that nobody could stop. Extra dates seemed to be continually
added and, despite there being no plans to extend the tour outside
Australia, word of mouth created huge demand in Britain. Rumour had
it that Kylie would be ... *performing Stock Aitken Waterman hits!* Gay fans

went into meltdown. As a result Kylie was obliged to tack on three dates at London's Shepherd's Bush Empire nearly four weeks after the tour had concluded back home.

So what exactly did fans get? A very simple set, John Farnham's rock 'n' roll band, two beatific go-go boys dressed in cod-pieces and Stetsons, and Kylie descending the stage on a short flight of stairs. The minimal tour design was conceived by William Baker, Kylie's loyal confidant and 'gay best friend' whom she first met in 1994 when he was working at Vivienne Westwood's boutique in London's Conduit Street. Their relationship blossomed from their very first meeting ('He did all the talking and nothing's changed,' Kylie later remarked) and Baker was rapidly installed as her personal stylist. From overseeing the look of her album artwork to TV appearances and live shows, Baker has been the constant in Kylie's life.

As ticket-holders entered the concert venues a gigantic pair of Kylie eyes surveyed them from a video screen, looking left to right, then up and down. The effect was deliberately unnerving. Kylie made a teasing silhouette behind the pink polyester tent which had graced the sleeve of 'Impossible Princess' before silently appearing beneath the spotlight. This was Indie Kylie – dressed in black blouse and pedal-pushers, hair scraped off her face and only the barest smudge of make-up on her cheeks. Unusually, Kylie looked cool and somewhat detached, setting the scene with an impassioned rendition of 'Too Far'. When she wailed 'Help me' during the song's chorus some fans might have been moved to think she needed actual assistance. The tension continued with a crunching version of 'What Do I Have to Do' and a static 'Some Kind of Bliss', the urban angst only dissipating with the sweet calm of 'Breathe', prompting Kylie's face to break into a toothy grin and allowing her spellbound audience to exhale.

Immediately after the first costume change, when Kylie re-emerged from her black chrysalis as a beautiful butterfly in a sparkling showgirl outfit, the atmosphere changed. The torch song version of 'I Should Be So Lucky' delivered with simple piano accompaniment was stunning, although it was her cover of ABBA's 'Dancing Queen' (Kylie now wearing a plume of ostrich feathers on her head and flanked by her two muscle Marys) which finally broke the palpable feeling of trepidation in both audience and performer alike. The rockier interpretations of some of her older pure pop hits weren't, to be truthful, wholly satisfying (with three guitarists, no less), but the real shocks of the *Intimate and Live* tour were provided by the little-heard deConstruction material – namely the smooth Balearic guitar of beautiful non-album track 'Take Me with You' and the frenzied drumming of the Celtic 'Cowboy Style'.

Each show ended with the loud gay bang of 'Better the Devil You Know', ferocious mortars firing streamers and glitter across the stage. This was Kylie's epiphany, her self-fulfilling prophecy, if you like; the instant the performer awoke from pop exile. She knew what her audiences had always known: Indie Kylie had been a fascinating, exhilarating experiment, but glitzy, camp, star-spangled Kylie was the undisputed truth. 'It has become the stuff of legend,' recalled Baker of the tour. 'It was a truly iconic moment. Suddenly among that blur of pink feathers and sequins, everything seemed to make sense.' It also paved the way for Kylie's future. Thanks to *Intimate and Live* the Impossible Princess was finally pronounced dead; all hail the re-birth of the Showgirl. 'She's small, she's sassy, she's the new Shirley Bassey,' announced the *Observer*.

A film of Kylie's 1 July date at the Capitol Theatre, Sydney, was screened peak time on Network Ten in Australia and then released on DVD as *Kylie: Intimate and Live*, directed by Mark Adamson and produced by David Wilson. It also featured Kylie performing at the 1998 Sydney Gay and Lesbian Mardi Gras. In November 1998 Mushroom Records in Australia released a live double album of the tour, produced by Steve Anderson and also called *Intimate and Live*. The album featured all 21 tracks which Kylie had performed on stage.

'Cowboy Style'

Released August 1998 (Australia)
Written by Kylie Minogue, Dave Seaman and Steve Anderson
Produced by Brothers in Rhythm
Highest Chart Position #39 (Australia)

Flipside: 'Love Takes Over Me'
Video directed by Michael Williams

As a result of the meagre UK sales of 'Impossible Princess', deConstruction could not justify releasing another track off the largely misunderstood album, despite the fact that fans had clamoured for the collection's opening track 'Too Far' to be the next single.

However, the céilidh-versus-sitar 'Cowboy Style' became the album's final hurrah, released exclusively on the Mushroom label in Australia. A cool, bouncy Country 'n' Western favourite, the song featured prominently on Kylie's last tour and is allegedly about her relationship with French ex-boyfriend Stéphane Sednaoui. 'I'm frightened. I'm aroused,' Kylie sings cryptically.

In Europe the inevitable happened and Kylie's fears were finally realised. Struggling to keep Kylie a profitable property, deConstruction waved goodbye to their most famous artist. By November 1998 it was reported that Kylie's 'Impossible Princess' had sold only 47,000 copies. On the 25th of that month it was announced to the newspapers that she had been 'sensationally dumped', although Kylie claimed the split was purely 'amicable'. 'It had been in discussion for the past few months,' said a spokesperson for the label. The British press, always delighted at a public figure's downfall, seemed gleeful at the news. Their knowing 'told-you-so' attitude echoed throughout the gossip columns, predictably laying the blame squarely at Kylie's vain attempt to re-invent herself as a rock star.

'We want pop stars to know their place,' wrote the London *Evening Standard*. 'If you're going to move from pop into more credible music it takes more than a change of wardrobe. It takes new tunes, and good ones.' The *Independent* noted, rather snottily, that 'in attempting to come over as a 'serious artiste' she has forfeited the very audience that has kept her in fluffy frocks for nearly a decade.' For Kylie herself, the very public break-up with her record company was a painful experience. Initially she had no idea what she would do next, blithely telling reporters that she'd probably take 'baby steps' back into acting. 'Oh, I'm the first to admit I am useless at making long-term plans,' she told the *Observer* in 1998. 'My manager is always desperately trying to pin me down and I'm like, "No, I'll think tomorrow!" By all rights, I shouldn't be here. That's the thing that keeps crossing my mind. It's written in the tablets by the gods that a pop star in 1988 shouldn't still be here in 1998...'

'GBI (German Bold Italic)'

Released October 1998 (UK)
Written by Towa Tei and Kylie Minogue
Produced by Towa Tei
Highest Chart Position #63 (UK), #50 (Australia)

Flipside: 'GBI' (Sharp Boys Deee-liteful Dub Mix)
Video directed by Stéphane Sednaoui

'GBI' may well be the only song ever written about a typeface, that's to say a distinctive alphabet of letters, numerals and punctuation. German Bold Italic is one such typeface, and it's doubtful that when Kylie was hitting #1 throughout the world with 'I Should Be So Lucky' she ever thought ten years later she'd be singing about such a thing. Released on the little-known independent Arthrob label, 'GBI' is the most obscure and quirkiest single of Kylie's career; co-written and produced by Japanese-born artist and musician Towa Tei, whose love of jazz and electronica first brought him to public prominence in the early nineties. As one third of the multi-cultural dance group Deee-Lite, Tei scored his biggest international hit with the perennially popular 'Groove is in the Heart', followed by a string of US dance chart smashes until the group disbanded in the mid-1990s.

Tei continued as a solo artist and in 1996 approached Kylie to provide vocals for a track which would eventually appear on his 'Sound Museum' album the following year. 'GBI' is a seriously deranged, inexplicably random choice of sounds and lyrics in which Kylie sensuously asserts to her audience that 'My name is German Bold Italic. I am a typeface which you have never heard before.' The track bursts open like an aural cartoon, full of blips, bumps and scratches punctuated with some sleazy jazz beats, crazy snatches of 'Groove is in the Heart' and, for want of a better expression, 'supermarket muzak'. Undoubtedly, Tei's song is a witches' brew of hypnotic Japanese madness, but fabulous fun nonetheless. First released in Japan in 1997, where it tickled the Top 20, it was a further year before 'GBI' hit the lower reaches of the British and Australian charts. Hardly a mainstream radio track, 'GBI' has remained a capricious collectors' piece for Kylie's fans ever since.

The equally unhinged video follows a hyper-unreal Kylie tip-toeing around freezing New York streets, dressed up as an elegant Geisha girl with a heavy platinum wig. The promo was directed by Kylie's ex-boyfriend Stéphane Sednaoui, whom she had broken up with in the autumn of 1997 but had remained on good terms with. 'I never expect relationships to last,' she told the *Daily Mail* in 1998, 'which is probably one reason why I don't fall out with boyfriends. Of course I love being in love.'

☆   ☆   ☆

Towa Tei's curious song marked the end of Kylie's bravely experimental but less-than-auspicious era of different musical styles. The rest of 1998 saw Kylie doing a variety of more mainstream work, including modelling a new range of sexy underwear in a campaign for Swedish clothes retailer H and M, and performing at the Mushroom 25 Live concert at Melbourne's cricket club on 14 November. It was here she did a medley of predominantly Stock Aitken Waterman material to celebrate the silver anniversary of her Australian record company, including 'Celebration', 'Shocked', 'Turn It Into Love' and 'Hand on Your Heart'. Mushroom released the concert (also featuring Jimmy Barnes, INXS, Peter Andre and Dannii) on DVD and CD. After years on the outside refusing to look back, there were now tentative signals that Kylie was happy to embrace her poppy persona again.

However, as 1998 drew to an end there were no definite plans for any new material. 'I parted with deConstruction after a long and mainly happy time together because we didn't achieve what we wanted to achieve with 'Impossible Princess',' asserted Kylie, in an attempt to reinforce her current position. 'I made mistakes, they made mistakes. At no point do I consider it to be the end of my musical career.' All a weary deConstruction spokesperson could add was, 'Kylie is currently in discussions with several record companies for her next album, probably due in 1999.' Fans awaited the news with bated breath.

'Kylie'

Published October 1999 (UK)
Edited by Chris Heath
Published by Booth-Clibborn Editions (UK)
Pan MacMillan (Australia)

Well, there was no new album in 1999; there wasn't even a solitary single. Instead, all ardent Kylie fans, especially those with £25 to spare, had to contend with was a pink monolith of a book containing over 100 sumptuous images of the princess of pop. Originally announced in March 1999 as *Kylie Evidence*, the new book,

with a frustratingly shortened title, finally hit
the shelves in October 1999, with Kylie doing a
signing session at Selfridges in London.

This huge coffee-table slab (nearly 40
centimetres high and 26 centimetres wide)
of anonymous cerise, presented in a glossy
removable sleeve showing a life-size photo
of Kylie's dainty forearm and fist, took 14
months to compile. Described as merely 'self
indulgence' by some of Kylie's detractors, she
actually found it to be a therapeutic experience
putting together the volume. 'It was born out of
a moment of boredom,' explained Kylie in an
interview with the *Sunday Times*. 'I was sat in
my kitchen with a friend, having just finished
Intimate and Live, and I was in need of a project
to get me through the lull.'

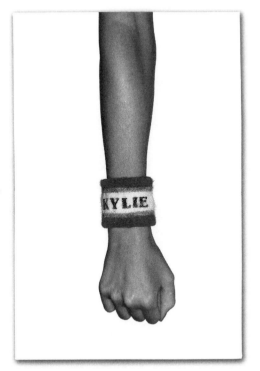

Kylie's book is a photographic study of
the singer's professional life, with a section
of opinions and thoughts written by, among
others, Barry Humphries, Nick Cave, Julie
Burchill, Elton John, Pete Waterman, Baz
Luhrmann, Boy George and William Baker.
'Kylie herself reminds me of the silver strip which runs through every
genuine currency note of the realm,' writes Burchill. 'She makes modern
music at once more shiny and more authentic, more truly itself.'

While some of the fancy words border on pretentiousness, far
more revealing are the photographs. Intriguingly, the book opens
with a frankly terrifying close-up of Kylie's first wax effigy at Madame
Tussauds from 1989, all teeth, gums and eyeliner, and ends with her
more sedate, pouting 1998 re-model. Sandwiched in between is a
startling portfolio of colourful images by Anton Corbijn, Pierre et Gilles,
Stéphane Sednaoui, her ex-flatmate Katerina Jebb and the legendary
American portrait photographer Bert Stern, the latter claiming that he'd
never met a star who 'related' to his camera like Kylie, at least not since
his sessions with Marilyn Monroe in the 1950s.

Alongside the professional glossy photos are more candid and
intimate snaps, such as Kylie the little girl on the set of *The Sullivans* or
Kylie the big girl, butt naked backstage, after an appearance at London
club G-A-Y. 'The reason I included that shot was because I remember

the moment it was taken and I was so happy,' she said, responding to the media's fixation with the photo. 'But it's not there to shock, it's tasteful. It's a nipple. Big deal!' More shocking perhaps are the numerous other visualisations of Kylie, particularly an amusing sketch by Chris Cunningham of her sitting on a lavatory, knickers round her ankles, while she studiously examines a picture of a huge erect phallus and a hairy vagina. On the opposite page is a teenage Kylie joyously promoting 'Got to Be Certain'.

What it all means is a matter of interpretation; probably even Kylie doesn't understand what it's all about. 'In this book I am both spectator and participant, objective and subjective...' she wrote. The *Evening Standard* just cut to the chase. 'It's a bit vain, isn't it Kylie?' journalist Simon Mills asked. 'Well, yes!' Kylie happily concurred.

Sample People

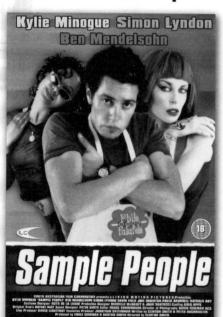

1999 / A Living Motion Picture Production / Australia / 97 minutes / cert 'MA' (Australia) cert '18' (UK) / Opened May 2000 (Australia)

Directed by Clinton Smith / Written by Clinton Smith and Peter Buckmaster / Produced by Emile Sherman and Barton Smith / Cinematography by David Foreman / Original Music composed by Raphael May

Cast: Kylie Minogue (*Jess*), Ben Mendelsohn (*John*), Simon Lyndon (*Andy*), Nathan Page (*Len*), David Field ('*Two T*'), Joel Edgerton (*Sem*), Paula Arundell (*Cleo*), Nathalie Roy (*DJ Lush Puppy*), Justin Rosiak (*Joey*), Mathew Wilkinson (*Gus*), Gandhi MacIntyre (*Phil*), Dorian Nkono (*Shiva*)

With no album to promote in 1999 Kylie returned home to Australia and began work on two low-budget movies, shot in quick succession. Her first feature film for two years could be described as the Australian *Human Traffic* (minus the laughs); at worst it's more like an unpalatable MTV trawl through the grimy gutters of Sydney. First-time director Clinton Smith rips off elements from every 1990s poster film – a little bit of *Go*, a little pinch of *Run Lola Run*, a nod to *Pulp Fiction* and a massive dollop of *Trainspotting*.

The opening sequence even has the audacity to introduce each character, freeze the frame and then caption their names on screen.

Rash, derivative and sloppily constructed, *Sample People* invites a voyeuristic audience to take a 97-minute peek at the seedy underbelly of Australian nightlife, exposing drug-taking, gun culture, promiscuous sex and bloody violence. Surprisingly, it ain't much fun to watch. Clinton (who also co-wrote the script) presents a parade of tired urban stereotypes, none of whom is the slightest bit convincing. Len is an introspective fantasist working in a falafel snack bar. 'Baby, just look at yourself,' the owner's bisexual son tells him, 'you're white, you're straight and you're employed. In this neighbourhood you're a weirdo!' Indeed, Len is *supposed* to be a weird, virginal geek, yet the part is played by actor Nathan Page, a handsome, muscular, head-turning six-footer with perfectly styled hair and razor-sharp sideburns. It just doesn't add up that he can't get laid.

Len secretly lusts after a superstar DJ called Slush Puppy – the main attraction at über-trendy nightclub Sample People ('If you can boogie, you can get in!'). The cavernous club is run by cardboard crook, and professional nose-biter, 'Two T' (David Field) – 'Twat' would be a more appropriate name – who is being double-crossed by square-jawed drug peddler Andy (Simon Lyndon). The plot, such as it is, explodes into an orgy of coke snorting and blood letting, winding up in a messy gorefest at the falafel shop. For some light relief Kylie's *Henderson Kids* co-star Ben Mendelsohn pops up as a gender-bending Marilyn Manson lookalike who smokes joints for breakfast and, in the movie's single running 'joke', endures regular and brutal beatings.

Poor Kylie is rather sidelined as tortured Jess, the gangland boss's moll, who, despite being top-billed, makes only relatively fleeting appearances on screen. However, for die-hard Minogue fans looking for something a little different, *Sample People* is just what you've been waiting for. If you want to see a more adult Kylie snorting coke, romping in bed with her lover (Lyndon) and very possibly enjoying some cunnilingus, handling a gun and saying 'Fuck you!' very loudly then this is the movie for you. Kylie's character despises her despotic, twitchy boyfriend and dreams of escape. In one particularly nasty scene the vile gangster spits a bullet right into her mouth.

But what doesn't kill you only makes you stronger and she fights back, both physically and verbally. Thinking he's the Mr Big Shot of the Sydney underworld, 'Two T' boasts that the guy down the falafel shop even mistakes him for Scarface. 'He calls me Mr Al, as in Al Pacino,' he boasts. 'I like that. "You talking to me?"' 'That's De Niro,' says a scornful Kylie. And that's the best dialogue in the entire movie.

Kylie, who's never looked more severe and scary (even more than the record sleeve for 'Some Kind of Bliss') in big red wig, enormous 1960s sunglasses and sporting elaborate snake tattoos on her arms, is totally wasted (in more ways than one) in *Sample People*. The actress doesn't look like she's having much fun and only manages to crack a smile at the movie's conclusion, which is probably a similar reaction to the audience's.

The trouble with *Sample People* is that it just tries way too hard to be trendy, tying itself up in knots in a vain attempt to tick all the Generation X boxes. Pretentious in the extreme, the movie portrays a fantasy world where drugged-up loony losers inhabit apartments decorated in pop art, where sex invades every corner ('Mmm, cool, cable porn,' says Mendelsohn, wetting his knickers) and 1950s-style refrigerators are customarily customised in spray paint. Clinton's film, actually shot on location in Adelaide, wants us to believe this is what Sydney is really like, but whereas *Trainspotting* was edgy, intelligent and terrifying, *Sample People* is devoid of atmosphere or message (although, bizarrely, the movie's credits do find time to thank the Church of Scientology, so perhaps there's something subliminal going on).

David Foreman's brash cinematography is sometimes quite arresting, but is spoilt by the clichéd direction and the slung-together central performances. The only performer to get out alive is trumpet-tooting Sem, played by Joel Edgerton (better served in 2005 Britflick *Kinky Boots*), who struggles with his own, and his girlfriend's, definition of 'open relationship'. 'Let's not fuck anyone else then, OK?' he pleads. 'Let's just fuck each other!'

Kylie bravely struggles with the hackneyed script and looks uncomfortable throughout, although, to be fair, she was happy to be exploited as the big 'name' to carry this hedonistic car crash. *Sample People*, which ironically holds the distinction of being Kylie's second-worst film, opened to universally bad reviews in Australia on its May 2000 release; in the UK it emerged straight-to-video in August 2002. Unsurprisingly, the salivating British tabloids were obsessed with Kylie's image in the film. 'KYLIE IS A TART' screamed the *Sun*. 'Here's pop princess Kylie Minogue as you've never seen her before – as a cocaine-addicted PROSTITUTE!' Quite where they got the prostitute thing from is anybody's guess. Needless to say it didn't do much to boost the film's chances.

Among the sometimes hallucinatory visuals and less-than-pumping soundtrack of unrecognisable 'club' tunes, there pops up a new recording by Kylie, heard over the closing credits. 'The Real Thing', produced by Josh G Abrahams (later to co-ordinate the soundtrack for *Moulin Rouge!*), is a cover version of Russell Morris' rocky #1 Australian hit from 1969. It was written by Johnny Young, the singer-turned-DJ who later went on to present TV's *Young Talent Time*, the series that had made Dannii Minogue a household name in Australia. Kylie's version of the song appeared on *Sample People*'s soundtrack, released in 2000 on Best Boy records.

Cut

2000 / A Mushroom Pictures-Beyond Films Production / Australia / 82 minutes / cert 'MA' (Australia) cert '18' (UK) / Opened March 2000 (Australia)

Directed by Kimble Rendell / Written by Dave Warner / Produced by Bill Bennett and Martin Fabinyi / Cinematography by David Foreman / Original Music composed by Guy Gross

Cast: Molly Ringwald (*Vanessa Turnbill*), Kylie Minogue (*Hilary Jacobs*), Jessica Napier (*Raffy Carruthers*), Frank Roberts (*Brad Walker/Scarman*), Geoff Revell (*Professor Lossman*), Sarah Kants (*Hester Ryan*), Stephen Curry (*Rick Stephens*), Matt Russell (*Paulie Morrelli*), Erika Walters (*Cassie Woolf*), Cathy Adamek (*Julie Bardot*), Steve Greig (*Jim Pilonski*), Sam Lewis (*Damien Ogle*), Phyllis Burford (*Martha*)

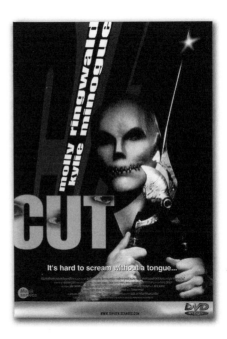

Hot on the bloody high heels of *Sample People*, Kylie's next movie was another threadbare Australian exploitation flick. For *Cut* she was reunited with her *Hayride to Hell* director Kimble Rendell, this time helming his first feature-length production. In an interview before the film was released Rendell, who has subsequently gone on to work on big Hollywood pictures like *Matrix Reloaded* (2003), *I, Robot* (2004) and *Ghost Rider* (2006), said he deliberately didn't want to make any more so-called 'arthouse' movies but wanted to concentrate on something much more commercial.

The script for *Cut* was commissioned in January 1998 by producer Martin Fabinyi, who knew instinctively that Rendell was the man with the creative energy to make Australia's answer to the *Scream* trilogy of slasher movies. To get the project off the ground Mushroom needed a big name to help raise the money from backers. The first person they called was Kylie, and much to everybody's surprise she said yes without hesitation.

'It's the first film for Mushroom Pictures,' Kylie commented in 1999, 'and I've got such a history with Mushroom Records that it just seemed like a good thing to do. Plus I guess Kimble and I always thought that one day we'd work on a feature together.' *Cut* is a brutal, funny horror movie but despite her experiences with blood in *Sample People*, Kylie admitted she wasn't confident with gory scenes. 'I am my own soundtrack to those films,' she admitted. 'I make all the right noises, aarrgh!' Unfortunately for Kylie, her character in *Cut* meets an especially grisly end. Like the movie's tagline says, 'It's hard to scream without a tongue.'

Filmed during April and May 1999 primarily on location in the Adelaide Hills, *Cut* is one of those postmodernist scary movies, very much in the vein of *Scream* and *Urban Legends*. The movie's prologue takes us back to the 1980s – and when Kylie first saw the script she was 'initially horrified'. The idea of dressing up in stretch denim and wearing blue eyeliner would be taking her right back into *Neighbours* territory again. ('I thought, "It's the eighties. Oh no!"' she said.) Back in 1987 a film crew are working on a new Australian horror film called 'Hot Blooded', starring visiting American actress Vanessa Turnbill. When baddie-in-the-mask Brad (former stand-up comedian Frank Roberts) continually messes up his scenes, the movie's tyrannical director, played by Kylie, has just about had enough. 'You idiot!' she screams. 'I told you *not* to go for the throat straight away. You've got to rip her blouse off first!'

Humiliated in front of the rest of the crew, Brad turns up at the director's chalet later that night demanding an apology. He doesn't get one. Kylie, displaying uncharacteristic venom, chastises him for being unprofessional on set. 'I could put a monkey in that suit and it'd do a better job,' she screams. Oh dear, maybe she shouldn't have said that. Brad puts on the rubber fright mask and starts wielding his trademark gardening shears. First off he prunes one of his *own* little pinkies (the man is quite obviously insane) and then Kylie's tongue gets ripped out. Considering how tiny Kylie is in real life the pink prosthetic tongue is bizarrely out of proportion. Kylie's character then finally gets her comeuppance when she is violently pierced to death on a sofa.

Fast forward 12 years and we learn that 'Hot Blooded' was never completed. The ensuing tabloid scandal surrounding the movie means that the three remaining reels of film have been left untouched in a vault. One of the original crew now teaches Film Studies at a Sydney college, but when several of his students start haranguing him about the infamous movie his own blood starts to boil. 'That movie was a nightmare,' he explodes,' and you don't go playing with nightmares.' Professor Lossman (an excellent Geoff Revell) acts as the conscience of Kimble Rendell's film, incessantly warning of the perils of playing with dead things. Naturally enough his protestations all come to nothing when eager beaver student Raffy Carruthers (Jessica Napier) buys the rights to 'Hot Blooded' and vows to finish her mother's work, since it emerges that little Raffy is Kylie's daughter.

With a crew of dim-witted students ready to get the cameras rolling again and the original star contracted to reprise her part in the movie, 'Hot Blooded' resumes shooting at a very creepy, very gloomy old house. Along with a tongue-less Kylie the other 'name' in *Cut* is American actress Molly Ringwald, best remembered from her mid-1980s trilogy of John Hughes so-called Brat Pack movies, *Sixteen Candles* (1984), *The Breakfast Club* (1985) and *Pretty in Pink* (1986). By the dawn of the new millennium Molly's star status had waned, but she was happy to accept the lead role in the Aussie film; she is terrific as faded actress Vanessa Turnbill, a Diet Coke-swilling LA diva, sacked from a daytime soap and reluctant to face the demons from 12 years before. Spoilt in the extreme, and forgetting she's appearing in a low-budget production, Vanessa refuses point blank to do any of her own 'stunts', even something as simple as driving a car ten yards.

Ringwald puts in an energetic performance and, unlike poor Kylie, her tongue remains firmly in her cheek. Predictably enough, as soon as filming recommences the killer reappears in his creepy alien mask and starts picking off the dim-witted film crew one by one. Innocents in the audience coerced into buying a cinema ticket for a comedy starring Kylie Minogue might be slightly perturbed by the steady flow of blood from sundry beheadings, disembowelments, stabbings, throat slashings and impalements, culminating in one young innocent getting her head squashed in a log splitter. *Cut* is blessed with far better special effects than many reviewers gave it credit for and the disgusting denouement, where the killer's face melts over cute little Raffy, is really something to be savoured.

It's all schlock of course, but a refreshing change from the knowing excesses of *Scream* and its other American imitators. *Cut* was far better received than Kylie's previous movie and did respectable business in Australia, where the Red Cross Blood Service supported the movie's marketing campaign by giving promotional packs and free tickets for the premiere to prospective blood donors. Released theatrically in most European countries, most notably in France where it reached #2 at the box-office, *Cut*, like *Sample People*, only limped to a straight-to-DVD release in Britain. Critics weren't kind. Stan James in the *Observer* wrote, 'No film in which Kylie Minogue is brutally murdered can be wholly bad,' which is a throwaway comment in worse taste than the movie itself.

✻   ✻   ✻

The commercial failure of the 'Impossible Princess' album proved Kylie's audience had been reluctant to accept her new 'rockier' direction. Churlish though it may sound, fans wanted the 'old' Kylie back; simply put, they wanted her to record pop songs again. There were persistent, but unsubstantiated, rumours in many of the British tabloids that Pete Waterman had offered to 'save' her freefalling career, but Kylie had other ideas. 'Musically, I won't be foolish and go back to somewhere I've already been,' she explained. Her apprenticeship as an 'indie girl' now officially over, Kylie had proved her vocal versatility; nobody could ever accuse her of being the 'singing budgie' anymore.

In February 1999 she recorded a new duet with Pet Shop Boys for their forthcoming album 'Nightlife'. Called 'In Denial', the song was backed by a full orchestra and choir, with string arrangements provided by Craig Armstrong of Massive Attack. 'The Pet Shop Boys are so talented and the offer came out of the blue,' Kylie said. 'It was no pressure because it wasn't for my album. It's quite theatrical and I'm singing in a fairly dramatic way!' The song, about a gay father coming out to his daughter, has Kylie singing: 'You're not admitting you should be quitting these queens and fairies and muscle Marys.' Although not a disco song per se, 'In Denial' gave Kylie's fans a taste of what they had been missing for the past few years.

Two months later Kylie's cover of 'The Real Thing', the lead song from the *Sample People* movie soundtrack, oozing with Beatles-style flower power flourishes and hallucinatory vocals, proved to be a big club hit when released on white label promo to Australian DJs. The public, sensing Kylie was starting to embrace her pop roots once again, weren't surprised to hear in April 1999 that she had signed to

Raising temperatures
in Glasgow during
KylieFever, May 2002

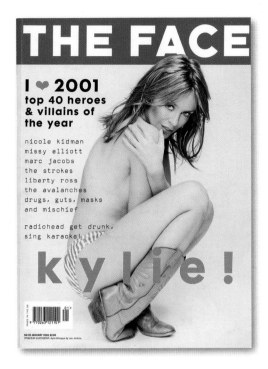

THE FACE

I ♥ 2001
top 40 heroes
& villains of
the year

nicole kidman
missy elliott
marc jacobs
the strokes
liberty ross
the avalanches
drugs, guts, masks
and mischief

radiohead get drunk,
sing karaoke!

k y l i e !

NO 60 JANUARY 2002 £2.90
PRINCESS SUPERSTAR: Kylie Minogue by Lee Jenkins

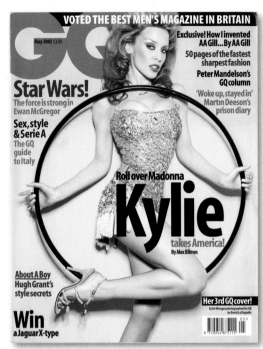

VOTED THE BEST MEN'S MAGAZINE IN BRITAIN

GQ May 2002 £3.00

Exclusive! How I invented
AA Gill...By AA Gill

50 pages of the fastest
sharpest fashion

Peter Mandelson's
GQ column

'Woke up, stayed in'
Martin Deeson's
prison diary

Star Wars!
The force is strong in
Ewan McGregor

**Sex, style
& Serie A**
The GQ guide
to Italy

Roll over Madonna
Kylie
takes America!
By Alex Bilmes

Her 3rd GQ cover!
Kylie Minogue photographed for GQ
by David LaChapelle

About A Boy
Hugh Grant's
style secrets

Win
a Jaguar X-type

Q

Britain's Biggest Music Magazine

PUNKS not Dead!

Sex Pistol Whipped!
The Readers vs John Lydon

From Gob To Glory!
Punk's Lost Years

Plus
**OASIS
BOWIE
DOVES**

**HELL's
BELLS!**
IT'S THE
OSBOURNES

KYLIE GOD
SAVE THE
QUEEN!

PLUS DR FOX SAVAGED BY BABOON | IS LIAM BROKE? | LOSTPR

attitude

WORLD EXCLUSIVE
KYLIE & WILL

A GAY BOY
IS A GIRL'S
BEST FRIEND

DEC 2003 £2.75
WHERE IT'S @

put yourself in my place

Justin Timberlake gets to grips with Australia's finest bottom, BRIT Awards, 2003

Top: Attending the World Sports Awards in Monte Carlo, May 2003

Bottom: Promoting 'Body Language' in Cologne, October 2003

Priceless Kylie. Onstage for *Money Can't Buy*, November 2003

Kylie arrives for the *Top of the Pops* relaunch party, November 2003

LoveKylie
OfficialCalendar2004

ULTIMATE**KYLIE**

NME
NEW MUSICAL EXPRESS

Kylie
rides again
The world exclusive interview

MORRISSEY
THE CURE

THE '80S
POSTER
COLLECTION

Courtney Love
jail drama!

Coldplay: Why
they've scrapped
four albums!

Rock
'n'Roll
Riot
your

Jet and The Hiss
Brawling their way
across the UK

The full report!

RYAN ADAMS SQUARES UP TO HIS CRITICS HAR MAR RIDES A PINK HORSE
HUNDRED REASONS ON THE EDGE OF THE WORLD AND A SHED SEVEN TRIBUTE (KINDA...)

VOTED MAGAZINE OF THE YEAR

January 2005 £3.30

GQ

HITS! HEADLINES! HYSTERIA!

Kylie

OUR FAVOURITE POP
STAR IS BACK. ARE YOU
READY FOR HER?
BY ALEX BILMES

'DRUGS RIGHT
HOOKERS LEFT'
120 MORE
MOVIE QUOTES
YOU CAN USE
IN REAL LIFE

WE HAVE
LIFT-OFF!
GQ IN SPACE

HASSLE-FREE SEX!
HOW TO STEAL
ANOTHER MAN'S
MISTRESS
BY TONY PARSONS

SPECIAL
REPORT!
WHAT YOUR
PENIS SAYS
ABOUT YOU

BUSINESS SPECIAL! **TRADE SECRETS, TRAVEL TIPS AND OUT-OF-OFFICE SEX** the Pet Shop Boys record label, Parlophone, part of the EMI group.

'At several points in my career, it's true, I've tried to create images that just weren't right, that just weren't me,' Kylie admitted, referring to her time at deConstruction. 'But my fans just say, "Oh, it's Kylie going through one of her phases. Don't worry, she'll get over it." They seem to appreciate that I tried something and it didn't work. But at least I tried! I guess it was part of me growing up. I feel that now I've realised where I belong and what I excel at.' Later, Kylie was even more candid about the experience. 'I learnt that you can run but you can't hide. I'd been running away from my old images, my history, pretending it wasn't the real me. All those different styles I had was just me trying to work out who I was and experimenting with different versions. What I came to understand was that I was *all* those people, the sum of those parts. Now I'm proud of who I am and what I do.'

After the Parlophone announcement Kylie was in particularly buoyant mood and indicated from the outset that she would be giving the fans exactly what they wanted. 'I took my time in choosing a new label,' Kylie admitted. 'There is much I hope to achieve with my next album and I believe that anything is possible with my new partnership. I have learnt a lot in the last couple of years and I am very enthusiastic to make a record that is unmistakably *Kylie*.' Parlophone itself echoed her sentiments: 'Kylie is undeniably the most successful female solo artist of our time,' they wrote in their press release. 'She wants to make a pop album and we found that we have a shared idea of what the next record will be like. Kylie is raring to go and I'm sure we'll get the Kylie record that everyone has been waiting for!'

'Spinning Around'

Released June 2000 (UK)
Written by Ira Shickman, Osborne Bingham, Kara DioGuardi and Paula Abdul
Produced by Mike Spencer
Highest chart position #1 (UK), #1 (Australia)

Additional tracks: 'Cover Me with Kisses' and 'Paper Dolls'
Video directed by Dawn Shadforth

Fans had to wait over 12 months before the first fruits of Kylie's Parlophone partnership were ready. As a naughty tease, however, in Spring 2000 Kylie released a strictly limited, one-sided white label of a new tribal-pounding disco track to the clubs. Intrigued music

journalists immediately embraced the mysterious new song, entitled 'Butterfly', and began heralding a new beginning for Kylie.

But even better was just around the corner. In June Kylie appeared at Essential in Manchester and then at G-A-Y in London's Tottenham Court Road, where she performed 'Better the Devil You Know', 'Step Back in Time' plus a cover of Donna Summer's 'I Feel Love'. It was the strongest indication yet of Kylie's new musical direction, further compounded by a rendition of 'Butterfly' plus two totally fresh songs, 'Spinning Around' and the anthemic 'Your Disco Needs You', perhaps the campest song Kylie had ever recorded. *NME*, not always Kylie's biggest supporter, must have blushed when it wrote, 'The pint-size princess of pop has returned to what she knows best. Indie chancers throw away your hair slides and take note, this is the sound of somebody enjoying themselves. Does it scare you?'

The first single from Kylie's new album became 'Spinning Around', a track co-written by ex-pop star and soon-to-be *American Idol* judge Paula Abdul. Allegedly about Abdul's divorce from her second husband, the song is a powerful feminist tirade about moving on from a useless relationship; in that respect it has much in common with Gloria Gaynor's 1979 classic 'I Will Survive'. 'I found a new direction,' Kylie sings in her new song, 'and it leads me back to me.' The number was actually penned by a total of four songwriters, none of whom was Kylie. This marked a distinct change from Kylie's previous life at deConstruction, where she insisted on having more control over songwriting duties on her music. 'I enjoy the period of being in the studio, starting the day with nothing and going home with something you made; it's a thrill,' said Kylie at the time. 'But I said my concern with this album is that it has to be song driven and if I don't write the songs, I don't mind. Let's just get the best songs we can.'

It was one of Parlophone's A & R men, Jamie Nelson, who finally found a demo of 'Spinning Around' in New York in 1999. 'He went over there,' reported Kylie, 'and arrived home waving his arms about saying, "I've got this great song here. I think it would be perfect for you!" And we all listened to it and loved it straight away, even in demo form. It had something! I panicked and said, "Quick, call them and don't let them let anyone else have it!" We all wanted that song.'

Smoothly produced by Mercury Award-nominated Mike Spencer, 'Spinning Around' fizzes with flirty effervescence; a deliberate homage to Kylie's PWL days but infused with an ironic 1970s disco sensibility and lashings of sexual energy. Kylie sings with unrestrained glee as though she's finally free of her rock chick shackles and is doing what she loves best. (Interestingly, though, the song's two B-sides, 'Cover Me with Kisses' and 'Paper Dolls', are more akin to her deConstruction work than her new disco sound.) 'Spinning Around' became an instant radio airplay hit throughout Europe and Australia before entering the British charts at #1, the first time Kylie had done so. It was Kylie's sixth UK chart-topper and her fifth in Australia, where it also debuted at #1. It also hit the Top 10 throughout the world, giving Kylie her biggest international seller for nearly six years.

The now-fabled video, directed by Sheffield-born Dawn Shadforth, shows Kylie flirting with some sexy boys and confidently strutting her stuff in a hedonistic London club. Looking her best on celluloid since 1994's 'Put Yourself in My Place' – totally carefree, happy and shimmering with St Tropez fake tan – it was her bottom that fixated fans and journalists alike. But the video's budget, reputedly £400,000, was dwarfed by a 50 pence pair of second-hand gold lamé hotpants which Kylie wore throughout. As the song's cheeky lyrics state, 'Threw away my old clothes, got myself a better wardrobe,' yet it was the ruched shorts from a flea market which were credited for helping relaunch Kylie's career. 'Most of my clothes are second-hand,' Kylie admitted. 'I like a bargain and it also makes sure I have something no one else has.'

The hotpants had been bought some years earlier by a friend of the singer's and the day before the 'Spinning Around' video shoot Kylie's stylist William Baker was hunting round her flat trying to find something she could wear. 'They leapt out at me as just the job for the image we were going for,' Baker said in an interview with the *Sunday Mirror* in 2002. 'We knew the hotpants looked good but we didn't realise how it was going to take off. When she wore them I was panicking that the pants were going to disappear up the crack of her bum, which would have been very embarrassing. No one thought we were creating an icon. It was a total fluke.'

Several copies of the original sparkly hotpants were made, but Kylie safely kept the original, which later went on display (in a protective glass case, no less) for the 2005-08 travelling exhibition of her stage outfits. Some fans were alarmed to see just how worn they had become, despite their being insured for a staggering £1 million. 'I was so self-conscious in them,' Kylie admitted, 'but it's not like my bum can actually do anything, except wiggle!'

From 'Spinning Around' onwards Kylie's peachy derrière became a huge public talking point. The *Sun* newspaper recommended that her bottom be recognised as an official 'national treasure', with readers voting it the world's best 'pert posterior'. Two years later the tabloid was alleging that 33-year-old Kylie must have had a 'bum lift' after flashing her perky rump at the BRIT Awards. Such was the popularity of Kylie's backside that even an unofficial *Hotpants Workout* DVD was hastily released with the strap-line: '*For a bum like Kylie's!*' Regardless of Kylie's physical attributes, 'Spinning Around' was still an absolutely crucial song in her career. In more ways than one it marked the beginning of Kylie's second Golden Age.

'On a Night Like This'

Released September 2000 (UK)
Written by Steve Torch, Graham Stack, Mark Taylor and Brian Rawling
Produced by Graham Stack and Mark Taylor
Highest chart position #2 (UK), #1 (Australia)

Additional tracks: 'Ocean Blue' and 'Your Disco Needs You'
Video directed by Douglas Avery

Kylie first performed 'On a Night Like This' at the London Mardi Gras on 1 July 2000, when it met with unanimous approval from the predominantly gay crowd. At that time Parlophone hadn't made a final decision on what the follow-up to the mammoth-selling 'Spinning Around' would be; they were toying with several options. In August Kylie flew to Monte Carlo to shoot the video for the song and a few weeks later was singing it at Radio One's 'Big Sunday' roadshow on Plymouth Hoe in front of an estimated 60,000-strong crowd. The public's positive reaction to the new track convinced Parlophone they had made the right choice.

'On a Night Like This' was released in the UK in early September, immediately debuting on the charts at #2. In Australia it shot to #1 (her sixth chart topper), cheerfully knocking Madonna's 'Music' off the peak. The song was co-written by Steve Torch and Brian Rawling and co-produced by Mark Taylor, the team who had orchestrated Cher's unprecedented worldwide comeback two years previously with her awe-inspiring single, 'Believe'. That song had hit pole position in 23 countries, earning itself a Grammy Award and becoming officially recognised as the most-played song on radio for the whole of 1999. Part of the single's universal appeal was the way Cher's vocals had been digitised, creating a unique fluctuating sound, which became much copied and lampooned.

Because of the huge global success of 'Believe', and Cher's subsequent album, the team behind the song became hot properties and Parlophone were keen to work with them on Kylie's new material. If they could propel a 52-year-old American rock star back to the top with disco, then they could certainly do it for a 32-year-old Australian pop singer with a solid-gold posterior.

Few people realise that 'On a Night Like This' was not actually written with Kylie in mind, nor was she the first performer to take it into the studio. In 1999 the track was recorded by controversial Swedish disco diva Pandora, with Mark Taylor producing; then it was covered by celebrated Cypriot singer Anna Vissi in early 2000, who went on to perform the song at the *Miss Universe* TV beauty pageant, held in Nicosia in May of that year.

Both versions were entirely different but it is Pandora's Europop mix which Kylie's version most closely resembles. Kylie's weightless vocals slip effortlessly over the thumping disco beat, yet Mark Taylor's deluxe production is as dreamy and polished as any pop lullaby can be. The backing vocals, also provided by Kylie, replicate the digital effects of Cher's hit with her trancelike 'on a, on a, on a...' slinking between the tranquilising keyboards and plucky strings. The full-lipped lyrics also present Kylie at her most libidinous: 'You touch me, I want you. Feels like I've always known you.'

A production as ambrosial as 'On a Night Like This' deserved an equally sophisticated video, and director Doulgas Avery's Monaco-set promo is the most cinematic of Kylie's entire pop career. Inspired by Martin Scorsese's movie *Casino*, Kylie plays a beautiful moll to Rutger

Hauer's creepy underworld boss. Dutch-born Hauer, best known for his intense performances in movies such as *The Hitcher* (1986) and his eccentric appearances in the 1990s Guinness advertising campaign, is as deranged and detached as ever, responding to sinister concerns about his dodgy business dealings. 'What you find difficult,' he says, menacingly, 'I find simple.' Kylie is left neglected by her older lover, resorting to scare tactics to perk his romantic interests, going so far as to play dead, face down, in their villa's floodlit pool. Lonely, frustrated and bored, she strips off and tosses her wet clothes at Hauer's window, but to no avail.

Later, dripping in £2 million worth of diamonds especially borrowed for the shoot, her character goes to the casino and proceeds to fling all her chips into the air over the gaming table, much to the shock of the other patrons. 'I've never been a jewellery type,' said Kylie, 'but as soon as I got that lot on I was a different woman. They were so heavy and I've got to say I felt like running away with them. However, the two security guards didn't look that keen, so I reluctantly handed them back.' Gems aside, it is the video's last scene which has proved to be most iconic. Disrobing again to just knickers and high heels, she steps slowly back into the pool, while a solemn Hauer looks on passively, raising the question: who really holds the power in this relationship, the kept woman or the man who keeps her?

The velvety video is as spine-tingling as the music that accompanies it and the combination arguably makes 'On a Night Like This' one of Kylie's greatest ever dance-pop moments. Her reinvention as a disco diva, after years shying away from pop, prompted the *Daily Mirror* to ask what had suddenly come over her. 'Don't ask me why I'm seen as hip these days,' she said. 'I honestly don't know. Times have changed and maybe people are just ready to enjoy some unashamed pop music again. I just want to be completely true to myself, to be what I am. I do pop, I do disco. I'm a show pony. I'm a bit campy and very showy. Oh, and I love to have fun!'

'Light Years'

Released September 2000 (UK)
Parlophone / Mushroom Records
Produced by Mike Spencer (track 1), Graham Stack and Mark Taylor (track 2), Johnny Douglas (tracks 3, 4 and 6), Guy Chambers and Steve Powers (tracks 5, 7, 12 and 13), Richard 'Biff' Stannard and Julian Gallagher (track 8, 11 and 14), Steve Anderson (track 9), and Mark Picchiotti (track 10)

Highest chart position #2 (UK),
#1 (Australia)

Track listing:
'Spinning Around'
'On a Night Like This'
'So Now Goodbye'
'Disco Down'
'Loveboat'
'Koocachoo'
'Your Disco Needs You'
'Please Stay'
'Bittersweet Goodbye'
'Butterfly'
'Under the Influence of Love'
'I'm So High'
'Kids'
'Light Years'

Kylie's rebirth as a dance icon took her way back beyond
the deConstruction years, even 'Let's Get to It', dropping her right into
the fertile early 1990s wonderland of 'Better the Devil You Know'.
'Light Years' is everything 'Impossible Princess' isn't – 14 frothy Studio
54 rhythms topped with a heavy dusting of Eurotrash decadence –and
it's Kylie pulling out all the populist stops here because this is an album
that just yearns to be adored. Ditching Manic Street Preachers' stream
of consciousness in favour of fluff from contemporary pop masters Guy
Chambers, Robbie Williams, Mark Taylor, Johnny Douglas and Richard
'Biff' Stannard, Kylie delivers a very commercial-sounding album
packed to the nightclub roof with instantly catchy modern filtered-disco
– not necessarily an easy thing to do.

Ostentatious singles 'Spinning Around' and 'On a Night Like
This' set the pace with their unstoppable likeability. Chambers and
Williams quickly nail it with the holiday romance fiesta of 'Loveboat'
and the easygoing beat of 'I'm So High', although Kylie is at her
most unashamedly frivolous on the boys' 'Your Disco Needs You': a
kitsch, and clever, 'YMCA' pastiche complete with a male voice choir.
Village People, Donna Summer and Gloria Gaynor are all afforded due
reverence along the way, and accordingly Kylie delivers a light and airy
retro cover of Barry White's 1974 disco standard 'Under the Influence
of Love'. Best of the new tracks is the pounding, unrufflable 'Butterfly'

– a tough-talking floorfiller and the album's missed opportunity as a single release.

It's not all sweaty vests and poppers though. Nestling among a virtual hour of mirrorball anthems is 'Bittersweet Goodbye', a moving ballad laden with strings and emotion (produced by deConstruction's Steve Anderson) and the pomp rock of 'Kids', Kylie's camp, high-octane duet with Robbie himself. The album winds down with the trance dreamscape of Biff Stannard's ace-in-the-pack title track, where Kylie takes on the mantle of pink-hued trolly dolly, thanking her hedonistic passengers for taking the trip with her. 'Thank you for flying KM Air. We hope you had a pleasant flight,' she says. 'Please fly with us again'. Kylie, you don't even have to ask.

'Light Years' proved to be the regeneration Kylie had dreamt of and Parlophone had banked on; selling in excess of two million copies worldwide. Complimenting the massive success of her later *On a Night Like This tour*, the album was reissued in Australia in March 2001, featuring a bonus disc of remixes plus her version of Olivia Newton-John's 'Physical'.

FOOTNOTE: some listeners noticed a slight 'hiccup' at the beginning of the original European release of the album. When rewinding the CD from 'Spinning Around' a 'secret' track is revealed, the funk-filled 'Password', later to appear as the B-side to the Aussie release of 'Your Disco Needs You'.

✳   ✳   ✳

The whopping success of 'Light Years' was undeniably dwarfed by Kylie's next great public performance. On 16 October 2000 she appeared at the closing ceremony of the Sydney Summer Olympics, performing to an estimated global audience of four billion people. Arriving at the stadium atop a giant flip-flop carried by a bevy of buffed Aussie lifeguards, she changed into a pink sequinned showgirl outfit and sang a spirited version of ABBA's classic 'Dancing Queen'. If that wasn't quite camp enough, the ceremony continued with a troupe of drag queens in an *Adventures of Priscilla, Queen of the Desert* tribute and then Kylie returned to the stage to perform, appropriately, 'On a Night Like This'; the result was by far the most ludicrously swanky Olympiad party in living memory. 'For the week leading up to it, I was a complete wreck,' confessed Kylie.

In absolute contrast, for the opening ceremony of the Paralympic Games two days later, Kylie gave a surprisingly low-key performance, wearing just a long overcoat, singing a spellbinding, and surprisingly intimate, version of 'Waltzing Matilda' before discarding her coat to reveal gold jeans and halter-neck top and throwing herself into an energetic rendition of 'Celebration'. As a result of the huge TV exposure, Kylie's 'On a Night Like This', which had dipped from the top spot in the Australian charts, rightly reclaimed its position at #1.

'Kids'

Released October 2000 (UK)
Written by Robbie Williams and Guy Chambers
Produced by Guy Chambers and Steve Power

Additional tracks: (performed by Robbie)
'John's Gay', 'Often', 'Karaoke Star' and 'Kill or Cure Me'
Highest chart position #2 (UK), #14 (Australia)
Video directed by Simon Hilton

Kylie's next single was penned by Robbie Williams and his longtime songwriting collaborator Guy Chambers, both at the peak of their powers. Having just had a worldwide smash with 'Rock DJ', and with a string of MTV and BRIT awards behind him, it seemed like Robbie could do no wrong. Duetting with a performer as legendary as Kylie would just be another notch on his musical belt. 'Kids' originally appeared as a cut on Robbie's August 2000 album 'Sing When You're Winning' before appearing, albeit in an edited form, on Kylie's 'Light Years'. The song was originally envisaged as a solo track; odd since it was a wordy duel detailing a person's apparent incompatibility with a potential partner. Robbie liked the song so much he suggested a duet between him and Kylie, each taking a lyrical line in a musical battle of words.

'I basically fancy her,' Robbie boasted in an interview in the *Daily Mirror*. 'I always have and it's a kick for me. She's such a fantastic singer. I was like, "Kylie, I fancy you, can you sing on my record, please?" I was really nervous when we got it together to sing it. I couldn't even speak to her.' Kylie had also been an admirer of Robbie ever since his Take That days. In July 1995 Kylie was asked on the *Steve Wright People Show* which member of the band she most fancied.

Without hesitation she answered, 'Robbie!'

More so than any of Kylie's previous duets, the chemistry between her and Robbie is tantalising throughout and is never more in evidence than in the *Grease*-inspired video, where the two performers weave and skip around each other in an MTV mating ritual. In a rare break from filming, the pair jumped on the back of tour manager Sean Fitzpatrick's white Vespa and tore off round the Pinewood Studios backlot, much to the amusement of the crew. The press desperately wanted to believe the couple were dating in real life, but Kylie revealed that he hadn't even made a pass at her. 'He's quite see-through sometimes,' she told the *Sun*, 'but he's the first to admit he can be Robbie Williams the showman, the ego. Underneath he's quite vulnerable and complex. We got on well, but we're not best mates or anything.'

The duo performed the track on a Robbie Williams *Top of the Pops* special in Britain and then a raunchier funked-up version for the MTV Europe Music Awards, held in Sweden in the autumn of 2000. The fact that Robbie was suffering from gastroenteritis didn't stop him from flirting with Kylie and the dozen or so ostrich-feathered pole dancers. Their provocative performance tore the roof off the Stockholm Globe Arena. Madonna was also in attendance, famously performing her hit single 'Music' while wearing a t-shirt with a golden 'Kylie Minogue' emblazoned across the front. 'I wonder how much an advertisement on Madonna's breasts would cost?' laughed an obviously flattered Kylie. 'It would be pretty expensive, so I was really taken aback. I was absolutely floored by that!'

The choppy percussion and buzzy electric guitar of 'Kids' perhaps seem more at home on a U2 song, so it was ironic that Bono should duet with Kylie on 'Kids' for her *Showgirl Homecoming* tour. Their performance ended up on Kylie's 2007 concert movie *White Diamond*, with Bono cheekily emulating Robbie's swagger and thrusting arrogance. 'How does Robbie do it?' asked Bono sarcastically. 'He's my inspiration.'

The version of 'Kids' which appears on Kylie's 'Light Years' album differs from the recording on Robbie's LP. The longer version of the song features a tongue-in-cheek rap by Robbie, which taunts the British press for its obsession with the possibility that he may be bisexual. He retorts, 'Press be asking do I care for sodomy? I don't know, yeah, probably!' Parlophone had the rap removed for Kylie's album version, mindful that her younger fans might not care for references to anal sex, but forgetting that her gay audience might well have enjoyed it.

'Please Stay'

Released December 2000 (UK)
Written by Kylie Minogue, Richard 'Biff'
Stannard, Julian Gallagher and John Themis
Produced by Richard 'Biff' Stannard and Julian
Gallagher
Highest chart position #10 (UK), #15
(Australia)

Additional tracks: 'Santa Baby' and 'Good Life'
Video directed by James Frost and Alex Smith

In November the newly marketable
Kylie filmed an Australian commercial
for Pepsi, having switched allegiance
from Coca-Cola, which she had previously
promoted in the early 1990s. The new
Pepsi advert featured an adolescent boy
watching Kylie singing 'On a Night Like
This' on television. The boy's remote control suddenly comes to life,
meaning he can 'switch off' his moaning family and transport Kylie
into his living room, where the petite singer lands on his lap and
starts cuddling up to him suggestively. The commercial upset a few
puritanical viewers and Pepsi promptly withdrew it.

On much safer ground, Kylie's festive release for December 2000
was not 'Your Disco Needs You' or 'Butterfly' as some fans had hoped,
but instead the flamenco-flavoured 'Please Stay', taken from the 'Light
Years' album. Not the most obvious choice for a single, it nevertheless
showed off Kylie's rediscovered pop versatility. The lyrics are a poignant
plea to a much-adored love ('I lose it every time I'm near to you'),
drifting lazily over gorgeous gipsy guitar and clicking castanets. 'Please
Stay' was co-written and produced by Richard 'Biff' Stannard, better
known, at that point, for his work with Gabrielle, Gary Barlow and Spice
Girls. Kylie's song has a definite Spice Girls vibe to it, reminiscent of
the beautiful Spanish-accented 'Viva Forever' from 1997.

The single was backed with two new recordings – the squeakily
laidback Balearic groove of 'Good Life' and Kylie's cover of the 1953
standard 'Santa Baby', originally a hit for Eartha Kitt but also released
by a variety of artists over the years, including Madonna in 1987. Kylie
seductively performed the song, dressed in a red fur-trimmed dressing
gown, on the Christmas Day *Top of the Pops*, which was enough to give

anybody indigestion after turkey, sprouts and stuffing. 'Please Stay' reached #10 in the UK charts, giving Kylie her best run of consecutive Top 10 hits since 1990-91.

'Your Disco Needs You'

Released March 2001 (Australia)
Written by Kylie Minogue, Robbie Williams and Guy Chambers
Produced by Guy Chambers and Steve Power
Highest chart position #20 (Australia)

Additional tracks: 'Password' and 'Please Stay' (7th District Club Flava mix)
Video directed by Todd Cole

First released in Germany in January 2001, where it reached a lowly #31, the fifth track from the 'Light Years' album never became a single in the UK, despite a campaign by some of Kylie's most fervent British fans. Discounted as a single because it had already been included as a bonus track on the British CD release of 'On a Night Like This', with hindsight the non-appearance of a 'You Disco Needs You' single was a serious misjudgment by Parlophone. However, it is understandable that Kylie wanted to release the totally un-disco-ish 'Please Stay' instead, in a bid to promote the variety of the 'Light Years' album. Perhaps a double A-side December release of 'Please Stay' and a new mix of 'Your Disco' would have been the sensible compromise, especially since the latter song was destined to be a party favourite throughout the festive season.

In March 2001 'Your Disco' eventually emerged as a limited edition single (just 10,000 copies) in Australia, where, despite its ultra-camp Village People feel, it still only managed to climb to #20, ultimately a casualty of everybody already playing it death off the album. Featuring extended and radio edit mixes by dance outfits Almighty and Casino, the song gained a second wind in the gay clubs where it has remained a staple ever since. The sparkling track was co-written by Kylie in conjunction with Robbie Williams and Guy Chambers, and its saucy title is a pastiche of the iconic 1914 British army recruitment poster featuring moustachioed Lord Herbert Kitchener, imploring young men to join up and fight. The 'Your Country Needs You' slogan was much parodied over the ensuing century, but never more cheekily than when Kylie called up her legion of gay fans to step onto the world's dancefloors, from 'Soho to Singapore...'

Because of the single's relative obscurity, the fabulous 1970s-style video, shot in LA and featuring an army of beguilingly busty Kylies, has been largely unseen. The song was a concert favourite during the original *Showgirl* tour, but the frustration that it was denied a wider audience seems to have persisted. Even as late as 2006 the *Sun* newspaper incorrectly predicted that a new remix of the song would spearhead Kylie's comeback after beating cancer. As it is, 'Your Disco Needs You' might just be the greatest #1 Kylie never had and quite possibly the only pop song ever to name-check Scrabble.

On a Night Like This Tour

Creative Director – William Baker / Music Producer – Steve Anderson / Choreography by Luca Tommassini / Tour Manager – Sean Fitzpatrick / Stage Manager – Phil Murphy / Set Designer – Jonathan Perry / Wardrobe by Julien MacDonald

Musicians: Steve Turner (keyboards), Chris Brown (bass), James Hayto (guitar), James Mack (percussion), Lurine Cato and Sherina White (backing vocals)

3-28 March 2001 (Europe)
14 April-30 May 2001 (Australia)

Set list: Love Boat, Koocachoo, Hand on Your Heart, Put Yourself in My Place, On a Night Like This, Step Back in Time/Never Too Late/Wouldn't Change a Thing/Turn It Into Love/Celebration (medley), Can't Get You Out of My Head, Your Disco Needs You, I Should Be So Lucky, Better the Devil You Know, So Now Goodbye, Physical, Butterfly, Confide in Me, Kids, Shocked.
First Encore: Light Years, What Do I Have to Do.
Second Encore: Spinning Around.

It seemed oddly appropriate that Kylie's latest tour came steaming into harbour on a giant 1950s cruise liner. Calling in at several British ports, then Denmark, Germany and France before setting sail for Australia, this was the biggest tour of Kylie's career to date. Inspired by *South Pacific*, *Anchors Aweigh* and American burlesque theatre – also incorporating elements from her performance at the Sydney Olympics and a splash of Tiki high camp – the tour promised the best bits of 'Light Years' mixed with some sexy new interpretations of Kylie's greatest hits.

Each night the singer was lowered onto the stage on HMS Kylie's giant sparkly anchor, not something, it later transpired, Kylie was totally comfortable with. ('Teetering on tiny heels high up in the air isn't fun!') The show launched with a glittering version of 'Love Boat' as Kylie danced with grass-skirted hula girls and some very unconvincing butch sailors. After a luscious and smoothly intimate version of 'Put Yourself in My Place', everything stepped up a gear with Kylie donning her flaming red leather Julien MacDonald flares and getting a huge roar from the audience for 'On a Night Like This'.

For the medley of SAW's greatest moments, Kylie became a disco guru with her American football armour-wearing dancers on their knees swaying around her in worshipful obedience. The rearranged version of 'Turn It Into Love' in particular was a hypnotic treat, as was the poignant ballad version of 'I Should Be So Lucky' with Kylie dressed in top hat and tails. The laidback jazzy mix of 'Better the Devil' was also mesmerising, demonstrating how Fred Astaire might have performed it had it been his song.

This was also the tour when Kylie debuted 'Can't Get You Out of My Head' – here a strangely low-key performance of what was yet to become her all-time anthem. On stage Kylie performed the song as a duet with bass guitarist Chris Brown, before launching into a super-charged version of fan-favourite 'Your Disco Needs You'. A cover of Olivia Newton-John's 1981 hit 'Physical' proved to be a showstopper, with Kylie writhing around a cage-like contraption with four near-naked pole dancers, a favourite moment of the tour for her.

But it was the dirty electro version of 'Butterfly' which really got pulses racing. William Baker took advantage of every hardcore S & M gay porn cliché, with Kylie's nymphomaniac dancers dressed in Tom of Finland leathers, grinding their crotches and sweaty abdominals all over her petite female form. Kylie was the dominatrix in charge, strutting eroticism and enjoying every second of her descent into Frankie Goes to Hollywood territory. During 'Kids' she even sang the controversial Robbie Williams rap, sticking out her pert little bum during the risqué 'sodomy' lyric. This was Kylie at her most wantonly provocative.

For the encores of 'Light Years' and 'What Do I Have to Do' Kylie emerged from a huge art deco alien spaceship, the jerking and twisting robotic dancers providing the template for the iconic 'Can't Get You

Out of My Head' video. As an extra-special treat the show climaxed with a second encore: a euphoric, and exhausting, version of 'Spinning Around'.

1998's *Intimate and Live* had whetted Kylie's appetite for live performance again, but *On a Night Like This* was on a wholly different scale, and the first mega-tour of Kylie's career was not without its problems. The female dancers were so sweaty during the show that by the time they performed the pole dance during 'Physical' they kept slipping down their equipment. William Baker was dissatisfied with the technical elements of the show; there were several 'wardrobe malfunctions' and, to top it all, Kylie caught the flu during the Melbourne leg of the tour and a doctor was installed silently in the wings with an oxygen mask and a hypodermic needle full of anti-nausea drugs. One night during her performance of 'I Should Be So Lucky' the crew were convinced an ashen-faced Kylie might even topple off the grand piano. Understandably, by the end of the 43rd concert on 30 May 2001 everybody – Kylie, her dancers, her band and her crew – was ready for a holiday.

Among the ecstatic reviews, the *Independent* noted that 'As well as a formidable singing voice, she has personality all her own and it shines best amid Hi-NRG beats, silver tassels and six inch stiletto heels!' And for the *Daily Mail*, 'Kylie is in her element, revelling in her status as the queen of pop – a woman at the apex of her career.'

Kylie: Live in Sydney

A Terry Blamey Management (TBM) – Done and Dusted Production / 107 minutes + 25 minutes of extra footage

Directed by Hamish Hamilton / Produced by Ian Stewart / Executive Producer – Terry Blamey / Distributed by Warner Music Vision

The *Live in Sydney* DVD – recorded at the 30 May Sydney concert (the final date of the tour – features Kylie's entire set. All the songs, including the sheer raunchy kinkiness of the S & M 'Butterfly' routine, are presented in full, but it is the backstage footage (which can either be viewed as nine individual vignettes, or incorporated into the actual concert) that is most illuminating.

A tongue-tied Kylie shows her obvious discomfort in being caught off-guard by the camera on several occasions. 'I feel exhausted. I can't concentrate before a show,' she complains during a wardrobe fitting. 'There are not normally camera people in here at this point!' Later when Kylie comes off stage she is unexpectedly greeted by an eager film crew. 'What are you guys doing here?' she asks, rather frustrated. Little did she dream what a huge imposition William Baker's camera would be making five years later for the feature-length *White Diamond* documentary.

Amid the hunky Italian dancers splitting their pants ('They fill their trousers quite well!' says the anonymous cameraman), the DVD's most candid moments involve the tour's mischievous technical boys trying to distract Kylie while she performs 'Better the Devil You Know', culminating in a cheeky full monty. 'I suspected the final night might involve a little nudity,' Kylie says wearily.

Moulin Rouge!

2001 / A Bazmark Film Production / Australia-USA / 127mins / cert 'M' (Australia) cert '12' (UK) / Opened May 2001 (USA)

Directed by Baz Luhrmann / Written by Baz Luhrmann and Craig Pearce / Produced by Baz Luhrmann, Martin Brown and Fred Baron / Cinematography by Donald McAlpine / Original Music composed by Craig Armstrong

Cast: Nicole Kidman (*Satine*), Ewan McGregor (*Christian*), Jim Broadbent (*Harold Zidler*), Richard Roxburgh (*The Duke*), John Leguizamo (*Toulouse-Lautrec*), Kylie Minogue (*The Green Fairy*), Garry McDonald (*The Doctor*), Jacek Koman (*narcoleptic Argentinean*), Matthew Whittet (*Satie*), Kerry Walker (*Marie*), Caroline O'Connor (*Nini Legs in the Air*), Christine Anu (*Arabia*), Natalie Mendoza (*China Doll*), Lara Mulcahy (*Madame Fromage*), David Wenham (*Audrey*), Keith Robinson (*Le Pétomane*), Deobia Oparei (*Le Chocolat*), Peter Whitford (*stage manager*)

Considering Kylie is so tiny in real life it comes as no surprise that in the most commercially successful movie of her career she plays a six-inch tall fairy, albeit one with green skin. The role was earmarked for her by visionary Australian director Baz Luhrmann, for what he now calls the third part of his 'red curtain trilogy' – following *Strictly Ballroom* (1992) and *William Shakespeare's Romeo + Juliet* (1996).

Based very loosely on the 1952 British-made *Moulin Rouge*, which starred Zsa Zsa Gabor and José Ferrer, Baz Luhrmann's re-imagining of the subject matter manifests itself in multi-coloured camp theatrics of the very highest order. Shot between November 1999 and May the following year, *Moulin Rouge!* (note the added exclamation mark) proudly displays every single penny of its $52 million budget, making it the most expensive Australian movie of all time – that is, until production was bumped out of Sydney's Fox Studios to make way for *Star Wars: Episode III – Attack of the Clones*.

Luhrmann is well known for his love of bold, beautiful and often gratuitous visuals and it could be argued that *Moulin Rouge!* is contemporary filmmaking at its most self-indulgent. Audiences were split between those who adored every moment of the director's glittering, big-busted musical epic and those who just found the whole sugar-coated exercise a little too rich to stomach. Certainly if your liking is for loud, OTT, retro-styled extravaganzas fit to bursting with sparkling sequins, bulging corsets, frilly pink knickers, belly-dancing dwarves and Bollywood glamour then *Moulin Rouge!* is just what the doctor ordered.

As with his previous two movies, Luhrmann continued with his favoured theme of forbidden love. Set in 1900, Ewan McGregor stars as Christian, a naïve, penniless writer who dreams of perfect, everlasting love and finds it in the Moulin Rouge's elegant, fragile Satine (a career-defining performance from Nicole Kidman). From the movie's inventive *Pink Panther*-esque opening titles through to its heart-stopping conclusion, *Moulin Rouge!* races along at a relentless pace, liberally pinching endless snippets of popular songs and presenting them in the most unethical way. From choice cuts of Queen, T.Rex, Dolly Parton, LaBelle, Marilyn Monroe, The Police and even Nirvana, Luhrmann re-packages some of the most instantly recognisable tunes of the late 20th century.

However, some viewers may be forgiven for being disorientated by the sheer bombardment of pop tunes. There's a spine-tingling moment when McGregor sings excerpts from Elton John's 'Your Song', but the couple's rapid-fire medley of love songs (The Beatles, U2, Wings, David Bowie etc), delivered while standing in Satine's elephant-shaped bedroom, is almost too intoxicating to swallow in one sitting, proving to be both comforting and distracting at the same time. Undoubtedly, the movie's musical highlight is seeing a rubicund Jim Broadbent delivering an eardrum-splitting rendition of Madonna's 'Like a Virgin', surrounded by fey waiters wobbling breast-shaped jellies on plates.

Oddly enough it is Kylie, the only professional singer in the principal cast, who actually has the least amount to warble. Despite recording a new version of Olivia Newton-John's worldwide #1 single 'Physical', which was subsequently cut from the final film, Kylie delivers only one vocal performance – a weird amalgamation of T.Rex's anthemic 1972 hit 'Children of the Revolution' and 'The Sound of Music' from the musical of the same name.

Although little more than a cameo, Kylie enjoys the most emblematic role in *Moulin Rouge!* Throughout 19th century Europe, absinthe, a highly alcoholic (sometimes 80 per cent proof) aniseed-flavoured beverage, was widely believed to be the inspiration behind (and ruin of) writers, poets and artists. The favoured tipple of young French bohemians, absinthe naturally makes an important early appearance in Baz Luhrmann's film. When Christian meets up with Toulouse-Lautrec's free-and-easy gang of misfits he submits to a few glasses of the drink, popularly dubbed *La Fée Verte* ('The Green Fairy). The tipple is known for its hallucinatory powers and after Christian and his cohorts have imbibed vast quantities they imagine the pretty little pixie on the side of the bottle come to life.

A winged Kylie leaps from the label, zipping around the room, trilling 'The hills are alive...' and doing a sexy, bum-wiggling dance. 'I'm the Green Fairy' she says cheekily, giving Christian come-hither looks before replicating herself into 11 identical pixies in a miniature pastiche of a Busby Berkeley musical number. Eventually she flees from the window spelling 'freedom, beauty, truth and love' in her slipstream, all words central to Luhrmann's original concept for his film. Unfortunately, for her role, Kylie didn't meet any of her co-stars during filming, not even Richard Roxburgh (her *Hayride to Hell* victim) or Peter Whitford, who had been her gang's arch nemesis in *The Henderson Kids*.

Images of Kylie in her iconic fairy costume were used extensively to promote *Moulin Rouge!* prior to its release. The film finally premiered at the Cannes Film Festival on 9 May 2001 as the event's opening title and met with instant adoration from audiences. The film became a massive international hit for distributors 20th Century Fox (it made $13 million during its opening US weekend alone) and was eventually nominated for eight Oscars. It won two, for art direction and costume design, yet Luhrmann received absolutely no recognition from the Academy for his dazzling directorial duties. Even so, screenings were invariably greeted with wild, rapturous applause.

An enthralled *Washington Post* called the movie a 'wonderful post-modern hug', while *Rolling Stone* likened watching the film to being 'mauled'. Both reviewers are spot on. It's a heady, lascivious mix of the familiar and the frivolous, a modern-day pantomime for lovers of old-fashioned romance. But immerse yourself too deeply and you might just make yourself sick.

'Can't Get You Out of My Head'

Released September 2001 (UK)
Written and Produced by Cathy Dennis and Rob Davis
Highest chart position #1 (UK), #1 (Australia)

Additional tracks: 'Boy' and 'Rendezvous at Sunset'
Video directed by Dawn Shadforth

Just when everyone thought Kylie's comeback couldn't get any bigger, up popped 'Can't Get You Out of My Head'. Kylie had premiered the track on her *On a Night Like This* tour, which opened in Glasgow on 3 March 2001, and it was the only completely new number she performed during the concert dates. The song had been recorded just weeks before the tour commenced, Kylie little knowing at the time that it was to become her signature tune and the biggest selling single release of her career.

'Can't Get You' was written by two unlikely musical bedfellows – a dance diva from the 1990s and a Glam Rocker from the 1970s, respectively Cathy Dennis and Rob Davis. Norfolk-born Dennis had enjoyed genuine transatlantic success as the million-selling singer of 'C'mon and Get My Love' (a US dance chart #1), 'Touch Me' and 'Too Many Walls'. 'It never crossed my mind that I could be a pop star, because I came from Norwich,' said Dennis in a rare interview in 2001. 'Pop stars don't come from Norfolk. All my friends were farmers!' After becoming a household name in America and Japan, Dennis lost her addiction to being a singer and found her real niche as a songwriter for other artists including Spice Girls, S Club 7 and Will Young, always keeping a dictaphone by her bedside in case inspiration came in the middle of the night. Coincidentally, years before she met Kylie, she co-wrote Dannii Minogue's minor 1992 hit 'Love's on Every Corner'.

Two decades earlier Rob Davis had also enjoyed considerable fame as the permed, gaudy guitarist with glitter legends Mud, whose brand of Teddy Boy rock 'n' roll had endeared them to the British public during the mid-seventies. Their biggest success was 1974's 'Tiger Feet', which became that year's bestseller. Years later Davis became immersed in the club scene after a chance meeting with superstar DJ Paul Oakenfold, who lived near his Surrey home. He went on to write lyrics for two of the biggest club tunes of 2000: 'Toca's Miracle' for Fragma and 'Groovejet (If This Ain't Love)' for Spiller, proving Davis' special skill was adding high street accessibility to cutting-edge dance tunes.

The odd combination of Dennis and Davis might not have looked good on paper, but on radio they were irresistible. 'Can't Get You' is a narcotic blend of obsessional lyrics mixed liberally with a deliriously simple, but effective, 'la la la la' hook; a sweet melody counterbalanced by a hard-edged chorus. The demo of the song (with Davis on guitar and Dennis singing) was originally offered to Sophie Ellis-Bextor, who passed on it, and then was played to Kylie in late 2000. Her reaction was immediate. 'When can I do it? When?' she screamed. Months later Kylie told the *Sun* why she had adored the song so much. 'I fell in love with it the first time I heard it,' she explained. 'Like Cinderella's slipper, it was a perfect fit!'

Dennis and Davis also produced the song, giving it a very contemporary, electro sound, full of punchy robotic beats and snip-snappy percussion reminiscent of German synthpop pioneers Kraftwerk. 'It was so simple. It was cool. It was pop!' Kylie enthused. The accompanying video, shot in July 2001 by 'Spinning Around' director Dawn Shadforth, shows Kylie in a futuristic urban world, driving a smooth yellow sports car and dancing atop a skyscraper with a brilliantly choreographed (by dancer Michael Rooney) troupe of jerkily moving androids.

Her white hooded jumpsuit with ridiculously plunging neckline, dipping well past her cute little navel, was almost immodest in comparison to her dancers and created much debate in the press. The Grace Jones-inspired outfit was designed by unknown dressmaker Fiona 'Fee' Doran. 'What can I say about Kylie, apart from the obvious?' said Fee in 2005. 'She's lovely, and for a little bird, she's one tough cookie with a body and face sent from heaven.'

The tabloid's preoccupation with Kylie's 'sexy body' seemed to bemuse, and frustrate, the modest star. 'To be honest my so-called sexiness is more like a *Carry On* film,' she admitted. 'I do these videos to entertain people. They're only supposed to be fun. I mean if people would prefer it I've still got my Charlene dungarees from *Neighbours*. I could wear them for my videos. Oh god, can you imagine!' Irrespective of Kylie's protests, the video for 'Can't Get You Out of My Head' became one of the most requested promos of all time on MTV Europe, demand for the song gradually rising to near-unprecedented levels. Parlophone were sure they had a massive international hit on their hands.

In August it was revealed that 'Can't Get You' was to be released the same day as Victoria Beckham's debut single. Since the break-up of Spice Girls, Posh had brushed the charts again in a clubby duet with dance outfit True Steppers, but the mid-tempo R'n'B-styled 'Not Such an Innocent Girl' was to be her first solo effort. The tabloids went wild, forecasting which high-profile diva would win the coveted #1 spot, desperately trying to stir up a bitchy feud when it really didn't exist. 'I met Victoria once and we just sort of acknowledged each other,' said Kylie. 'You don't wish any ill towards the other, but of course you still want to be number one. I've heard her song. It's all right, but I'm a bigger fan of mine!' Cathy Dennis had other ideas: 'I'm sure Victoria's the first to admit that the only reason she's doing it is so she can keep shopping,' she told the *Sunday Express*.

In the end it was a scarily one-sided contest anyway; Kylie totally demolished all the competition in the Top 10. 'Can't Get You Out of My Head' sold an incredible 306,648 copies in just one week and hurtled into the top spot. All Posh could manage was a paltry 35,000, and a disappointing #6 position. 'It's been a really interesting week with all the media frenzy about chart battles,' Kylie told reporters afterwards. 'It can only be good for the record industry. I want to say a special thanks to everyone who came up to me on the street and told me they loved the single and the video. It means such a lot to me.' Posh graciously accepted defeat through gritted teeth, saying a brief 'Well done, Kylie' to her opponent.

Just like in the UK, Kylie's fabulous new single also entered the Australian charts at #1 (selling 100,000 copies in one week) and thereby starting an almost implausible domino effect throughout the rest of the world. Italy, Germany, France, Denmark, Belgium, Sweden, Ireland, Austria, Portugal, Poland, Greece, Luxembourg and Holland

Kylie, live at
the BRITS

all succumbed to the song and by
the end of the summer 'Can't Get
You Out of My Head' had hit the top
spot in an incredible 40 countries. It
was the bestselling single in Europe
for 16 consecutive weeks, while
in America the track hit #7 on the
Billboard Hot 100 and took pole
position on the US Dance Charts,
making it Kylie's first major Stateside
hit for 13 years. Back in the UK the
song remained at #1 for four weeks,
finally selling over one million copies
by the end of the year and becoming
the most played radio hit of 2001. In
one week alone the song was played
over 3000 times on British radio.

In an interview with the *Guardian*,
Rob Davis tried to shed some light
on why his song had such strong
crossover appeal, from the teenage
bedrooms of Newcastle to the
underground clubs of New York.
'The missus was saying to me the
other day, "It's strange how 'Can't
Get You Out of My Head' is so
big, yet so credible." I think that's
because it's got the club element in
it. We're trying to get it where we've got a little bit of credibility with the
writing, where it's not total cack. I wouldn't have let it out of the house
unless I thought the song was really tasty!'

Throughout the world, from Argentina to Turkey, the unshakable
'Can't Get You Out of My Head' gained platinum sales status, winning
multiple awards wherever it went. 'It is as complete a representation
of a great pop song as it is possible to get,' enthused journalist Paul
Morley, 'and you can imagine Elvis singing it!' At the 47th Ivor Novello
Awards in London, 'Can't Get You' was nominated for four gongs:
Bestselling UK single, the Dance Award, Most-Performed Work and
International Hit of the Year award. Official, and unofficial, club
remixes of the song popped up everywhere, including a magnificent

mash-up of Kylie's hot hit and New Order's groundbreaking 1983 single 'Blue Monday'. Kylie performed the retitled 'Can't Get Blue Monday Out of My Head' (mixed by Stuart Crichton) at the 2002 BRIT Awards, arriving on stage in a Dolce & Gabbana mini-dress atop a giant compact disc; naturally, flashes of her bottom made the showbiz pages of every European tabloid the following day. And such was the popularity of the remix it was released as an additional track on the CD single of 'Love at First Sight'.

The massive global success of 'Can't Get You Out of My Head' caught everybody on the hop, particularly Kylie herself. 'I am totally shattered,' she confessed. 'The whole comeback thing has been totally crazy.' On doctor's orders Kylie was ordered to take a week off work. The punishing schedule of touring, recording a new album and then promoting 'Can't Get You' around the world was taking a serious toll on her health. 'It was exhaustion,' Kylie told the *Daily Mirror.* 'I thought my body was invincible, but I ignored the warning signs. I'm the worst culprit; I just work, work, work. Well, it finally caught up with me. I had to take a week off and spend it in bed. It turned out to be a blessing in disguise. The world didn't cave in, everything still got done. And people's attitudes towards me changed from "She's a machine, she can keep going" to "Oh, and actually, she can't". I had to be reminded of that myself. Career-wise, I'm going up the ladder two rungs at a time right now.'

'Fever'

Released October 2001 (UK)
Parlophone / Mushroom Records
Produced by Tommy D (track 1), Richard 'Biff' Stannard and Julian Gallagher (tracks 2, 8 and 10), Cathy Dennis and Rob Davis (track 3), Greg Fitzgerald (track 4), Mark Picchiotti (track 5), Rob Davis (track 6), Cathy Dennis (track 7), Steve Anderson (track 9), Pascal Gabriel and Paul Statham (track 11), and Greg

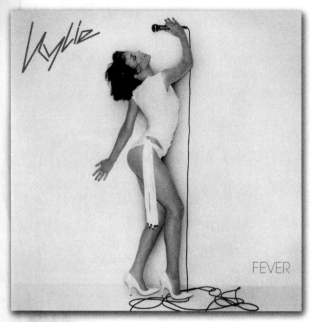

Kylie

FEVER

Fitzgerald and Tom Nicholls (track 12)
Highest chart position #1 (UK),
#1 (Australia)

Track listing:
'More, More, More'
'Love at First Sight'
'Can't Get You Out of My Head'
'Fever'
'Give it to Me'
'Fragile'
'Come Into My World'
'In Your Eyes'
'Dancefloor'
'Love Affair'
'Your Love'
'Burning Up'
Bonus tracks: 'Tightrope' (Australia),
'Good Like That' and 'Baby' (Japan),
'Boy' and 'Butterfly' (USA)

Just over 12 months on Kylie made a triumphant return to the club where 'Light Years' had strutted its stuff, only this time she'd moved away from the illuminated crush beside the DJ booth and was now sipping cocktails in the VIP lounge. 'Fever' steps up a gear from its sisterly predecessor, being an altogether more sophisticated, quality electronic production. On the surface it might appear it's just more of the same, but you'd be mistaken.

Opener 'More More More' isn't just a lazy cover of Andrea True Connection's beddable 1976 dance hit, but a lusty new composition full of funk and fun. Naturally, there are some retro discotheque elements wiggling their butts, like the super stomping 'Dancefloor', and there's a palpaple element of pure Chic-ism on the supremely invigorating 'Love at First Sight', one of the greatest ever songs Kylie has recorded, but overall the feeling is far more contemporary than reverential. The all-conquering global phenomenon of 'Can't Get You Out of My Head' does tend to dominate, if you allow it, but the album is much more than a one-slick trick. With its relentless energy and innovation 'Fever' is the most cohesive and satisfying album of Kylie's career, sizzling with genuine sex appeal, particularly on the rampant, bleeping Moloko-like 'Give It to Me' ('like I want it...' she demands) and the lovesick title track ('So now shall I remove my clothes?').

The breathlessly upbeat tempo is maintained throughout, although it temporarily slows for 'Fragile', a beautiful heartbreaking lament sadly overlooked as a prospective single. Sad and shimmering, 'Fragile' is a highly accomplished piece of thoughtful pop, composed with great sensitivity by Rob Davis and sung with poignancy by a star who obviously believes in what she's doing. Edgier numbers like 'Love Affair' and the minimal Madonna-esque 'Burning Up' insidiously get under your skin, while 'Come Into My World' and 'In Your Eyes' just get better and bigger with continued listens.

Indeed, 'Fever' is a rare thing, a dance album which stands up to repeated plays, revealing a new energy and emotion every time; the sort of game ABBA was so damn good at. With the help of a globally adored lead single, 'Fever' met its critics head-on and blew them away. Selling nearly seven million copies worldwide it is, to date, Kylie's biggest selling album, hitting #1 in Australia, Germany, Ireland, Brazil and the UK and going Top 10 in virtually every pop territory in the world. In America it shifted over a million units alone, becoming her most commercially successful album there and, temporarily, revitalising her profile across the Atlantic.

'Fever' was reissued in Europe in November 2002 with a bonus disc of ten remixes and the additional Japanese tracks.

An Audience with Kylie Minogue

An LWT Production for ITV / 59 minutes / First broadcast (UK) 6 October 2001
Directed by Tony Gregory / Produced by Andi Peters / Musical Director – Steve Anderson / Creative Director – Will Baker / Choreography by Dan Karaty & Michael Rooney

Starring: Kylie
With special guests Adam Garcia and Stuart Whitmire (as Kermit the Frog)

Featuring Pete Waterman, Frank Skinner, Boy George, Julian Clary, Anne Charleston, Cat Deeley, Edith Bowman, June Sarpong, Dane Bowers, Patsy Palmer, Claire Sweeney, Melinda Messenger, Sam Fox, Katie Price, Jenny Frost, Stuart Manning, Jennifer Ellison and Dannii & Brendan Minogue

Track listing: Spinning Around, In Your Eyes, Step Back in Time, The Loco-motion, On a Night Like This, Especially for You, I Should Be So Lucky,

Better the Devil You Know, Put Yourself in My Place, Fever, Can't Get You Out of My Head, What Do I Have to Do-Shocked-Never Too Late-Wouldn't Change a Thing-Celebration (medley)

The *Audience with...* Saturday night specials have become something of a British television institution for the past three decades. The format is simple – a big name performer tells jokes, recalls amusing anecdotes, sings a few songs (or in Bruce Forsyth's case, tap dances) and takes pre-picked questions from a celebrity audience. The series began in December 1980 with *An Audience with Dame Edna Everage* (later invited back for two more raucous instalments) before making way for other such luminaries as Dudley Moore, Kenneth Williams, Joan Rivers, Billy Connolly and Bob Monkhouse.

The first all-singing *Audience with...* was Shirley Bassey's show in 1995 which led the way for specials by the Spice Girls, Elton John (both 1997), the Bee Gees (1998) and Diana Ross (1999). However, not all the nominated stars have such auspicious track records of enduring fame, considering the series is intended to showcase the talents of 'entertainers admired and loved by the British public'. On 10 February 2001 ITV broadcast the lacklustre *An Audience with Ricky Martin*, starring the titular Puerto Rican vocalist who had enjoyed a brief period of international success from 1999-2001 when he began recording in English. For the special Martin performed his cheesiest song (and worldwide #1) 'Livin' La Vida Loca'. At the point in the song when he changes the famous sing-a-long lyrics to 'Woke up in London city...' the stage explodes with pyrotechnics and Kylie appears wiggling her bottom and sliding up and down a pole before joining him on cheek-to-cheek vocal duties. On face value it's a fun performance, although unsurprisingly characterised by a total lack of sexual chemistry between the two singers.

Ricky Martin's show was not one of the most memorable *Audiences...* but, if nothing else, it did provide Kylie with a dry run for her own ITV special, recorded at the London Studios on 22 September 2001 and broadcast two weeks later. Kylie's first ever British TV spectacular was directed by Tony Gregory who had previously overseen *An Audience with the Spice Girls*. The show opens with a scary looking Kylie (resplendent with giant black crow wings attached to the top of her head) emerging from the back of the stage surrounded by dancers and acrobats and belting out 'Spinning Around' to an audience up on their feet and loving every moment. The crow wings disappear for a

Top hat and tails for *An Audience with Kylie Minogue*

performance of 'In Your Eyes', the first of a trio of brand new songs including 'Fever' (sung on a hospital bed) and 'Can't Get You Out of My Head', which coincidentally hit #1 on the day Kylie recorded the TV special.

The rest of the show sticks to totally-reworked interpretations of more familiar classics which she had previously aired on the just-ended *On a Night Like This* tour. These include the jazzy 'Better the Devil You Know' (sung here as a duet with West End star Adam Garcia) and the magical slowed-down version of 'I Should Be So Lucky', after which Kylie looks out into the crowd and says a sincere 'Thank you, Pete' to her most famous music producer. Unfortunately for Kylie there are too few Pete Watermans in audience and a dreary excess of wannabes from *Big Brother*. The rent-a-crowd which populates the front ten rows is predictably depressing – ex-cast members from *Emmerdale*, *Coronation Street*, showbiz parasites like Victoria Hervey and Tara Palmer-Tomkinson and a bevy of bouncing Page Three girls – Sam Fox, Melinda Messenger and Katie Price.

At the start of the show Kylie explains that the celebs in the audience are people who she has 'admired for many years' and the camera comes to a juddering halt on ex-*Blue Peter* presenter Tim Vincent. Even more discomforting is when *Big Brother* champion Brian Dowling asks, rather conceitedly, how he should avoid media attention. Kylie simply says: 'Stay in as much as possible!' It goes without saying none of this banality is Kylie's fault; she obviously has no idea who half of these non-entities are. A few recognisable faces are conspicuous like Anne Charleston (aka Madge Ramsay) who, referring to the fact her *Neighbours* character was killed off the previous April, cheekily asks Kylie, 'Why didn't you make an appearance at my deathbed?' as well as an obviously embarrassed Boy George remembering to sound unscripted when he goads Kylie: 'Do The Loco-motion, girl!'

In an excruciating moment, which Kylie has subsequently blanked from her mind, she is encouraged to drag cocky stud muffin Philip Olivier (*Hollyoaks*), imbecilic fantasist Paul Clarke (*Big Brother 2*) and Olympic boxer Audley Harrison out of the audience to strangle her first hit. You can almost see Waterman fighting back the tears. 'I've obviously got the cream of the crop here,' a sarcastic Kylie tells her new backing group. Mercifully Kylie is wise enough to let her own performances do the talking.

Highlights include the thrilling version of 'Can't Get You Out of My Head' (performed with the robotic dancers from the video) the energising break-dancing thrills of 'Step Back in Time' and Kylie's charming duet with her childhood hero Kermit the Frog on 'Especially for You' ('a more than adequate replacement for Jason Donovan' wrote Ally Ross in the *News of the World*). The show climaxes with a slick medley of Kylie's greatest SAW moments, ending with a captivating rendition of 'Celebration'. Self-publicising reality TV pond-life notwithstanding, Kylie seems to be having a wonderful time (as did over seven million British viewers). 'I've always loved the UK,' she said later, 'but until now I didn't realise how much you guys loved me. This has got to be one of the best nights of my life!'

FOOTNOTE: As part of an exclusive deal with ITV, following her *Audience with...* Kylie was persuaded to record the theme tune for the network's unfairly maligned late-night soap opera *Night and Day*, starring Joe McGann, Lysette Anthony and Glynis Barber. It was Kylie's first involvement with soap since leaving *Neighbours* some 13 years earlier. As it turned out the taboo-breaking serial was cancelled after just 80 episodes, and Kylie's haunting song 'Always and Forever (Tears Will Fall)', written by David Arch and Toddy, has remained a curio ever since.

*   *   *

As 2001 drew to a close, Kylie's last single seemingly refused to go away. In the UK charts 'Can't Get you Out of My Head' remained in the Top 60 for an incredible 25 weeks solid, beating her previous record of 19 weeks, set by 'Kids' a year earlier. Kylie continued to promote the song with high-profile appearances at the V2001 Music Festival in Chelmsford (18 August), BBC Radio 1's One Big Sunday in Leicester (2 September), the *GQ* Awards (5 September) for which she won the jokey 'Services to Mankind' accolade, the MTV Europe Awards in Frankfurt (10 November), the German BAMBI Awards (15 November), the Spanish Music Awards (26 November), the inaugural *Top of the Pops* Awards (30 November), the *Smash Hits* Poll Winners Party (9 December) and the Italian Dance Music Awards (11 December). Phew!

Back in Britain, Kylie's new album 'Fever' made the #1 spot, becoming her first UK chart-topping album since 1992's 'Greatest Hits' compilation. For a while it seemed like Kylie didn't actually have enough hours in the day to promote any more music. 2001 had been a colossal year for her. In May she had even launched her saucy *LoveKylie* lingerie range in Australia, dovetailing with Melbourne Fashion Week.

Speaking about her new collection of specially designed bras, knickers and silky camisoles, she wryly commented, 'There's nothing wrong with a little indulgence no and again!'

'In Your Eyes'

Released February 2002 (UK)
Written by Kylie Minogue, Richard 'Biff' Stannard, Julian Gallagher and Ash Howes
Produced by Richard 'Biff' Stannard and Julian Gallagher
Highest chart position #3 (UK),
#1 (Australia)

Additional tracks: 'Tightrope', 'Good Like That', 'Never Spoken' and 'Harmony'
Video directed by Dawn Shadforth

Following up a hit as colossal as 'Can't Get You Out of My Head' was never going to be an easy task. With 'Fever' awarded triple platinum status in the UK and quadruple platinum in Australia, Parlophone announced that 'In Your Eyes' would be Kylie's new single. It had originally been scheduled for January release in Britain (as it was in Australia), but the determined and ongoing European popularity of 'Can't Get You' had created a delay. With over one million copies of that single sold so far, Kylie's record company seriously doubted whether they'd ever be able to top it. Eventually 'In Your Eyes' was released to tie in with the 2002 BRIT Awards (held in February), of which Kylie was nominated for four gongs, winning two: 'Best International Female' and 'Best International Album'.

The song, co-written by Biff Stannard, now one of Kylie's favourite collaborators, has an almost decaffeinated deep house sensibility with powerful, sexy beats diffused with some subtle Latino elements in its chorus. The lyrics refer to a mesmerising encounter between Kylie and a mysterious man on a packed dancefloor: 'In this crowded place there is only you.' Kylie also makes a rather waggish reference to her 2000 comeback hit, when she name-checks 'Spinning Around' during the bridge. 'In Your Eyes' entered the Australian charts at #1 (her fourth number one there since the start of the new millennium) and scored healthy Top 10 places throughout most of Europe. It also crashed into the MTV Europe Top 20 at #4, with the video becoming the most requested clip on MTV UK and Ireland. Kylie went on to win 'Best Dance Act' and 'Best Pop Act' at the 2002 MTV Europe Awards, held in Barcelona in November.

KylieFever Tour

Devised and Designed by William Baker and Alan MacDonald / Music Producer – Steve Anderson / Choreography by Rafael Bonachela / Tour Manager – Sean Fitzpatrick / Stage Manager – Steve Martin / Wardrobe by Dolce & Gabbana

Musicians: Steve Turner (keyboards), Chris Brown (bass), James Hayto (guitar), Andrew Small (drums), Lurine Cato and Sherina White (backing vocals), DJ Ziggy (turntables)

26 April-18 June 2002 (UK)
2-16 August 2002 (Australia)

Set list:
Silvanemesis: The Sound of Music (intro), Come into My World, Shocked, Love at First Sight, Fever.
Droogie Nights: Spinning Around.
The Crying Game: The Crying Game, Put Yourself in My Place, Finer Feelings.
Street Style: GBI, Confide in Me, Cowboy Style/Double Dutch, Kids.
Sex in Venice: On a Night Like This, The Loco-motion, In Your Eyes/Please Stay/Rhythm of the Night (medley).
Cybertronica: Limbo, Light Years/I Feel Love, I Should Be So Lucky.
First Encore (Voodoo Inferno): Burning Up, Better the Devil You Know.
Second Encore: Can't Get Blue Monday Out of My Head.

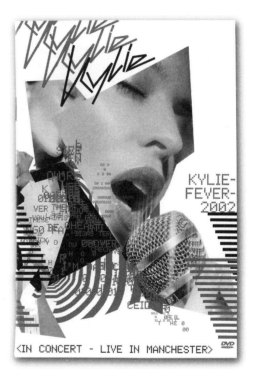

KYLIE-FEVER-2002

‹IN CONCERT – LIVE IN MANCHESTER› DVD

What the *On a Night Like This* tour had begun *KylieFever* continued, in spectacular style. Staged to coincide with Kylie's latest album and elaborately directed by William Baker and acclaimed cinema designer Alan MacDonald, *KylieFever* became one of the most celebrated tours of the singer's career.

Coming less than a year after her last record-breaking tour, Kylie was obviously desperate to get back in front of a live crowd. 'I can perform till I'm blue in the face; to myself or to a camera or in the studio, but you're missing a part of the equation if there's no audience there,' she said. 'The audience isn't stupid. They respond with their instinct and instinct is always right. I can't fool anybody in a live show. If they like it then I know straight away that they like it.' If an immediate reaction is what Kylie wanted then the grand unveiling of *KylieFever* would be everything she desired and a whole lot more besides. This was the live show every Kylie fan had been waiting for.

From the very opening chords of 'The Hills Are Alive', adapted from the *Moulin Rouge!* soundtrack, Kylie set the scene by ascending from the stage floor, clad in beautiful silver robotic armour (reputed to have cost £40,000). Reminiscent of the android beauty from Fritz Lang's 1926 movie classic *Metropolis*, or a super-sexy female Cyberman, Kylie's outrageous costume was simply breathtaking. Named 'Kyborg', the figure remained motionless for a moment before the metal plates slowly began to peel off, revealing Kylie dressed in a crystal-sparkling Dolce & Gabbana miniskirt and bra. Kylie became a futuristic sorceress controlling the marionette movements of her dancers with a flick of her hand, lunge of a buttock or thrust of an elbow.

The amazing choreography by Rambert Dance Company graduate Rafael Bonachela had the silver-clad dancers leaping about like giant mechanical insects, yet their faceless sci-fi look (created by the use of huge, curved motorcycle helmets) was inspired by the lightning-quick Raston Warrior robot from a 1983 episode of *Doctor Who* called 'The Five Doctors', an image which had stayed with William Baker since his childhood. Later Kylie commented that her dancers had a very difficult job performing with partial visibility and in very hot costumes. 'They're all excited to do my tour,' she laughed, 'and then they realise they're dancing with a bucket on their heads!'

KylieFever kicked off at Cardiff International Arena on 26 April, with the singer (suffering from a sore throat) teasing her predominantly Welsh audience. 'I'm very pleased to be opening here because many of my relatives are from round here. It's the home of my mother's family. Are there any Joneses out there?' Kylie then invited the audience to, appropriately, 'Come into My World' and thus began a two-hour extravaganza of stunning visuals and dazzling music.

Again the British tabloids obsessed over Kylie's skimpy stage costumes and the amount of flesh she was revealing. The *Daily Mirror* printed a full-page photo of her bum with the headline: 'OFFICIAL – this wiggles 251 times every night', which indicated that some lucky hack sat in the audience with a pen and paper making a tick every time Kylie shimmied her backside. 'Apparently, it says in the paper today that I wiggle it 251 times in a show,' a bemused Kylie told the audience at the Manchester Evening News Arena during her 1 May concert. 'It's news to me, but I'm going to try and up that tonight!'

The new show reverberated with sexuality throughout, both male and female. For Kylie's plucky performance of 'Fever' she was flanked by a couple of British sex comedy popsies in bodystockings, writhing about on mattresses, an image inspired by Stanley Kubrick's *A Clockwork Orange*. This led directly into a vicious, hard-hitting interpretation of 'Spinning Around' with a masculine Kylie taking on the Malcolm McDowell role as chief 'Droog', dressed in bowler hat, white jumpsuit and alarming codpiece. It was an immediate showstopper, but with a show as extraordinary as this it would be difficult to select the most heroic highlights. Special mention must go to Kylie's intimate trilogy of ballads, comprising 'The Crying Game' (popularised by Boy George in 1992), a Cocteau Twins-inspired version of 'Put Yourself in My Place' and 'Finer Feelings'. Kylie had never appeared more powerful, particularly on the latter song; a tiny figure standing alone on a giant stage, being showered with red rose petals.

Less well-known tracks like 'GBI' (making its debut on any tour), 'Cowboy Style' and 'Limbo' showed Kylie taking chances and instructing her audience not to take her for granted. But the sexed-up version of 'The Loco-motion', complete with cross-dressing male dancers, was a reminder that, however much you rearrange the original, it still sounds like the most dated and cheap song in her entire repertoire. A mind-blowing medley of 'Light Years' segued into its spiritual disco grandmother 'I Feel Love' was utter perfection; as was the soft, dreamy Ibiza milkshake mix of 'I Should Be So Lucky'. Kylie closed the show in a mountainous, vertigo-inducing red dress, towering over the stage and delivering a blasting second encore of 'Can't Get Blue Monday Out of My Head'. Like the frock, the sheer size and scale of *KylieFever* was astounding, leaving the audience in no doubt that the show used every penny of its £4 million budget.

A 120-minute film of the 4 May date at Manchester's Evening News Arena was released on DVD as *KylieFever2002 – Live in Manchester*, directed by William Baker, Alan MacDonald and Chris Keating. It also featured an additional behind the scenes documentary. A limited edition package came with a CD of 14 live tracks, all recorded in Manchester.

Kylie: La La La
(aka Feel the Fever)

Part Kylie, part Kyborg

A Blink TV-TBM Production / 30 minutes / 2002 / Narrated by Jack Davenport

Directed by Alan MacDonald and William Baker / Produced by Claire Oxley / Executive Producers – Terry Blamey and Bill Lord / Edited by Guy Harding and Michael Baldwin

Kylie's backstage 'Fever' documentary, excitably narrated by actor Jack Davenport, illustrates just how hard the singer pushed herself emotionally and physically. 2002 was *the* big year for Kylie and, as a result, she often appears stressed and over-worked, stuck in an exhausting cyclone of video shoots, photo-calls, radio promotion, TV interviews and concert rehearsals. Since the deConstruction days Kylie has often been aware of her own fragility and the fleeting nature of fame obviously plays on her mind. 'I'm suddenly on this wave and it feels good, but obviously being on a wave is quite dangerous at the same time,' she says. 'I'm trying to look cool and graceful while I do it, but I'm aware I could tumble under this at any minute.'

The success of 'Fever' in America caught her totally by surprise and the documentary crew followed her to New York in February 2002, where she did an album signing at the Virgin Megastore in Times Square. We can see her discomfort as she is forced to appear on several inane radio shows where the bonehead DJs only recognise her from her hit 'The Loco-motion' some 14 years earlier. 'Wow! You've come a long way, darling!' says one corpulent, patronising US jock. Almost as fascinating is Kylie enjoying her 34th birthday party in London in May 2002 and her extravagant Dolce & Gabbana party held in Milan in July.

The documentary also provides a few glimpses of the infamous Kylie mineral water. The *KylieFever* tour was sponsored by Evian, which specially printed 200,000 new bottle labels substituting the red Evian name with Kylie's. The French drink was handed out to fans as they entered the concert venue and within hours of the shows finishing the newly branded refreshments were appearing on eBay.

Feel the Fever was later broadcast on Channel 4 on 27 October 2002, preceding a showing of edited highlights from the tour.

'Love at First Sight'

Released June 2002 (UK)
Written by Kylie Minogue, Richard 'Biff' Stannard, Julian Gallagher, Ash Howes and Martin Harrington
Produced by Richard 'Biff' Stannard and Julian Gallagher
Highest chart position #2 (UK), #3 (Australia)

Additional tracks: 'Baby' and 'Can't Get Blue Monday Out of My Head'
Video directed by Johan Renck

In June, during a two-week break from her latest tour, Kylie found enough energy to promote her latest single, 'Love at First Sight', the third superb cut from the 'Fever' album. The track, once again co-written by Biff Stannard, erupts with unrestrained ecstasy and is one of the most joyously summery tracks Kylie has ever recorded. Like its predecessor, 'Love at First Sight' documents Kylie's encounter with a man in a club, this time the archetypal superstar DJ. Far from being love at first sight it is more 'love at first listen' for Kylie as the 'stars come out and fill the sky'. The brilliantly simple playground rhyme of the chorus and the song's uplifting feel-good sentiment, coupled with the cleverly fluctuating muffled quality of the middle section, made the song incredibly popular with radio stations, which played it to death.

Recorded in Dublin in 2001, and heavily influenced by the club music Kylie had been listening to, the song turned out every bit as good as 'Can't Get You Out of My Head' and actually out-performed 'In Your Eyes' in the European charts, finding a Top 10 placing in over 20 countries and topping the Billboard Hot Dance Club Play charts in America with a radically funked-up remix. In the UK the song debuted at #2 and smashed the airplay record of 'Can't Get You Out of My Head' by racking up an astounding 3,116 radio broadcasts in just seven days.

As with Kylie's previous two hits, the video for 'Love at First Sight' continued a futuristic theme, with unnerving robotic dancers set against a metallic computer-generated background of rolling geometric patterns. Over this background a totally uninhibited Kylie rushes around like she's having the best time of her life. The crisp direction and smart visuals are all credit to Swedish filmmaker Johan Renck, one-time pop star in Stakko Bo, who scored a worldwide hit with the homemade hip hop sound of 'Here We Go' in 1993. Subsequently he has helmed promos for New Order and Suede, although his big breakthrough video was for Madonna's 1999 hit 'Nothing Really Matters'. However, it is Renck's experience working with Kylie that he cherishes most. 'I walked around with a strange smile for weeks after completion,' he told a journalist.

'Love at First Sight' definitely wants to make you beam; it is nothing short of Kylie delirium.

'Kylie La La La'

Published November 2002 (UK)
Written by Kylie and William Baker
Published by Hodder and Stoughton

La La La is the nearest thing to an official Kylie autobiography. The singer has always been resistant to putting pen to paper and writing her life story, partly because she openly confesses to having an 'appalling memory' and also because there is much she would prefer to keep to herself. 'I have long successfully avoided the almost inevitable biography,' she said. 'This is because I feel so much of it deserves to be private.'

That's not to say Kylie hasn't been pissed off by other people's books about her. In the late 1990s an especially poorly researched biography came out, which was enough to rile even the ostrich feathers in her wardrobe. 'It was so wrong,' she angrily told the *Sunday Times*. 'I never read it, but I've had parts of it relayed to me, and, as diabolical as my memory is, I do remember how I lost my virginity and it wasn't how it happened in that book!'

Kylie has been approached by several publishers over the years to do a 'tell-all' book but so far she has resisted, and quite properly so.

However, in 2001 she and her creative director William Baker accepted an offer from Hodder and Stoughton to compile a retrospective of her changing image, including photo shoots, contact sheets, magazine covers, album artwork and some previously unseen family snaps and polaroids. The honeyed visuals are punctuated by Baker's intelligent text and additional handwritten commentary by Kylie. 'My life story will have to wait,' she writes. 'Please enjoy and know that it is your enjoyment that has played a major part in allowing me to come this far.'

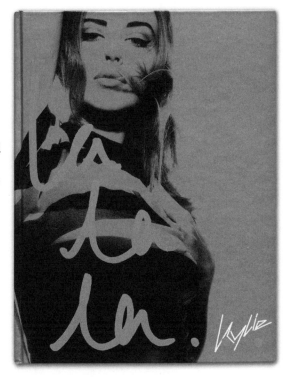

Behind the sexy silver cover (featuring Robert Erdman's beautiful Bardot-inspired image of Kylie from the 'What Do I Have to Do' record sleeve), *La La La* is divided into ten chunky chapters in which Baker provides an illuminating insight into the life of Kylie, or more accurately life *with* Kylie. The book is a collaborative effort in every sense, but it has something of the wedding album about it, with the obvious love between the international pop star and her superstar stylist frothing over on every page – candid snaps of the couple hugging, cuddling, kissing, laughing... even posing by a TARDIS police box in Glasgow's Buchanan Street. 'We are partners in crime,' writes Kylie, without irony.

Stuffed with over 300 memorable photos, *La La La*'s highlights include Katerina Jebb's saucy monochrome study of Kylie, aged 26, as a Playboy bunny girl and John Rankin's seductive shots of Kylie in black bra and knickers sprawling on a pool table. Unsurprisingly, the British tabloids loved the book but the broadsheets did not. 'Kylie bares almost every centimetre of flesh, but not a millimetre of soul,' wrote the *Independent*.

La La La had an initial print run of 217,000 copies, reaching #3 in the British Bookscan charts. In autumn 2003 an updated paperback edition was published, featuring a complete re-design, additional photos and a new afterword by William Baker discussing life during the 12 months subsequent to the *KylieFever* tour. Kylie herself contributes a coda at the end of the new edition: 'In re-reading the book for the purpose of the paperback edition, I found myself going through a great range of emotions. Amongst the feelings of pride, embarrassment, elation, longing, inspiration and nostalgia, the main thing I found myself doing was laughing.'

'Come into My World'

Released November 2002 (UK)
Written and Produced by Cathy Dennis and Rob Davis
Highest chart position #8 (UK), #4 (Australia)

Additional tracks: 'Love at First Sight' (Live) and 'Fever' (Live)
Video directed by Michel Gondry

After the light-headed hedonism of 'Love at First Sight', Kylie decided to wind down with a more laidback slice of pop from her 'Fever' album. Subtly remixed and with re-recorded vocals, 'Come into My World' became Kylie's fourth international hit in just over 12 months. Written by the geniuses behind 'Can't Get You Out of My Head', Cathy Dennis and Rob Davis, the song's lyrics encourage the man of Kylie's affections to submit to her kisses and touches, and take her heart that 'will beat for two'. It's a silkily passionate song with a slight Celtic flavour and a 'na na na na' hook. Kylie herself likened it to a 1970s Fleetwood Mac track, although it's far more technically glossy than that. The original version of the song had been a late addition to the 'Fever' album but was so wildly popular as the opening number on the *KylieFever* tour that Parlophone were encouraged to earmark it for future single release.

The song's stunningly complex video, directed by award-winning filmmaker Michel Gondry (famous for his work with Daft Punk), was shot on location at Point du Jour in the Boulogne district of Paris on 8 September 2002. The camera follows the star as she strolls through a busy market intersection, singing the song's romantic lyrics. Each time she completes a circuit of the area yet 'another' Kylie appears and the extras in the background duplicate too. By the time the video nears its complicated conclusion there are four Kylies weaving between each other, dodging ladders, flying mattresses, traffic wardens, wheelchairs and aggravated motorists. The promo fades with a fifth Kylie emerging from a shop, indicating that's one shot too far, especially as it had taken over 15 individual takes to create the incredible effect.

Helped by its video, 'Come into My World' comfortably found Top 30 places throughout Europe but was most successful in Mexico and South Africa, where it hit #1. Over in the US Kylie took the unusual step of performing the song with a totally live band on *Good Morning America*, but her sexy dance moves probably proved too much for the show's conservative audiences. The track only made the lower reaches of the America Dance charts, so it was something of a surprise when 'Come into My World' was nominated for, and won, a prestigious Grammy Award as 'Best Dance Recording' in February 2004. Kylie had been nominated the year previously for 'Love at First Sight'.

For several European promotions of 'Come into My World', Kylie performed a remix of the song, prepared by New York electroclash pioneers Fischerspooner. It is this buzzier, banged-up version which Kylie sang on *Top of the Pops*. Much sought after, it eventually became available as a bonus track on the repackaged limited edition version of 'Fever'.

*   *   *

Just before the release of 'Come into My World', Kylie was given the ultimate accolade by the Australian music industry when she won an unprecedented five gongs at the ARIA Awards, held at the Sydney Super Dome on 15 October 2002 – two for the international success of 'Can't Get You Out of My Head' and two for her album 'Fever', plus the 'Outstanding Achievement Award' for becoming the most successful Australian recording artist of all time. 'I am pretty much astounded,' said a visibly moved Kylie. 'Who could have thought this would happen?'

Rather unpredictably, Kylie then ended 2002 dressed up as a fat, balding monk for a cameo appearance in Kenneth Branagh's West End farce 'The Play What I Wrote', celebrating the comedy careers of Morecambe and Wise. The play was famous for its nightly 'Mystery Guest' slot and on 21 November it was Kylie's turn, dressed up in uncharacteristically frumpy male garb. 'It's the first time I've trodden the boards in the West End and I'm a bit lost for words,' she gushed. In the audience was Prince Charles, who praised her acting as 'fantastic'. When the two spoke again backstage after Kylie headlined the Royal Variety Performance on 2 December, Charles said to her: 'We must stop meeting like this!' Kylie responded: 'That's just what I was going to say to you!'

The start of 2003 was marked once more by the media's obsession with Kylie's bum. On 20 February Kylie appeared with Justin Timberlake at the BRIT Awards. The singers duetted on a cover version of Blondie's 1981 hit 'Rapture' and, although neither performer was nominated for a gong, they both got more column inches the following day than all of the winners combined. During their song Timberlake repeatedly ground his crotch into Kylie's posterior before giving it a lustful caress beneath her stunning Julien MacDonald dress.

Photos of the grope made the front pages of all the tabloids the following day. Even the usually highbrow *Guardian* was prompted to comment that the young American singer 'got a piece of arguably the most desirable bottom in pop'. It was alleged that Kylie's petulant on-off model-turned-photographer boyfriend James Gooding was suitably unimpressed, causing a fraças backstage. Kylie was unrepentant, admitting she loved flirting with Timberlake. 'We had to rehearse that,' she told reporters afterwards. 'I was like, "Wait, I don't think we got that quite right. I think we should do it again!"'

Also in February, Kylie attended the UK launch of her *LoveKylie* underwear range at Selfridges on London's Oxford Street. She modelled the sheer designs in a suggestive video shown in the shop's window, prominently wiggling her bum. 'All I had to do was jump up and down in my underpants,' she said, excitedly. The promo wasn't quite as raunchy as the advert she filmed the previous year for Agent Provocateur, which had her straddling a bucking bronco in bra and panties. That commercial could only be shown in UK cinemas with an 18 certificate. 'Personally I'm into the fuller brief,' admitted Kylie at the *LoveKylie* launch, 'though I don't have any proper Bridget Jones pants!'

As well as her bum the tabloids again started analysing Kylie's romantic entanglements. Gooding sold a pathetic kiss 'n' tell story about his infidelities during their three-year relationship to the *News of the World*. Kylie responded by telling him to 'grow up'. By this stage she had already started dating French actor Olivier Martinez and was concentrating on her new album. By the following year she and Martinez were living together in Paris, Kylie's 'second adopted home'.

'Slow'

Released November 2003 (UK)
Written by Kylie Minogue, Dan Carey and
Emiliana Torrini
Produced by Dan Carey and Emiliana Torrini
Highest chart position #1 (UK), #1 (Australia)

Additional tracks: 'Soul on Fire' and 'Sweet
Music'
Video directed by Baillie Walsh

Kylie had spent much of 2003 working on new material at Biff Stannard's Dublin studios, Biffco, and the first new song to go public surprised her fans almost as much as 'Confide in Me' had done back in 1994. On 29 September 'Slow' debuted on radios stations across Europe with some DJs doubting it was even her singing it.

Produced by Dan Carey and Emiliana Torrinis (aka production duo Sunnyroads) and co-written by them with Kylie, 'Slow' is a sophisticated piece of minimalist electro-pop, bubbling with sly beats and breathless American-sounding vocals. Spikier than any of her previous Parlophone output, the single is a brave, sexually charged hymn to Kylie's new love of deviant techno. The angular sound is heightened by the song's intricate lyrics, which Kylie deliberately delivers with crystal clarity. When she sings 'Skip a beat and move with my body' there's not a hair on the back of the listener's neck that's safe from her abundant sexuality. 'Slow' is Kylie's first out-and-out seduction spectacular, almost frighteningly so.

The song's eye-wateringly hypnotic sound was a gift to radio, and it immediately leapt to the top of the airplay charts both in the UK and Australia. Kylie's debut live performance of the single was on *Top of the Pops* on 17 October, featuring her startling new Brigitte Bardot image to coincide with the artwork on the single sleeve. The following day she announced a special one-off concert called *Money Can't Buy* to showcase the single and her new album, 'Body Language'.

However, it is the mesmerising Helmut Newton-inspired video for 'Slow' which created the most media interest. Shot on location in Barcelona over three wet September days, at the swimming pool purpose-built for the 1992 Olympics, the promo creates an astonishing kaleidoscope effect by filming Kylie directly from above, writhing around on a beach towel surrounded by 60 sunbathing hunks in Speedos and perfectly proportioned girls in bikinis. William Baker described the concept as a sort of 'fantasy lido', an idea which Kylie adored. 'It's a very glamorous location,' she commented, 'filled with very *hot* people!'

Using a brilliantly simple concept, and choreographed by Michael Rooney, 'Slow' is probably the first pop video where the dancers don't actually get up off the floor. The song entered the Australian charts at #1, seeing off all competition, and did the same in the UK, giving Kylie her 20th cumulative week in the top slot since 1988, a chart record for a female solo artist. 'Slow' became one of the most remixed singles of Kylie's career, both officially and unofficially. Most notably, the bootleg mix of 'Slow' combined with Kraftwerk's 1978 synth hit 'The Model' is an electro mash-up made in Heaven.

Money Can't Buy

Devised and Designed by William Baker and Alan MacDonald / Music Producer – Steve Anderson / Choreography by Michael Rooney / Concert Manager – Sean Fitzpatrick / Production Manager – Kevin Hopgood / Wardrobe by Jean-Paul Gaultier, Stevie Stewart and John Galliano

Musicians: Steve Turner (keyboards), Chris Brown (bass), James Hayto (guitar), Andrew Small (drums), Sara-Jane Skeet, Valerie Etienne, Jo Garland and Janet Ramus (backing vocals)

15 November 2003, live at the Hammersmith Apollo, London

Set list:
Paris By Night: Still Standing, Red Blooded Woman, On a Night Like This.
Bardello: Je t'aime/Breathe, After Dark, Chocolate.
Electro: Can't Get You Out of My Head, Slow, Obsession, In Your Eyes.
On Yer Bike: Secret (Take You Home), Spinning Around.
Encore: Love at First Sight.

Midway through her *Money Can't Buy* concert Kylie said to her audience, 'This is kind of a weird concept – one show!' Indeed it was; a £1 million one-off special at London's Hammersmith Apollo to launch the 'Body Language' album. As the name of the concert suggests admission was free, but try telling that to the dozens of touts selling tickets at vastly inflated prices outside on the pavement. Initially the 4000 tickets for the gig were given away to fans through competitions on the radio, TV and on the internet, although it is doubtful that the dozens of celebrities in the audience really won their tickets by answering Kylie-related questions on BBC Radio Cornwall.

There never was a 'Body Language' world tour. The *Money Can't Buy* show is the only record we have of Kylie actively promoting her 2003 album. Prior to the show Kylie attended a 30-minute press conference attended by 250 international journalists who, as the *Independent* newspaper commented, were 'serviced in one fell swoop.' Some commentators brazenly predicted that since 'Fever' had sold six million copies Kylie could now afford to put her feet up. Like *KylieFever*, the new 'Pucci-esque' show was created and designed by Alan MacDonald and William Baker.

Kylie was lowered onto the stage atop a giant metal girder, a rhapsody in black leggings, corset and black-and-white hooped jersey, all courtesy of Jean Paul Gaultier. With her mane of hair glowing bright Bardot blonde there was little question that this show was going to be French-flavoured; then a giant projection of the Eiffel Tower suddenly appeared behind her and the Parisian theme was immediately apparent. Kylie opened the show with 'Still Standing', a new number from her ninth album, an ironic song choice since she was suspended 30 feet in the air. The funky, vibrating electronic sound of the track set the scene for this darkly delicious performance. 'So beautiful to see you tonight,' she called out, obviously thrilled to see her fans.

Once on the safety of the stage floor Kylie and her troupe of hip-twisting Tour de France cyclists charged into a storming extended version of 'On a Night Like This', with Michael Rooney's ironic choreography giving a cheeky nod to Michael Jackson's 'Thriller' video but with much more toned flesh on display. Flashes of lightning and rumbles of thunder shattered the stage and the dancers slid around, twirling red umbrellas in a scene which would have made Gene Kelly proud. The computerised light display was incredible; the Eiffel Tower became a huge spurting fountain before merging into a giant foetal Kylie writhing about in mid-air above the dainty real one.

Kylie saddles up
for *Money Can't
Buy*

The Gallic feel continued when 'Breathe' intertwined with 'Je t'aime ... moi non plus', the saucy #1 which scandalised the British charts in 1969. It was a brilliantly smooth mash-up, portraying Kylie as cool and confident as ever. When she whispered 'It won't be long now ... breathe', you could have cut the atmosphere with a French bread knife. The crowd loved it and so did Kylie. 'I don't need to see you to know how gorgeous you all are,' she said, staring out into the blackness of the Apollo auditorium. 'If it's one thing my audiences are renowned for, it's their utter beauty!'

The wondrous costume changes whizzed by, from a multi-coloured pyjama two-piece which Agnetha and Anni-Frid would no doubt have adored, worn with fishnet stockings and their corresponding perfectly straight seams, to a white catsuit and kinky boots and a Pearly Queen cap. The new songs from 'Body Language' didn't fare as well as her 'classics' – obviously because the audience didn't recognise them yet, but also because most lacked a killer hook, something that several reviewers were acutely aware of. 'Where were all the huge choruses for which the nation loves her so?' wrote Craig McLean in the *Daily Telegraph*. Or, in the *Sunday Express*: 'The new material was at best lacklustre, at worst, dull.' Of the new tracks, Kylie's Sister Sledge-style performance of 'After Dark', teamed up with her backing singers, lacked punch but certainly not style, and the sensuous 'Obsession' was totally lost in the melée of terrific, twisting Saint Vitus Dance choreography.

'Slow' worked better, especially since it was happily sitting atop the charts and the crowd was baying for it. 'It is my sincere pleasure to introduce the #1 song in the country,' Kylie said proudly. The older hits got the Apollo shaking to its very foundations, particularly 'Can't Get You Out of My Head', sung against a solid wall of quickly evaporating blood-red visuals. 'Let me hear you,' screamed Kylie as the audience joined her for the 'la la la' chorus. 'Secret (Take You Home)', 'Spinning Around' and 'Love at First Sight' concluded proceedings with Kylie appearing on stage on the saddle of a Harley Davidson and rapping in a Texan drawl.

Throughout Kylie looked totally stunning, but her famous bum made less of a starring appearance. In an earlier interview Kylie claimed to be tiring of the media's obsession with her backside; it would be 'retiring' for now. Even the *Times* was complaining: 'She may have to rely on her looks more than ever if she wants 'Body Language' to be one of her biggest sellers,' it wrote. 'Hold that 'bum ban' for now then.'

British TV viewers saw an edited version of *Money Can't Buy* a week later on Saturday 22 November, introduced on ITV by presenter Cat Deeley. The concert was then released on DVD as *Body Language Live* (running time: 62 minutes) with an additional backstage documentary.

Body Language Live: Behind the Scenes

A Blink TV-TBM Production / 15 minutes / 2003

Directed by Russell Thomas / Produced by Philippa Pettett / Executive Producers – Bill Lord, Kylie Minogue and Terry Blamey

Featuring: Kylie, Edith Bowman, William Baker, Michael Rooney, Alan MacDonald and Sean Fitzpatrick

This short behind-the-scenes documentary especially filmed for the *Body Language Live* DVD follows Kylie during the four-month build-up to the release of her new album and the *Money Can't Buy* concert. Beginning with the 'Body Language' photo shoot on the French Riviera in August 2003, with Kylie looking ravishing in a Bardot bikini, and proceeding to larking about for the Barcelona video shoot for 'Slow' and the uncertain November rehearsals for the show, Kylie gradually seems to be getting more fed up. Whereas the band and dancers have had weeks of preparation, poor Kylie fits in rehearsals whenever she has a spare moment, which isn't very often.

Scenes of the press launch of the new album, with questions mediated by DJ Edith Bowman, are punctuated by brisk discussions with choreographer Michael Rooney and designers Baker and MacDonald, busy puffing away on their fags backstage (something Kylie probably doesn't put up with nowadays). The dress rehearsal is not a success ('That was awful,' she sighs), but there are lighter moments when Kylie is handed an enormous pair of leather trousers, selected for her to wear on stage. 'I'm expecting a growth spurt,' she giggles.

'Body Language'

Released November 2003 (UK)
Parlophone / Mushroom Records
Produced by Dan Carey and Emiliana Torrini (track 1), Baby Ash (tracks 2, 5, 9 and 10), Rez (track 3), Kurtis Mantronik and Johnny Douglas (Tracks 4 and 8), Johnny Douglas (tracks 6 and 7), Richard 'Biff Stannard and Julian Gallagher (track 11), and Cathy Dennis (track 12)
Highest chart position #6 (UK), #2 (Austr...)

Tr... list...

'Still Standing'
'Secret (Take You Home)'
'Promises'
'Sweet Music'
'Red Blooded Woman'
'Chocolate'
'Obsession'
'I Feel For You'
'Someday'
'Loving Days'
'After Dark'

Bonus tracks: 'Slo' Motion' (Australia and Japan), 'Cruise Control' (USA and Canada), 'You Make Me Feel (USA, Canada and Japan)

Released in Britain on Monday 17 November 2003, just two days after the *Money Can't Buy* concert, Kylie's ninth studio album deliberately veers away from the techno glitterball Euro-excesses of her last and into the low-lit R'n'B lounge of American hip hop beats and 1980s electro funk. The stark sophistication of 'Slow' opens the album and soon makes way for a fuller-bodied selection of highly polished, multi-layered urban sounds. At times it seems that 'Body Language' is less about delivering a collection of distinctive pop tunes and more about creating long cool swathes of homogenous sound. Anybody expecting the instant hit of 'Fever' is going to come away disappointed. 'It's my usual sound, but with curved edges,' explained Kylie cryptically.

The album gives tentative nods towards the experimentation of 'Impossible Princess' and rifles the wardrobes of Prince, Chaka Khan and Scritti Politti. In fact, Scritti's lead singer Green Gartside even turns in a sweet cameo on the deliciously disjointed 'Someday', where Kylie's vocals intermingle with Green's ethereal whispering and hark back to Scritti's seminal 1982 album 'Songs to Remember'. There's some old school hip hop frippery with the excellent frayed synth of 'Promises' and 'Obsession', both co-produced and co-written by Kurtis Mantonik, the British-based New York electro legend and so-called 'King of the Beats'.

The 1980s feel continues when Kylie blatantly plagiarises Lisa Lisa and Cult Jam's 1985 hit 'I Wonder if I Take You Home' on the richly dark 'Secret (Take Me Home)'. Co-written by Mercury Prize-winning Brit rapper Ms Dynami   track takes Kylie into the realms of noir-ish seduction and allow   hot at rapping. There's also a hair's-breadth of crunky rap during   tro to the luscious 'Chocolate', courtesy of Ludacris, although his original, complete rap was removed when Kylie felt it didn't work.

Sometimes Kylie's sweet vocals get too embedded among the bass and braces of tracks like 'After Dark' (where she's in particularly coquettish mood) and the initial tropical madness of 'I Feel For You' dissipates into a standard sugary R'n'B tune. Biff Stannard tries a different mood with the beautiful 'Loving Days', dripping with sparkling evening jewels, while 'Still Standing' and 'Sweet Music' pulsate with interesting sonic beeps, buzzing reverbs and provocative flavours but ultimately don't go anywhere. 'Body Language', loved and ignored in equal measure, is best enjoyed late at night, drinking a Rémy Martin and sprawled out among velvet cushions.

Inconsistent it may be, but 'Body Language' is never anything less than a luxurious listening experience.

✳ ✳ ✳

Where Take That and Spice Girls had gone before, Kylie followed: in January 2004 an officially sanctioned, fully posable 12" Kylie doll was released, available in two outfits and matching *LoveKylie* knickers. 'For years I have been asked about a Kylie doll,' the singer commented. 'Well, she has finally arrived and I'm delighted. I hope fans will agree it was worth the wait as we worked very hard to get every detail right.' Not everybody was convinced, however; some fussy fans complained that the doll's head was out of proportion with the body.

On 28 February the real 5' ¼" Kylie made a special appearance at G-A-Y at the London Astoria. In many ways, Jeremy Joseph's long-running club night has always been Kylie's spiritual home in the UK. It's traditional that every Saturday night at 12.30 am balloons are released from the ceiling to the strains of 'Better the Devil You Know', and Kylie could always be assured of a rapturous welcome when she appeared there. 'I am so excited to be performing once again at G-A-Y,' she announced before the gig. 'There is an atmosphere that is unlike anywhere else. Last time I performed there they had a huge clock counting down the minutes until the show and by the time I came on the crowd was at fever pitch.

It's a special venue for me and I have some amazing memories of gigs gone by. So many of the audience go to great lengths to make special outfits and they know the lyrics to the songs better than I do!'

Kylie's set included tracks spanning her entire career, from 'The Loco-motion' and 'Made in Heaven' right through to 'Slow'. As a special treat she performed an a capella rendition of 'Better the Devil' and a funked-up version of 'Red Blooded Woman', a fresh cut from the 'Body Language' album ...

'Red Blooded Woman'

Released March 2004 (UK)
Written by Karen Poole and Johnny Douglas
Produced by Johnny Douglas

Highest chart position #5 (UK), #4 (Australia)

Additional tracks: 'Almost a Lover', 'Cruise Control' and 'Slow' (Chemical Brothers remix)
Video directed by Jake Nava

Several weeks prior to its airing at Kylie's G-A-Y appearance on 28 February, the PPK 'Resurrection'-accented Narcotic Thrust Mix of 'Red Blooded Woman' had been released to clubs and propelled itself to the top spot in the UK dance charts. The commercially available single came out on 1 March (in its original album form), backed by the much sought-after Chemical Brothers electro mix of 'Slow', which had previously only been available on a very scarce yellow vinyl 12" promo.

The single debuted at #5 in Britain, but hit #1 in Hong Kong and South Africa (Kylie's seventh chart-topper there). The song failed to make inroads in the US Billboard Hot 100, despite being championed by several American record stations which embraced Kylie's more urban R'n'B sound, but made #1 on the US Dance Airplay Chart. The impressive video for 'Red Blooded Woman' is one of Kylie's most ambitious, shot by ex-Spice Girls director Jake Nava in Los Angeles in the autumn of 2003. Kylie plays a commuter stuck in a vast traffic jam, who eases her boredom by strutting among the stationary vehicles and swinging off the back of a fuel tanker.

'Red Blooded Woman' is also notable for name-checking the Stock Aitken Waterman-produced 'You Spin Me Round (Like a Record)', originally a worldwide smash in 1985 for Dead or Alive, and for its own catchy chorus in which Kylie pleads, 'Let me keep freaking around.' This was ruthlessly parodied in series three of Australian sitcom *Kath & Kim*, when naff Kel Knight (played by Glenn Robbins) attempts to get hip by listening to Kylie records and singing, 'I'm frickin' around.'

'Chocolate'

Released June 2004 (UK)
Written by Karen Poole and Johnny Douglas
Produced by Johnny Douglas

Highest chart position #6 (UK), #14 (Australia)

Additional tracks: 'City Games' and 'Love at First Sight' (Live)
Video directed by Dawn Shadforth

Kylie's third single from the 'Body Language' album is arguably one of the richest, most mellifluous releases of her career. 'Chocolate', as the name suggests, is a dark, velvety ballad with breathless vocals skimming over a delicate Middle Eastern-style production, touched by a certain Scritti Politti sensibility. For the single release Kylie re-recorded all her vocals at El Cortijo Studios in Spain, explaining that the song was technically one of the most difficult tracks she had ever laid down.

The video, helmed by one of Kylie's favourite directors, Dawn Shadforth, was filmed in London in June 2004, liberally plucking influences from MGM musicals of the post-war years, 1980s Kate Bush videos and Powell and Pressburger's 1948 movie *The Red Shoes*. Slow and seductive, with lusty 'Melt me slowly down, like chocolate' lyrics, 'Chocolate' sadly failed to sell in the same quantities as Kylie's previous two singles and Parlophone decided not to release any more singles from the largely misunderstood 'Body Language' album.

Kylie immediately began work recording new material with Scissor Sisters and hit-making production team Xenomania for her forthcoming greatest hits compilation.

'Ultimate Kylie'

Released September 2004 (UK)
Parlophone / Mushroom Records
Produced by Stock Aitken Waterman (tracks 1-11, 13 and 14), Stock and Waterman (track 12), Harding and Curnow (track 15), Jake Shears and Babydaddy (track 16), Cathy Dennis and Rob Davis (tracks 17 and 29), Richard 'Biff' Stannard and Julian Gallagher (tracks 18, 24 and 25), Dan Carey and Emiliana Torrini (track 19), Graham Stack and Mark Taylor (track 20), Mike Spencer (track 21), Guy Chambers and Steve Power (track 22), Brothers In Rhythm (tracks 23 and 30),

Johnny Douglas (track 26 and 28), Brian Higgins and Xenomania (track 27), Dave Ball and Ingo Vauk (tracks 31 and 32), and Nick Cave, Tony Cohen and Victor Van Vugt (track 33)
Highest chart position #4 (UK), #5 (Australia)

Track listing:
'Better the Devil You Know'
'The Loco-motion'
'I Should Be So Lucky'
'Step Back in Time'
'Shocked'
'What Do I Have to Do'
'Wouldn't Change a Thing'
'Hand on Your Heart'
'Especially for You'
'Got to Be Certain'
'Je Ne Sais Pas Pourquoi'
'Give Me Just a Little More Time'
'Never Too Late'
'Tears from My Pillow'
'Celebration'
'I Believe in You'
'Can't Get You Out of My Head'
'Love at First Sight'
'Slow'
'On a Night Like This'
'Spinning Around'
'Kids'
'Confide in Me'
'In Your Eyes'
'Please Stay'
'Red Blooded Woman'
'Giving You Up'
'Chocolate'
'Come Into My World'
'Put Yourself in My Place'
'Did It Again'
'Breathe'
'Where the Wild Roses Grow'
Bonus tracks: 'Turn It Into Love' (Japan), 'Your Disco Needs You' (Germany)

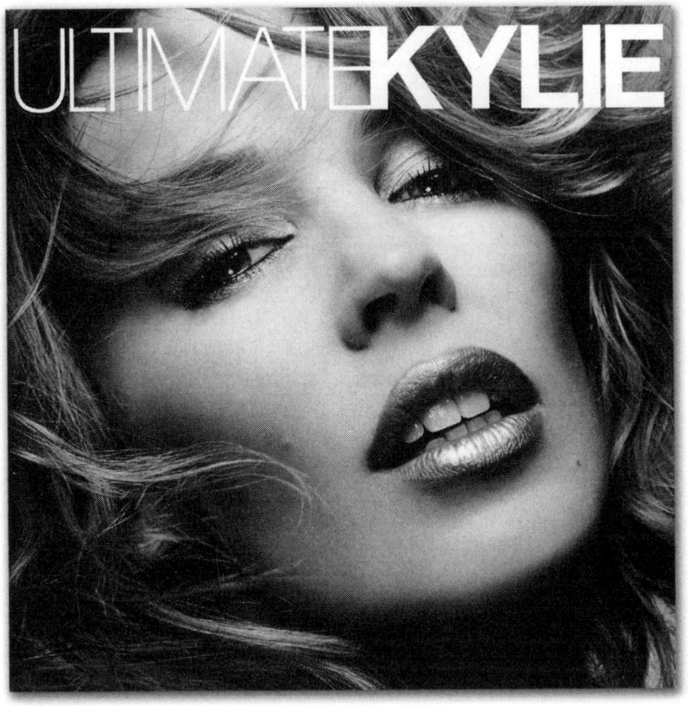

Not *quite* the ultimate but not far off, Kylie's second official greatest hits collection was the first time her best work from PWL, deConstruction and Parlophone had rubbed together on one disc, or two to be exact. The double-CD was released worldwide in the autumn of 2004, featuring 33 massive hits but at the same time neglecting 'What Kind of Fool', 'Word is Out', 'If You Were With Me Now', 'Finer Feelings', 'Where is the Feeling?' and 'Some Kind Of Bliss'. 'They are all missing,' Kylie explained mysteriously, 'for a good reason'.

Two new tracks – 'I Believe in You' and 'Giving You Up' – were especially recorded for inclusion, both becoming single releases. Seen as a reaction by Parlophone to the slightly disappointing international sales of 'Body Language', Kylie's new greatest hits album certainly cleaned up, selling over a million copies in the UK alone and hitting the Top 10 throughout the world, even reaching #1 in China.

'Ultimate Kylie' was also produced as a DVD collection, minus the video for 'Giving You Up' (which had yet to be filmed), but including Kylie's BRIT Awards performance of 'Can't Get Blue Monday Out of My Head'. There were also a couple of geographical amendments to the track listing for the album. The Japanese version also features 'Turn It Into Love', while the German edition dispenses with 'Please Stay' and replaces it with 'Your Disco Needs You'. The album was also reissued in 2006 to coincide with the Australian leg of *Showgirl Homecoming*, repackaging the greatest hits DVD with the two CDs.

Kath & Kim

Season 3, Episode 7 **'Foxy on the Run'**
Season 3, Episode 8 **'99% Fat Free'**

ABC Network / A Riley Turner Production / 25 minutes episodes / Episodes first broadcast (Australia) 18 and 24 November 2004
Created and Written by Jane Turner and Gina Riley / Directed by Ted Emery / Produced by Jane Turner and Gina Riley / Original music composed by Jeremy Smith

Starring: Jane Turner (*Kath Day*), Gina Riley (*Kim Craig*), Glenn Robbins (*Kel Knight*), Peter Rowsthorn (*Brett Craig*), Magda Szubanski (*Sharon Strzelecki*) with Kylie as *herself / Eponney Rae*

Taking its lead from observational British sitcom *The Royle Family* and the unintentionally funny Aussie fly-on-the-wall docu-soap *Sylvania Waters* (1992), *Kath & Kim* provides a hysterical insight into one working-class household in the fictional Melbourne suburb of Fountain Lakes. Premiering on Australian television in May 2002, *Kath*

& Kim follows the outrageously superficial lives of 40-something poodle-permed divorcee Kath Day (Jane Turner) and her whingeing, spoilt, 25-year-old daughter Kim (Gina Riley).

The series' crass, embarrassing humour, coupled with strangulated vowels and terrible fashions, made *Kath & Kim* a pop culture phenomenon in Australia, much akin to the impact *Absolutely Fabulous* had on British audiences a decade earlier. Such was *Kath & Kim*'s explosive popularity that the show twice won the 'Most Outstanding Comedy Award' at the Logies. Overseas *Kath & Kim* became a hit in England and America, and has enjoyed sustained, and inexplicable, success in Finland. Because of its cult appeal *Kath & Kim* has boasted several cameos from prominent Australian celebrities, including Rachel Griffiths, Eric Bana and Geoffrey Rush.

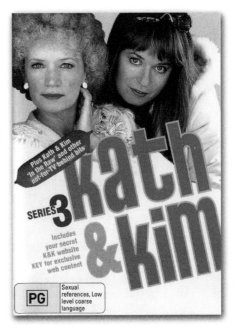

Kylie was also a great admirer of the show and famously begged Turner and Riley to let her appear. 'Come on guys, give this young actress a role!' she implored in a Sydney radio interview. It probably came as no surprise when, in early 2004, she was announced as the series' latest high-profile recruit. Originally only contracted for one episode, Turner and Riley were so excited to have Kylie on location that they trumpeted her upcoming appearance in the season three finale by giving her an unexpected cameo at the end of the penultimate episode.

In *Foxy on the Run*, Kath's beau, Kel, is approaching his 50th birthday with considerable trepidation. Fearing a loss of his virility and manly looks, Kel indulges in a hysterical makeover, suddenly preferring, for instance, to sing along to Kylie's 'Red Blooded Woman' than to (his usual preference) 1970s Prog Rock. Kylie appears, inexplicably as herself but dressed in a fetching tracksuit, at the episode's end, enjoying a glass of wine in the family garden.

The following episode, *99% Fat Free*, sees Kim desperate for her baby daughter – the delightfully named Eponney Rae – to be on *Neighbours*. However, baby Eponney spews all over Harold Bishop during her first scene and Kim is crestfallen. Fast forward 30 years and the baby is now a young woman preparing for her wedding day. Enter Kylie as the older, although not necessarily brighter, Eponney. In a hysterically perverse reimagining of Charlene's wedding day, Kylie is decked out in a ghastly white polyester mini-dress with abundant train, thigh-length leather boots and frilly garter. With her hair in dreadful permed ringlets and her make-up caked on with a spatula, she proves herself just as common and uncouth as her appalling mother. Kim, meanwhile, is more concerned that the not-so-blushing bride's dress is a little too revealing. 'Pull the back up,' she screeches. 'I can see your welcome mat. Why didn't you get it lasered when they did your 'tache?'

Kylie enjoys every minute playing the deluded Eponney, grimacing hard and relishing her sulky, conceited behaviour. You can't help but imagine this is how the *Neighbours* wedding really could have been. Resurrecting Charlene's characteristic Melbourne drawl, Kylie outdoes herself when the nuptials are deemed a failure. 'My marriage is over,' she wails. 'O-V-A-H!' A beautifully realised comic turn from Kylie proves, beyond all doubt, that she is a considerably more gifted actress than her critics would have us believe. And in surely one of the proudest moments of Kylie's TV acting career she is awarded the ultimate Australian accolade – to freely use the show's catchphrase and proudly say, 'Look at moiye!'

'I Believe in You'

Released December 2004 (UK)
Written by Kylie Minogue, Jake Shears and Babydaddy
Produced by Jake Shears and Babydaddy
Highest chart position #2 (UK), #6 (Australia)

Flipside: 'B.P.M.'
Video directed by Vernie Yeung

On 13 October 2004 Kylie announced details of her latest series of concerts, entitled *Showgirl – The Greatest Hits Tour*, to kick off in Scotland in March the following year. Demand for tickets was so astronomical that several websites selling tickets crashed. In conjunction with the tour, Kylie released her two-disc 'Ultimate Kylie' compilation, promoting it heavily on TV throughout France, Germany and Spain. In the UK Kylie performed a handpicked selection of her classic hits on TV – 'Spinning

Around' (*Saturday Night Takeaway*), 'Step Back in Time' (*BBC Children in Need*), 'Better the Devil You Know' (*Top of the Pops*) and 'Can't Get You Out of My Head' for the *Smash Hits Poll Winners' Party*. At the latter event Kylie also premiered her new single 'I Believe In You', a collaboration with New York glam pop group Scissor Sisters.

In fact, Kylie recorded a number of songs with lead singer Jake Shears and bassist Babydaddy (aka Scott Hoffman), including the funky 'Ooh (The Blues)' and the delicate 'Everything I Know', both unreleased but later leaked onto the internet, much to the consternation of their writers. 'I Believe in You' is intelligent Euro electro-disco with a demure soaring chorus, pulsing bassline and a hard-kicking drumbeat. 'I love it,' said Kylie in an interview with the Australian *Herald Sun* in November 2004. 'It does everything it's meant to do and then some! When the idea of working [with Scissor Sisters] came up I thought, "Well, I love their album, but it's not the music I make." However, we got on immediately; we were on the same wavelength.'

The single, backed by remixes by Scottish producer Mylo and a fabulous rush-hour disco tune called 'B.P.M.' ('I wanna lose myself in your beats per minute'), debuted on the UK charts at #2, beaten to the top spot by the new recording of 'Do They Know It's Christmas?' by Band Aid 20. Throughout Europe the single enjoyed Top 20 placings and in Australia it was nominated for an ARIA award for best pop release.

'I Believe In You' helped promote Kylie's new greatest hits collection, although it was her older songs which continued to spread the word. On the Christmas Day *Top of the Pops* special in 2004, Kylie performed an energetic medley of 'Step Back in Time', 'Shocked' (plus the rap), 'Better the Devil You Know' and 'What Do I Have to Do'. It was an upbeat end to another hugely successful year, but little could anybody have guessed what 2005 would bring.

Kylie: The Exhibition

15 January-25 April 2005 (Melbourne)
13 May-14 August 2005 (Canberra)
6 September-4 December 2005 (Brisbane)
26 December-7 May 2006 (Sydney)
8 February-10 June 2007 (London)
30 June-2 September 2007 (Manchester)
21 September 2007-23 January 2008 (Glasgow)

K ylie the album, Kylie the book, even Kylie the interview. What next? Kylie the exhibition? Well, yes, actually. Opening in Australia in January 2005, the exhibition of Kylie's outfits and memorabilia was inspired by the star's generous donation of nearly 600 items of clothing to the performing arts collection at the Melbourne Arts Centre 18 months earlier. The museum is also home to the Dame Edna Everage archive, of which Barry Humphries is patron.

'Kylie found it amusing that garments that had once been thrown on the floor between numbers were suddenly being handled with such reverence by specialists in white gloves,' commented collection curator Janine Barrand. Thankfully for the museum, nearly all Kylie's bespoke clothes had been carefully kept by her mother Carol and stored away since the late 1980s. 'Were it not for my parents I'm sure this collection would be the size of a suitcase rather than an exhibition space,' said a grateful Kylie.

Fifty of Kylie's most memorable costumes – 'from cobbled together to couture' – were liberated from cardboard boxes and black bin liners and placed on public display. From Charlene's *Neighbours* dungarees, complete with real oil stains and three garish patches, via the shapeless cotton muslin dress with kanga pouches from the 'I Should Be So Lucky' video and the pink ostrich feather and diamante tiara from *Intimate and Live*, right up to Fiona Doran's white jersey hooded jumpsuit with plunging neckline made iconic by 'Can't Get You Out of My Head', it was all here, displayed on specially made 5'1" mannequins.

'What I imagine people will want to see is the wear and tear, the ingrained make-up after 50 shows,' said Kylie. 'These are the things that for me bring costumes to life.' Fans were surprised to see priceless Karl Lagerfeld creations with velcro'd seams (for quick costume changes), the bulldog clips used for making a size 10 dress a size 6 for a photoshoot, the worn patches on the clothes where the microphone pack was hooked and the inevitable sweat stains. Wear and tear is certainly what fans got when they got up close and personal to the undoubted star of the show – the 50p gold lamé hotpants from the 'Spinning Around' video. Sealed in a glass box for their own protection, the legendary hotpants revealed their guilty secret – a very worn crotch.

The exhibition allowed Kylie to reminisce about the costumes; some had leading roles, others merely walk-ons. 'Each and every item in this collection evokes a myriad of memories and marks a time and place in my life,' admitted Kylie. Half a million people came to see the exhibition in Melbourne alone before it switched to Canberra, Brisbane and Sydney. After the abrupt end to Kylie's 2005 *Showgirl* tour, further items were added to the collection and the following year London's V & A Museum began negotiations with the Melbourne Arts Centre to bring the collection to Britain.

The British show opened on 8 January 2007 with the finest work of Dolce & Gabbana, Gaultier and McQueen all on display, plus a huge collection of tiny Manolo Blahnik shoes (a UK size four). The retrospective also provided an intimate portrait of how a girl became a woman: her dismissal of snow-washed denim in favour of Chanel by sheer force of will. The UK exhibition was divided into seven sections: clothes and stage outfits; shoes; awards (including the countless Logies, ARIAs and MTV gongs); record sleeves; silver, gold and platinum discs; video projections, and lastly a mock-up of Kylie's backstage dressing room from the *Showgirl Homecoming* concerts. Mascara, glitter and feather boas were spread out on the dressing table, fighting for space among bottles of Clinique, a stained 'Kylie Says Relax' mug and a stuffed 'good luck' kangaroo toy.

From the V & A the exhibition moved north to the Manchester Art Gallery and then Glasgow's Kelvingrove Museum, concluding in January 2008. A 160-page commemorative book, featuring a foreword by Kylie and colour photographs of all the outfits and accessories. was printed by V & A Publications in 2007.

The Magic Roundabout

2005 / A Pathé-Canal Plus Production / UK-France / 85 minutes / cert 'U' (UK) / Opened February 2005 (UK) / French title: *Pollux, le manège enchanté*

Directed by Dave Borthwick, Jean Duval and Frank Passingham / Written by Paul Bassett / Based on characters created by Serge Danot / Produced by Andy Leighton, Pascal Rodon and Claire Gorsky / Art Direction by Lilian Fuentefria / Original Music composed by Mark Thomas / Theme Tune performed by Kylie Minogue

Featuring: Tom Baker (*Zeebad*), Ian McKellen (*Zebedee*), Jim Broadbent (*Brian*), Joanna Lumley (*Ermintrude*), Bill Nighy (*Dylan*), Kylie Minogue (*Florence*), Robbie Williams (*Dougal*), Ray Winstone (*Soldier Sam*), Lee Evans (*Train*), Jimmy Hibbert (*additional voices*)

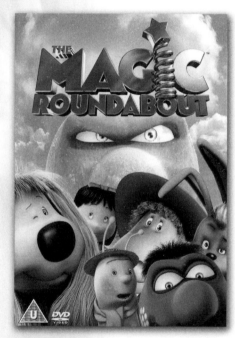

The Magic Roundabout started life as *Le Manège enchanté*, a stop-motion cartoon created in France by Serge Danot (and an uncredited Ivor Wood). Once it had been sold to an unconvinced British television, actor and writer Eric Thompson promptly removed the Gallic audio track, created his own interpretation of the crazy characters and recorded his own mellifluous narration. The result was rightly considered a masterpiece of Anglo-French popular culture, running for 441 episodes from 1965 to 1977. Thompson's witty scripts made the show must-see TV, both for children and adults alike, and his characterisations made stars of a laid-back rabbit, ravenous dog and hysterical cow, although from a strictly visual point of view the series' most enduring star was Zebedee – a red-faced, twizzle-moustached jack-in-a-box, who reminded younger viewers that bedtime was fast approaching as soon as the programme ended.

Three decades after the series ceased production, Bristol-based animators the Bolex Brothers announced a new take on *The Magic Roundabout*, but one still deeply indebted to the quirky original. Rather than a single narrator the new feature-length production assembled an impressive A-list voice cast, though some older fans couldn't help but wonder why Eric Thompson's actress daughter Emma wasn't involved. Critics suggested she would have been the ideal choice to play little girl Florence, but that honour went instead to Kylie. Frustratingly, however, Kylie was again denied an opportunity to shine on screen. Her voice is absent from a huge chunk of the film after her character is imprisoned early on in the frozen roundabout. When she *is* given some dialogue, though, Kylie has fun with it.

Delighted to have been invited to participate, Kylie was sent examples of the movie animation beforehand, along with storyboards, but voicing a cartoon was going to be very different from performing in front of thousands of fans during her recent *KylieFever* tour. 'I was thankful there was a voice coach there because I'm used to performing using everything I have and using the camera to your advantage,' she explained in 2003. 'Anything that's a challenge like that is interesting for me, and will lure me to a project!'

The casting of another singer, Robbie Williams, as the cowardly glutton Dougal ('a dim-witted draught excluder') is also a surprisingly clever touch. 'The relationship between her and Dougal is just so sweet,' said Kylie. 'I turned the pages of the script and thought, "Oh you're so cute". There's obviously a great understanding between the two of them. He knows he can get away with anything and she knows it too, but she loves him anyway.' It's pleasing to see the very obvious affection between Robbie and Kylie's characters in the movie, a counterpoint to their arrogant comic interplay on their October 2000 duet, 'Kids'. Dougal shows his undying devotion to his mistress and thankfully, unlike the hit single, there are no anal sex references here.

Unfortunately, the movie dispenses with the minimal white vistas of the TV series and replaces them with a quaint townscape oddly reminiscent of the BBC1 sitcom *'Allo 'Allo*. Even the incidental music distracts from the visuals. The lovely, creaky old barrel organ tune from the 1970s animation is replaced by a dizzying, and rather cynical, use of classic pop songs: 'You Really Got Me' by The Kinks, 'I Love to Boogie' by T.Rex, 'Mr Blue Sky' by The Electric Light Orchestra and the sublime 'Magic' by Pilot. In addition to these Kylie recorded a new theme tune – a bouncy singalong rhyme designed for the Teletubbies generation called, simply, 'The Magic Roundabout'. Written by Andrea Remanda and recorded with dodgy dance group Scaramanga X, the song features some of the most trite lyrics Kylie has ever had to sing, like 'So join in with the fun, the ride has just begun.'

Released a year later in America, the movie was retitled *Doogal* (their spelling) and much altered, even in storyline. All the characters, save for Kylie's and Ian McKellen's, were revoiced for the new version: Whoopi Goldberg became Ermintrude, William H Macy was Brian, Chevy Chase was the Train, etc. In addition, Judi Dench was installed as narrator, just in case US audiences were left scratching their heads as to what the hell was going on. The film did not translate well and performed disastrously, ultimately taking a nosedive into animation obscurity. For more discerning US viewers, however, the original British cut of the film was made available under the title *Sprung! The Magic Roundabout*. But, compared with the original series' four-minute chunks of charming inconsequence, even this unadulterated version tends to drag.

'Giving You Up'

Released March 2005 (UK)
Written by Miranda Cooper, Brian Higgins, Tim Powell, Lisa Cowling, Paul Woods, Nick Coler and Kylie Minogue
Produced by Brian Higgins and Xenomania
Highest chart position #6 (UK), #8 (Australia)

Flipside: 'Made of Glass'
Video directed by Alex and Martin

'Giving You Up', the second new track extracted from the 'Ultimate Kylie' collection, was produced and co-written by Brian Higgins, the mastermind behind Xenomania, the English production team responsible for Girls Aloud's string of European hits, as well as successes for Sugababes, Texas and New Order. Higgins, who also co-wrote Cher's international smash 'Believe', was an original member of dance outfit Motiv8, who worked extensively with Kym Mazelle and Jocelyn Brown and did the unforgettable 12" Vocal Slam Mix of Spice Girls' 1996 hit 'Wannabe', before going on to work with Dannii

Minogue on her superior mid-nineties material like 'All I Wanna Do' and 'Disremembrance'. From his base in Kent, Higgins presided over a hit-making empire not dissimilar to the glory days of SAW.

Recorded in late summer 2004, Higgins' Kylie track holds the record for most songwriters on one of her singles (seven). It's a tough-talking electro slinker with growling chainsaw keyboards and Kylie purring about her unconditional love for a man she just cannot give up: 'I lay intoxicated while angels circled high above.' The offbeat, and sadly seldom-seen, video features a giant, vampish Kylie striding through London's nightlife in a clever parody of the 1958 B-movie *Attack of the 50 ft Woman*. The promo's opening sequence, with Kylie marching through a road tunnel, was shot in the underpass beneath the iconic 1960s Barbican Estate on a chilly February evening, with choreography by Spaniard Raphael Bonachela.

The single's Xenomania-produced flipside, 'Made of Glass', is considered by many to be a superior track to 'Giving You Up'. Containing a whispered chorus with poetic lyrics about 'Bohemian boys and Brazilian girls', the song is indeed catchier than the A-side and in Australia gained more airplay than the official release. Unbeknown to everybody, 'Giving You Up' would become Kylie's final single for nearly two and half years.

Showgirl – The Greatest Hits Tour

Created and Directed by William Baker / Production Design by Alan MacDonald / Music Producer – Steve Anderson / Choreography by Michael Rooney and Rafael Bonachela / Tour Manager – Sean Fitzpatrick / Production Manager – Kevin Hopgood / Wardrobe by John Galliano, Julien MacDonald and Moschino

Musicians: Steve Turner (keyboards), Chris Brown (bass), James Hayto (guitar), Andrew Small (drums), Valerie Etienne, Jo Garland and Janet Ramus (backing vocals)

19 March-7 May 2005 (Europe)
Cancelled: 19 May-23 June 2005 (Australia and Asia)

Set list:
Showgirl: Overture, Better the Devil You Know, In Your Eyes, Giving You Up, On a Night Like This.
Smiley Kylie: Shocked (contains excerpts from Do You Dare, It's No Secret and What Kind of Fool), What Do I Have to Do (contains excerpt from Closer), Spinning Around (contains excerpts from Step Back in Time, Finally and Such a Good Feeling).
Denial: In Denial, Je Ne Sais Pas Pourquoi, Confide in Me.

What Kylie Wants, Kylie Gets: Red Blooded Woman (contains excerpt of Where the Wild Roses Grow), Slow, Please Stay.
Dreams: Over the Rainbow, Come into My World, Chocolate, I Believe in You, Dreams.
Kylesque: Hand on Your Heart, The Loco-motion, I Should Be So Lucky, Your Disco Needs You.
Minx in Space: Put Yourself in My Place, Can't Get You Out of My Head.
Encore: Especially for You, Love at First Sight.

'Essentially nostalgic, but ... really modern at the same time,' is how Kylie described her concept for the most ambitious tour of her career – 37 massive dates across Scotland, France, the Netherlands, Belgium, Austria, Switzerland, Denmark, Germany, Ireland, England, Australia, Singapore, Thailand and Hong Kong. Kylie's Showgirl personna, first unveiled during her 1998 *Intimate and Live* dates, would now be taking centre stage once again. *Showgirl – The Greatest Hits Tour* promised to outsparkle all that had gone before: more glitz, more glamour and more huge hits, plus a few surprises along the way.

William Baker and Kylie's idea for the tour was to catalogue the full spectrum of the singer's career. 'This is an opportunity to celebrate her finest musical achievements,' said Baker prior to *Showgirl*'s opening night in Glasgow on 19 March 2005. Kylie's 105-strong team were determined to make this her ultimate pop statement – a huge £1.25 million, five-part hydraulic stage with revolving elements (the largest ever built for an arena tour), £5 million worth of spectacular lighting effects and innovative video hardware, fantastic choreography (courtesy of Michael Rooney and Rafael Bonachela), 100 pairs of fishnet stockings, 500,000 individual Swarovski crystals and a full retrospective of Kylie's most memorable moments.

If *KylieFever* had been big then the *Showgirl* tour would be bigger; ferried from venue to venue, what's more, in 15 articulated trucks – with half of one such truck entirely devoted to feathers, if the rumours were to be believed. 'This show is not only a celebration of pop songs, and of my career,' Kylie commented, 'but also of a long-term relationship with my audience. This is my way of saying thank you.'

Production designer Alan MacDonald referenced Art Deco throughout (a favourite era of Kylie's), whereas Baker styled Kylie as the quintessential Las Vegas showgirl, dancing past the Moulin Rouge and Folies-Bergère via the backstreets of Soho; through disco diva, raver, Barbarella minx and torch singer, approaching every sequence of the show as if he were directing a 1940s MGM musical against the backdrop of an extravagant Busby Berkeley staircase.

'Are you ready for Kylie?' said a voice booming from the speakers. The resulting screams were enough to make even the hardiest of eardrums burst. And then she appeared, rising gracefully and motionless from centre stage, with peacock-like elegance, a vision in tight-fitting, jewel-encrusted Galliano corset ('A 16" waist? Wow! Even I would be amazed,' she quipped to the press), Manolo Blahnik heels and blue and white feathers – *lots* of feathers. Then the beats kicked in with 'Better the Devil You Know', the *fast* version. Muscular feathered men danced around her like a scene from *Flash Gordon* as 'In Your Eyes' made way for 'Giving You Up', this time joined by the female dancers in even more flamboyant feathered creations, straight off the streets of the Rio Carnival. The stage emptied, the audience hushed momentarily, leaving Kylie alone to sing 'On a Night Like This', twisting around the colossal arrangement of ostrich plumage attached to her tiny rump.

Showgirl continued at such a breakneck pace that it's hard to imagine how Kylie managed to endure seven costume changes and belt out hit after hit, barely pausing for breath. Displaying Supergirl powers rather than mere Showgirl high-kicks, Kylie leapt through the early-90s acid abandonment of 'Shocked', a fabulous extended, keyboard-heavy version of 'What Do I Have to Do' and a dynamic 'Spinning Around', her dancers whirling about like crazed circus performers against a backdrop of flashing smileys and CND signs. The myriad upbeat numbers – like a euphoric Hi-NRG mix of 'Please Stay' (referencing elements of Dario G's 1997 hit 'Sunchyme') and the SAW-faithful, retro mix of 'I Should Be So Lucky' (a version absent from so many of her recent concerts) crackled with excitement, particularly when Kylie deliriously spun round on the spot in a playful pastiche of the latter's 1988 video. 'There's no bubble bath tonight, I'm afraid,' she squealed.

'Lucky' was also intriguingly choreographed by Raphael Bonachela, with the dancers following the simple lyrics in sign language.

However, things got raunchier during 'Red Blooded Woman' when four semi-naked male dancers rose from the centre of the floor washing themselves under the YMCA showers, generating audible gasps from the audience. Kylie arrived, straddling a vaulting horse, and adopted the role of strict gay gym mistress, sending her workout bunnies into uncontrollable spasms. Kylie only got to wind down with an affecting, and unexpected, rendition of 'In Denial', featuring the disembodied tones of Neil Tennant, and the deep, sensuous beat of 'Dreams' from the 'Impossible Princess' album. And her impassioned Hollywood version of 'Over the Rainbow' from *The Wizard of Oz* once again provided her critics with something to mull over.

Surprisingly, each gig ended with an encore of 'Especially for You', sung as a duet with the enthusiastic audience, who were encouraged to sing along with lyrics displayed in gigantic letters on the screen behind her. 'The gig of the year?' queried the *Times*. 'No doubt about it.' The *Daily Telegraph*, meanwhile, summed up the show as 'A glitzy array of men with gleaming pecs doing hip-thrusts under some sort of electric firework display, and Kylie wagging her tail like an adorable Chihuahua at the centre.'

Behind the Feathers

A Blink TV-TBM Production / 21 minutes / 2005

Directed by Lauren Jones / Produced by Tom Colbourne / Chief Editor – Daniel Goddard

'I saw it as a film. That's how I approached it,' says William Baker of the *Showgirl* tour. In fact, a film of Kylie's debut at Earl's Court on 6 May was screened 24 hours later on British TV by Channel 4, then released on DVD as *Kylie Showgirl* in November 2005. Directed by Russell Thomas and produced by Philippa Pettett, the concert ran to 108 minutes and featured a backstage documentary entitled *Behind the Feathers*.

In its brief 21 minutes Lauren Jones' film examines just how massive an achievement the *Showgirl* tour actually was. From make-up and costume to choreography, set construction, lighting and eventual performance, it was nothing short of a 'Kylie industry'. The camera

Cuddling up to Dougal at the *Magic Roundabout*
première in London, January 2005

KYLIE

OFFICIAL 2005
CALENDAR

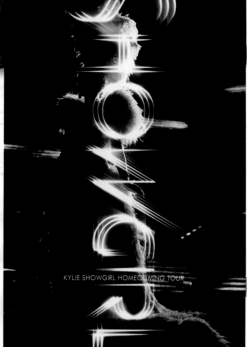

Kylie Showgirl tour programme, 2005

Opposite:
The Showgirl wows Sydney,
November 2006

attıtude

Exclusive!
Ky**lie**

PLUS
Bear Art Attack
Helen Mirren
Graeme Le Saux
Escorts In Love
and much more...

Q
Britain's Biggest Music Magazine

[World
Exclusive]

Kylie

Strewth!
Now *that's*
the way
to make a
comeback.

Kylie at the London première of
White Diamond, October 2007

Performing in Oslo at the Nobel Peace
Prize Concert, December 2007

UK 12" picture disc for 'Wow' (2008)

Kylie, January 2008

follows tour manager Sean Fitzpatrick from 6.30 am (when he leaves his London hotel) to 8.20 pm (when Kylie finally takes to the stage) and everything in between. The most telling moment comes when the hydraulic stage first appears, like a gigantic, revolving robot; it's so impressive even Kylie is blindfolded before she's allowed to take a peek. When she finally lays her eyes on it she is almost lost for words. 'That's a nice piece of kit,' she says, awestruck.

*   *   *

Kylie was in Melbourne taking a break before the Australian leg of her *Showgirl* tour when she was diagnosed with breast cancer. She had been feeling, as she described it, 'out of sorts' for some time and was suffering regular cold sweats and bouts of sickness. 'I distinctly recall going to my two sound guys and saying, "Maybe I'm too old for this. I'm so tired."'

Encouraged by her then-boyfriend, the actor Olivier Martinez, Kylie had tests done. When she returned for the results, accompanied by her parents and Martinez, she was apparently so dazed by the cancer diagnosis that her first reaction was to tell the doctor she was sorry but she had a plane to catch to Sydney. It was her father who told her that the plane could wait and she was just going to sit down. 'My relationship has always been close,' Kylie explained. 'My mother, in particular, has always been more like a friend to me, but when I was diagnosed it was like she needed to be my mother again. And it was as if I was her little girl again.'

Kylie had just one day's grace before an official announcement was made to a stunned press on 17 May 2005. It made front-page headlines around the world. Not only was the remainder of the *Showgirl* tour postponed indefinitely, but Kylie was also forced to pull out of her commitments to the Glastonbury Festival in June. 'I was virtually a prisoner in my own house,' Kylie recalled. 'I was completely thrown into another world.' Illustrating how well-respected Kylie is, Australian Prime Minister John Howard issued a statement supporting her and warning the paparazzi to leave her alone. Meanwhile distraught fans began to congregate outside the Minogue family home in Melbourne.

Kylie underwent surgery on 21 May at the private St Francis Xavier Cabrini Hospital in nearby Malvern. Kylie released a statement thanking her fans for their support and urging them not to worry unduly. For several weeks she totally disappeared from view, prompting a flurry of high-profile newspaper and magazine articles highlighting the importance of women checking their breasts for lumps. On 8 July Kylie made her first post-surgery public appearance, wearing a head scarf while visiting a cancer ward at Melbourne's Royal Children's Hospital. Straight afterwards she travelled to France with Martinez for chemotherapy at the Gustave-Roussy Institute at Villejuif, near Paris. 'I was lucky to have my mum with me in Paris throughout my treatment. I don't know how I would have got through that without her.'

Kylie recuperated in France for 14 months, a period she now likes to call her 'drama'. 'The days you didn't see me, or no one saw me, were the days that I simply couldn't get up or do anything,' she recalled. 'To walk to the corner was great ... I did it. I got to the café. And then went home.'

Much to her delight, Kylie received thousands of 'get well' cards from all over the world. 'I would receive so many sweet letters that would just be addressed to 'Kylie, Pop Princess, Australia',' she said. 'It was just incredible that these letters got to me. I thought, "Wow!" Some of the pictures children sent me made me look like Marge Simpson because the big blue feathered head dress I wore on the *Showgirl* tour looked more like hair!'

Kylie's final session of chemotherapy was on 18 December and she got the all-clear in January, although she faced a further six months of radiation treatment to help prevent the cancerous cells from returning. 'When your hair starts to grow back it's thrilling,' she said. 'There's an eyelash! There's an eyebrow!' In early June she announced that her cancer was in full remission and she was able to attend Elton John's famous white tie and tiara ball in Windsor. 'It was my official coming out party,' she laughed.

On Sunday 16 July 2006 SKY One broadcast an exclusive interview with Kylie conducted by Cat Deeley, later syndicated throughout the world. It was such a global media event that the programme was rather grandly entitled *Kylie: The Interview*. It presented a gamine-looking Kylie, sporting post-chemo blonde cropped hair, talking candidly, and movingly, about her ordeal. 'Having had cancer, one important thing to know is you're still the same person at the end, you are the same person during it,' she told Deeley. 'You're stripped down to near zero, but it seems that most people come out the other end feeling more like themselves than ever before. I'm more eager than ever to do what I did. I don't want to sound soppy, but that's the way it is. Try to enjoy the moment. Have a laugh. Swim in the sea. Hug and kiss...'

Kylie admitted that a lot had changed since her diagnosis. 'It is difficult for me to articulate the way in which things have changed,' she explained in an interview with the *Mail on Sunday* in September 2006. 'Before last year everything in my life was such a rush. I was travelling, I was touring, and I was recording; always moving from one thing to the next. Then I had a year when I was removed from that life, during which I went through this ordeal. I think that experience leaves you living more in the moment, with a stronger sense of your own identity. My friends say I am clearer, more defined now.'

The Showgirl Princess

Published September 2006 (UK)
Written by Kylie
Designed by William Baker and Swan Park
Published by Puffin Books

As Kylie regained her strength during her enforced year off it was something totally new which provided her with a much-needed distraction: her first attempt at writing a children's book. 'It's really funny because I love to write,' she said, 'but during that time there was so much whirring around in my head that the only other thing I actually wrote was a diary of my medication!' Writing something for children – more specifically, little girls – offered Kylie a gentle and rewarding way of getting back to work. She said, 'It was something different that wasn't physically challenging which I could do at that time. I couldn't do anything else.'

Kylie's debut novel, eventually titled *The Showgirl Princess*, tells the story of a character named Kylie who dreams of standing 'on a glittering stage and singing to a thousand people'. Unfortunately, her sparkly shoes go missing, but after some considerable panic they are discovered in the mouth of a Rhodesian ridgeback dog named Sheeba! 'A lot of the things in the book are true or based on true stories,' Kylie admitted, recalling the time her silver boots disappeared during the *KylieFever* tour, causing the wardrobe mistress to have a mini-breakdown. In fact, *The Showgirl Princess* is dedicated to her team of people working behind the scenes.

The fairy tale book features photographs of the 'real' Kylie (taken by William Baker) as the story's heroine, beautifully blended into pastel-coloured artwork by renowned Korean-born illustrator Swan Park. The artist even manages to paint a believable portrait of Sheeba, in reality Olivier Martinez's own dog. 'Sheeba was very important during my treatment,' confessed Kylie. 'There were many long hugs on the sofa during that time.'

The Showgirl Princess was published by Puffin in the UK and was launched at Waterstone's flagship store on London's Oxford Street on 20 September 2006, where Kylie signed copies for 250 young fans, most of whom had won tickets to meet her. A river of pink taffeta and golden sequins patiently queued to meet their idol, with several blushing fathers more excited than their offspring.

*   *   *

In November 2006, Kylie was back with her sales-lady hat on, launching her first signature fragrance 'Darling by Kylie', produced in association with Coty of New York and vying for a slice of the £600 million UK market. Smelling like Kylie proved to be irresistible for many women and the singer has gone on to produce two other bestselling fragrances ('Sweet Darling' in 2007 and 'Showtime' in 2008). At the same time Kylie was busy promoting her scent range in Europe and Australia, she was also heavily into rehearsals for her comeback tour and using the expertise she had gained from writing *The Showgirl Princess* to guest-edit, and appear on the cover of, the December issue of Australian *Vogue*. 'My energy's coming back now and I'm so revved up,' she said excitedly. 'I can't wait to get back to my day job!'

Showgirl – The Homecoming Tour

Created and Directed by William Baker / Production Designed by Alan MacDonald / Music Producer – Steve Anderson / Choreography by Rafael Bonachela, Akram Khan and Michael Rooney / Tour Manager – Sean Fitzpatrick / Production Manager – Kevin Hopgood / Wardrobe by John Galliano, Dolce & Gabbana, Gareth Pugh and Emilio Pucci

Tour programme cover for Showgirl Homecoming

Musicians: Steve Turner (keyboards), Chris Brown (bass), Mark Jaimes (guitar), Andrew Small (drums), Valerie Etienne, Hazel Fernandez and Janet Ramus (backing vocals)

11 November-17 December 2006 (Australia)
31 December 2006-23 January 2007 (UK)

Set list:
Homecoming: Overture, Better the Devil You Know, In Your Eyes, White Diamond, On a Night Like This.
Everything Taboo: Shocked (containing excerpts from It's No Secret, What Kind of Fool, Keep on Pumpin' It and I'm Over Dreaming (Over You)), What Do I Have to Do (includes excerpt from Closer), Spinning Around (contains excerpts from Step Back in Time, Finally and Such a Good Feeling).
Samsara: Confide in Me, Cowboy Style/Finer Feelings, Too Far.
Athletica: Butterfly, Red Blooded Woman/Where the Wild Roses Grow, Slow, Kids.
Dreams: Over the Rainbow, Come into My World, Chocolate, I Believe in You, Dreams (with When You Wish Upon a Star intro).
Pop Paradiso: Burning Up/Vogue, The Loco-motion, I Should Be So Lucky (with The Only Way is Up intro), Hand On Your Heart.
Dance of the Cybermen: Can't Get You Out of My Head, Light Years/Turn It Into Love.
Encore: Especially for You, Love at First Sight.

' The moment has arrived,' read the beaming press release. 'Pop's premier princess is back!' It only seemed proper that Kylie's long-awaited *Showgirl* comeback tour returned to the fans in Australia, who had missed out on it first time round. And for a determined Kylie it was a big deal – her long-awaited return to the stage for the first time since her breast cancer, a nerve-wracking but ultimately triumphant experience, not only for the singer, but also for the fans.

The re-titled *Showgirl Homecoming* concerts debuted on 11 November 2006 at the Sydney Entertainment Centre, where Kylie held court for three sell-out nights. Tickets from her cancelled 2005 concerts were still valid, something a self-deprecating Kylie made fun of. 'Sorry I was late,' she said humbly. After Sydney she travelled to Brisbane (three dates), then back to Sydney (three dates), Adelaide (two dates) and Perth (three dates) before climaxing with six further gigs at Melbourne's Rod Laver Arena. Each night Kylie was met with a standing ovation, which she responded to with tears in her eyes while blowing kisses to her fans. 'You have no idea how this makes me feel,' she commented on more than one occasion. 'I have waited for this for so long now.'

The spectacularly regenerated show stuck to much the same format as the 2005 original, but rather than just an updated 'tweak' here and there, much of it was totally re-designed by Kylie and William Baker. 'We try not to make two TV appearances exactly the same, so I'm not going to make the biggest tour of my life the same,' she said defiantly. Some dance sequences had to be changed out of necessity, courtesy of new choreographer Akram Khan. 'I actually can't do the same things as before,' Kylie admitted to *Hello!* magazine. 'I can't wear the same costumes. How can I replicate what that was, when I'm not the same person?' Kylie's mum Carol supervised all the new costume changes (sometimes lasting only 40 seconds), which her daughter admitted could be 'very stressful' and were akin to a Formula One pit stop.

The emotional Aussie debut of *Homecoming* saw a wasp-waisted Kylie rise, phoenix-like, from the centre of the stage and say, rather casually, 'Good evening, Sydney. How are you feeling tonight?' Her question was immediately greeted by a huge roar from the crowd. She kicked things off with a blistering version of 'Better the Devil You Know', but maybe accompanied by a few more feathers and a few hundred more sequins than last time.

The most notable inclusion on the updated set list was the previously unheard song 'White Diamond'. In February 2006 Kylie was in New York with Scissor Sisters, working on tracks for possible inclusion on her next album. Together they wrote and recorded several new tracks, the standout being the 'Xanadu'-inspired 'White Diamond', a magical, autobiographical slice of pop ('You're looking out from the darkness, feeling so alone...') and a spiritual paean to positivity. 'When I went back into the studio for the first time I was quite nervous,' admitted Kylie, 'but it was good to discover that everything was still working. I hadn't sung for nearly a year and it was reassuring to know nothing had changed.' As the tour progressed 'White Diamond' became an unexpected highlight, with fans naturally supposing it would be Kylie's comeback single; it wasn't.

A strangely emotional 'On a Night Like This' again led into a pulsating early 1990s megamix of 'Shocked' and 'What Do I Have to Do', featuring welcome snippets of 'Do You Dare?', 'It's No Secret', 'Keep on Pumpin' It', 'What Kind of Fool' and, most surprising of all, 'I'm Over Dreaming (Over You)' from Kylie's second album. Leaping forward a decade, 'Spinning Around' received a breathless workout via Ce Ce Peniston's classic 'Finally' and 'Such a Good Feeling' by Brothers in Rhythm, cheekily snuck in by ex-Brother – and Kylie's masterful musical director – Steve Anderson. This post-modern trawl through the best dance tracks of the last 20 years continued later on when 'I Should

Be So Lucky' brazenly pinched Yazz and the Plastic Population's happy house anthem 'The Only Way is Up' for its innovative intro. 'Who was at the disco in the '80s?' shrieked Kylie as her dancers energetically bopped around in custom-made *Kylie Says Relax* t-shirts.

Elsewhere the sparkly Showgirl made way for a brief reprise of the Impossible Princess for a moving version of 'Confide in Me', with attendant dancers dressed as Shaolin monks. Bollywood met Irish folk for a tireless 'Cowboy Style' and a lip-smacking, tough-talking 'Too Far', with Kylie at her most aggressive and bursting with attitude. Kylie's most talked-about costume change came for 'Red Blooded Woman', when she donned an outrageous D & G leopard-spotted catsuit and boxing gloves, vying for attention amid a hoard of sweaty, half-naked male dancers, doing synchronised push-ups, bench-presses and swarming over each others' muscular bodies in the most blatantly homo-erotic stage display since Kylie's 2001 *On a Night Like This* tour.

In homage to her heroine Madonna, Kylie mixed 'Burning Up' with 'Vogue', confident enough now to prove she doesn't need to ape anybody. An almost demented version of 'Kids' proved to be a real event even when Kylie sang it solo, but twice on the Australian leg of the tour, and four times more in England, she was joined by a rabble-rousing Dannii. Even better, in Sydney on 12 November Kylie was partnered by Bono from U2, an event recorded for posterity in William Baker's *White Diamond* documentary.

Baker's staging was again outstanding and never more spectacular than when Kylie performed 'Can't Get You Out of My Head' as a glitter-wigged Cleopatra commanding her armies of Cybermen descending in ranks from either side of the stage; silver males marching from the right and tottering shining females to the left. 'I've always loved the imagery of *Doctor Who*,' admitted Baker in 2007. 'I think that was what caught my attention when I was about four and has stayed with me for 30 years. *Doctor Who* has been a natural reference source for me because it's been such a huge part of my life.'

For *Homecoming* the classic *Doctor Who* baddies (replete with their iconic handlebar helmets) returned to Earth and fell to their knees before their glamorous, caped Cyber Controller before erupting into spontaneous dancing. Dialogue from the 2006 *Doctor Who* episode 'Age of Steel' eerily pervaded the stage, before Kylie delivered an absolutely mesmerising performance of 'Light Years/Turn It Into Love' as the noise of the Doctor's TARDIS dematerialised behind her. But this wasn't the Time Lord's moment of pop glory. 'My name is Kylie,' says the singer. 'I hope you had a pleasant flight, please fly with us again...'

With the Australian leg of *Homecoming* coming to an end on 17 December, Kylie had a few well-earned days off before flying back to London to perform a further 13 scheduled concerts to a lucky British audience, many of whom had already been fortunate enough to see the *Showgirl* tour first time round. The British tickets had sold out in barely six minutes, causing several websites to virtually implode. With expectation high, Kylie's debut UK date at Wembley Arena coincided with 31 December; 'I've been to some great New Year's parties over the years, but I can't wait to host what will be the biggest party of all,' the singer promised fans. Appropriately enough, on the night, she led the 12,000-strong audience in an extra-special countdown to 2007 and a midnight rendition of 'Celebration'. In addition, a specially constructed dancefloor with room for 3,500 sweaty revellers was built so fans could carry on dancing until 1.00 am.

Not all Kylie's Manchester shows went as smoothly as those in the capital. Her 13 January gig at the Manchester Evening News Arena was cancelled just 45 minutes into the show. Despite suffering from a bout of 'flu, Kylie had battled her way through the set list but the bug finally defeated her. 'This is what happens when you've been in sunny Australia and you come back to cold England,' she whispered to the audience, looking genuinely upset. Reluctant to leave the stage because she felt responsible for letting down the fans, Kylie could sense the shock in the auditorium. 'Don't worry, I've just got a cold, OK?' she said tearfully. She wrapped things up with an impromptu a capella version of 'Got to Be Certain' and then a duet of 'Kids' with sister Dannii, before bidding her worried fans a guilty adieu, and telling them not to fret. She was then carried off stage. 'The mood from everyone around was of concern for Kylie,' one fan told the *Manchester Evening News*.

The next day the tabloids were bursting with stories about Kylie over-doing it and pushing herself too hard so soon after beating cancer. 'Kylie has been diagnosed as having a moderately severe respiratory tract infection,' her steely spokesperson told reporters. 'It is nothing more sinister than that.' Kylie later admitted that she had briefly thought that her 'flu was in some way a resurgence of her illness, but she banished the thought to the back of her mind. The subsequent 15 and 16 January concerts were postponed while Kylie recuperated in Manchester's Malmaison Hotel, although they were both rescheduled a few days later, with an additional free show on the 23rd (taking her tally of British concerts up to 14) as a 'big thank you' to the fans who had

been disappointed on the 13th.

In January 2007 Parlophone released a double album called *Showgirl Homecoming Live*, produced by Steve Anderson, and featuring 29 tracks recorded live at the Sydney Entertainment Centre. The album reached #7 in the UK charts and #28 in Australia.

* * *

Prior to continuing the *Homecoming* tour in Manchester, Kylie's final day performing in London, 9 January 2007, was marked by her unveiling a bronze cast of her tiny hands at Wembley Arena's Square of Fame, and a day later her fourth mannequin at London's famous Madame Tussauds was revealed to the press. The wax figure, sitting on a crescent moon, was a far more demure version than Kylie's earlier incarnation from July 2002, when she had been captured on all fours, wearing a red basque and leather boots and with her famous bum poking up in the air. What Kylie had not banked on was that visitors to the museum would actually be able to walk around the model and take a sneaky peek at her knickers from behind. 'I was absolutely mortified,' she admitted five years later. 'I've done photo sessions like that before – on all fours, but I was thinking the model would be displayed from the front. I really didn't think it was funny. I'm still offended by it!'

Kylie's effigy courted further controversy in 2004 when Madame Tussauds dressed it up as the Angel of Annunciation, attached wings to it, and suspended it from the ceiling over models of Posh and Becks dressed as Mary and Joseph in a twisted celebrity version of the Nativity. Declared blasphemous by religious leaders, the exhibit was only closed after a furious member of the public attacked the display, decapitating Victoria Beckham in the process. Kylie had half-seriously requested that her old waxwork be 'melted down' and the 2007 version was far more to her liking, posterior well hidden by a red evening dress and doused in her signature perfume, Darling, making it the attraction's first scented figure. Interestingly, Kylie has been modelled four times by Madame Tussauds, with only Queen Elizabeth II enjoying more wax updates. 'I'm rather pleased about that,' Kylie commented, proudly.

White Diamond

2007 / A Blink TV Production for Darenote and Terry Blamey Management / UK / 111mins / cert '15' (UK) / Opened October 2007 (UK)

Directed by William Baker / Produced by Tom Colbourne / Cinematography by Justin Murphy / Edited by Reg Wrench / Music Produced by Steve Anderson / Executive Producers – Bill Lord and Terry Blamey

Starring: Kylie Minogue as *The Showgirl* with William Baker, Dannii Minogue, Olivier Martinez and Bono

Soundtrack listing: White Diamond, Finer Feelings, Sometime Samurai, Tears, I Believe in You, Burning Up, Vogue, Made in Heaven, Kids, Try Your Wings, Je t'aime, Dreams, Can't Get You Out of My Head, You Are There, Over the Rainbow, Come into My World, Alone Again, Light Years, Turn It Into Love, Diamonds Are a Girl's Best Friend

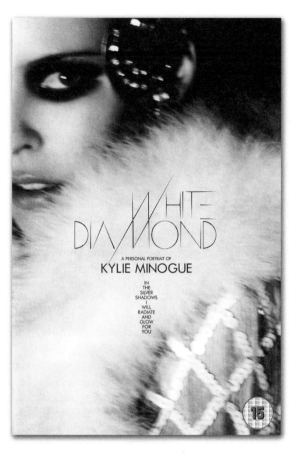

ommemorating the *Homecoming* tour, Kylie's performance in Melbourne at the Rod Laver Arena on 11 December 2006 was captured on film and coincidentally premiered on British television on the same night she was taken ill in Manchester. The concert was later screened on Australian TV on 4 March 2007. It was not released commercially until December that year, when it became one half of a two-DVD set alongside Kylie's documentary movie *White Diamond*. The 125-minute concert was directed by William Baker and Marcus Viner and also featured 21 minutes of re-edits of five tracks from her original 2005 Earl's Court show – 'In Denial', 'Je Ne Sais Pas Pourquoi', 'Confide in Me', 'Please Stay' and 'Your Disco Needs You'.

For those critical of Kylie's thespian abilities *White Diamond* was just what they'd been waiting for; here at last on the big screen was Kylie playing... well, Kylie. No acting required. Filmed between August 2006 and March 2007, *White Diamond* follows Kylie's journey as she resurrects her *Showgirl* tour. The documentary was directed by Kylie's longtime collaborator, stylist and confidant, and so-called 'gay husband', William Baker, the only man she would ever allow to film her 24/7.

The project was first announced in a statement released by Kylie's official website in May 2007. 'There are many funny and many tearful moments,' Kylie revealed to the press the following month. 'I was a little nervous to work on such a revealing project, but due to Willie's persistence, the film is now almost finished.' Just how revealing the project would be was a matter of frenzied speculation. Would fans see the aftermath of her much-publicised break-up with French actor Olivier Martinez? Would Kylie discuss her breast cancer ordeal in detail? Would there be any sibling spats between her and Dannii?

In reality, any similarities to *In Bed with Madonna* (1991), the fruity behind-the-scenes documentary which followed Madonna's record-breaking *Blonde Ambition* tour, stop with the music. While America's Queen of Pop had little problem being filmed having terrifying tantrums, fellating a Coca-Cola bottle and even sniping at a hopelessly uncool Kevin Costner, *White Diamond* is totally free of any such bitching or diva-ish behaviour. You don't even see Kylie get pissed and start swearing. But then that's *not* Kylie.

However, Baker promised something deeper and on that level the film doesn't live up to expectations. 'For most people *Neighbours*, Michael Hutchence, gold hot pants and cancer equal Kylie,' says Baker in his opening gambit. 'I want to rip that surface away.' Instead, what we see is Kylie as a genuinely lovely, thoughtful, slightly introspective woman, basically adored by everyone. The *Times* summed it up thus: 'Baker doesn't so much rip the surface away as gently caress it. He has obviously protected his best mate from some of the harsh realities of his camera and surely that proves the depth of feeling he has for her.'

There had been several rumours circulating that some of the most revelatory sequences had been left on the cutting room floor, at Kylie's insistence. A month before *White Diamond* was released the *News of the World* claimed Kylie had been shocked at some of the rough footage which Baker had shot. She allegedly axed a sequence where she rages about former fiancé Olivier Martinez and breaks down during an emotional phone call with the French actor. Another scene edited out supposedly showed a glimpse of Kylie's operation scar after her breast cancer surgery. 'Kylie wanted a warts and all documentary, but there are loads of scenes fans will never see,' reported the Sunday tabloid.

White Diamond was released in the UK on 16 October exclusively at Vue Cinemas and strictly for one night only. Kylie attended the première in London's Leicester Square alongside Baker, sister Dannii and several showbiz friends, including a bedraggled Rupert Everett. Over 1000 fans turned up to greet her as she stepped out of her limousine in a sparkling D & G gown. 'I said to William earlier, what if only six people turn up at the cinema?' she admitted to June Sarpong. The latter proceeded to conduct the most inept and unprepared interview ever committed to videotape, which was then, frustratingly, screened at 39 Vue cinemas around the country, prior to the actual film. 'So then, girl,' she gushed, 'you've had a really rough couple of years during the past year, yeah?' (Sic.) Kylie, as gracious as ever, explained that she hoped people would enjoy *White Diamond* as 'part road movie, part buddy movie and part behind-the-scenes drama.' And that in a nutshell is what it is.

Subtitled 'A Personal Portrait of Kylie Minogue', *White Diamond* opens with Kylie arriving for rehearsals for the newly dubbed *Showgirl Homecoming* tour at Sadlers Wells in London. She ends up crying when reunited with her troupe of dancers. 'It's like the first day back at school,' she sobs. Kylie explains that she was compelled to resume the tour in order to move on in her life and to tie up unfinished business; she is the eternal showgirl. 'It's naturally what I'm inclined to do,' she says of performing live. 'I would do it for two people out there. I would do it in the morning in my dressing gown. There will be part of me that will want to do it. That's all I've ever done ... I don't see why I should stop now.'

As with *In Bed with Madonna* the scenes of Kylie performing on stage are all filmed in colour while her one-on-one interviews with Baker are conducted in startling monochrome. Kylie explains she needed some convincing to make the movie and, at times, seems weary of the camera intrusion. Baker jokes that she nearly canned the project five times already, to which Kylie playfully retorts, 'I might can it again!'

Throughout the movie Kylie looks delicate and vulnerable, often melancholic, but she can suddenly spring to life at the flick of a switch, never more so than when she climbs back onto the stage (her 'other home') for the first time in Sydney. 'I'm used to being fashionably late, usually by ten minutes,' she tells the enraptured audience. 'Today I'm a year and a half late.' The fans whoop and cheer. Baker captures a shot of gay men waving an 'Our Disco Missed You!' banner. Kylie seems so fresh and alive on stage, internally combusting with sheer excitement, particularly during the spellbinding 'Dance of the Cybermen' medley of 'Turn It Into Love' and 'Light Years', one of the movie's memorable highlights.

Backstage she shows the reality of her stage gymnastics. 'It's physical and mental exhaustion,' she admits quietly, nursing her bruised knees while her make-up artist re-paints her tiny toenails. In *White Diamond*'s most distressing moments Kylie is reduced to tears on stage in Manchester when she tells her audience she cannot go on due to a respiratory tract infection. Her voice faltering, she manages to squeeze out an a capella 'Got to Be Certain' before being carried off stage. 'I felt so responsible and guilty,' she tells Baker.

The overriding feeling you get from watching *White Diamond* is the genuine love Kylie has for Baker. They constantly refer to each other as 'dear' like an elderly couple down at the British Legion snug. This public affection was first glimpsed in 2002's *Feel the Fever* documentary, but here the hugs and kisses come in waves. Elsewhere, Olivier Martinez makes a couple of fleeting appearances, but we don't learn anything about his break-up with Kylie. 'She's always 'Smiley Kylie' but she doesn't let the world see her pain,' says Baker, and nor does Baker's camera. What he thinks of Kylie's French boyfriend is not recorded, but what seems likely is that he protects her from most of the media attention she receives. If Baker was heterosexual he and Kylie would surely have walked down the aisle years ago.

White Diamond includes some very funny moments, namely Kylie's style meeting with Messrs Dolce & Gabbana, where she picks out a bizarre bespoke catsuit and boxing glove combo, and the launch of her perfume 'Darling' in Sydney, when her publicist sprays nearby shrubs with the scent. U2's sardonic lead singer Bono also makes a bravado appearance during a stage duet of 'Kids' and mocks Robbie Williams' strutting arrogance. Elsewhere Kylie looks bored in her dressing room, bemoaning the fact she can't just go for a leisurely stroll outside in the street. Stuck indoors she complains to Baker that 'It's a bit like *Big Brother* but without the tasks', before launching into an uncannily accurate impersonation of petulant Nikki Grahame's 'Who is she?' rant from *Big Brother 7*.

The movie soundtrack sizzles with Kylie tracks, old and new, including 'Confide in Me', 'Better the Devil You Know', 'Finer Feelings', 'Can't Get You Out of My Head' and 'Come Into My World', plus the beautiful slowed-down Scissor Scissors title track and a smattering of classics from Diana Ross, The Cure and Pet Shop Boys along with Liza

Kylie at the Cannes Film Festival, May 2007

Minnelli's heartwrenching version of 'Rent', which seems strangely appropriate here.

Baker said he hoped his film would show Kylie as 'not just a pop princess in gold hotpants'; whether he succeeded is a matter of opinion. Certainly Kylie looks genuine enough. Her intoxicatingly sweet personality cannot be questioned and her warm relationship with Baker is voyeuristically addictive. When the *Showgirl Homecoming* tour's super-computer blows a gasket, leaving Kylie floundering on stage and apologising to the crowd for not 'learning the second verses to her songs', Baker is backstage happily making male genitals out of blu-tak. 'Thanks for coming to my rescue!' she cheekily berates him.

The *Daily Mail* reported that Kylie spent most of the film première sitting at the back of the cinema 'either laughing out loud or sobbing' and was asked by reporters afterwards whether she was looking for love again. She joked: 'There's always a call to my office saying, "Who's she with?" and my manager's like, "Are you sure you're not with anyone?" and I'm like, "No, but if you can get me someone that'd be great!"' Truth be told, Kylie's biggest love is her career is the thrill of performing in front of her fans. The end of *White Diamond* sees Kylie bidding farewell to her Showgirl personna. 'I'm saying goodbye, but she's in me,' she says defiantly. 'She won't go too far.'

*   *   *

Ever since Kylie's post-cancer return to the public eye with the *Homecoming* tour, speculation concerning her new material had been widespread. Working with a variety of producers and DJs, Kylie had recorded in excess of 40 new tracks for possible inclusion on her next album. In March 2007 several numbers purporting to be hers were leaked to the internet, including the awesome 'Lose Control' and 'Excuse My French'. Then, in May, demos of three new songs – 'In My Arms', 'Stars' and 'Sensitized' – appeared on several file-sharing websites. Some cynical journalists claimed the leak was a deliberate attempt by Kylie's management to create a buzz about her new material, but this was strongly denied by Parlophone.

By September two more tracks, 'In the Mood for Love' and 'Spell of Desire', had escaped onto Scottish dance producer Mylo's MySpace page. He claimed he had recorded the songs with Kylie but they had 'sadly been rejected' by her record company. Within days both had been swiftly removed. 'It's really peculiar dealing with all that extra stuff – the leaked tracks,' Kylie admitted in an interview with *Attitude*. 'Which songs were, or were not, me, like 'Excuse My French'. To my knowledge it isn't me. I have no recollection of singing that song, which doesn't necessarily mean that it wasn't me! But there has just been so much that isn't correct, just this maelstrom of information that has nothing to do with me.'

One new song Kylie admitted to, however, was '2 Hearts' ...

'2 Hearts'

Released November 2007 (UK)
Written and Produced by Kish Mauve
Highest chart position #4 (UK),
#1 (Australia)

Additional tracks: 'I Don't Know What it Is' and 'King or Queen'
Video directed by Dawn Shadforth

'2 Hearts' received its unforeseen worldwide premiere at BoomBox, the ultra-hip, absurdist Sunday club night at London's Hoxton Bar and Kitchen. For one night only during September's London Fashion Week, Kylie appeared as BoomBox's superstar DJ, emerging from behind the mixing booth to the strains of 'Your Disco Needs You' before spinning discs by pop contemporaries Madonna, Spice Girls, Gwen Stefani and new kids on the block Girls Aloud. First highlight of the evening was Kylie playing SAW classic 'Respectable' by Mel and Kim and then doing an impromptu bar-top groove to 'What Do I Have to Do'. The unveiling of '2 Hearts' surprised everybody. 'I really wasn't meant to play it but I called my A & R man and he wasn't there,' Kylie confessed. 'I didn't hear back so I just went for it!'

A few weeks later Kylie was honoured by the Music Industry Trust at London's Grosvenor House Hotel for her 20-year pop career and for being the most played female artist on UK radio. She became the first woman in the event's 16-year history to receive the award. Sting, who was attending, called her an 'iconic beauty' and praised her 'courage and grace under pressure', but it was Dannii who was on hand to present her sister with the award. 'I am truly thrilled to be recognised in this way,' Kylie told the audience. Afterwards Kylie performed 'I Should Be So Lucky' with Jamie Cullum on piano and then her new single '2 Hearts' with a sparkly-suited Jake Shears. The number was written and produced by Kish Mauve, a British underground electro-punk duo, who, until the collaboration with Kylie, had failed to be noticed by the mainstream pop press.

The sultry, mascara-smudged tune wears its Scissor Sisters colours proudly, but perhaps more apparent is its similarity to the sound of British glam pop band Goldfrapp, particularly their 2005 hit 'Ooh La La'. Certainly Brit glitter is what '2 Hearts' is all about; the laidback, nonchalant drumming, plucky guitar and high-pitched backing vocals could also have come straight off anything by T.Rex or The Sweet. Kylie herself preferred the more succinct description: 'It's glam rock meets *Cabaret*.'

In Britain the video for '2 Hearts' was premiered on *GMTV* on 10 October, accompanied by a specially filmed clip of Kylie talking about the song. 'It's bizarre to me that it's even coming out,' she said. 'I've been through such a process to get here; not only personally, but just in terms of the record. There is always at this stage a sense of "Here we go again!"' Dawn Shadforth's promo presents Kylie in full-on glitter mode, strutting around in a rubber catsuit and Marilyn Monroe hair, in the midst of stomping platform heels, smashing guitars and speakers exploding with tinsel. It's almost like eccentric Australian glam legend Noosha Fox had never gone away.

'2 Hearts' was first released via digital download and then, a week later, to high street music stores. The song's initial #12 UK chart placing was bettered during its second week when it leapt to #4, helped no doubt by the broadcast of ITV's *The Kylie Show*, but it was not the number one UK comeback Parlophone had predicted. (In Australia, however, it debuted in the top spot, her tenth number one Down Under, equalling Madonna's tally.) *Pop Justice* commented that '2 Hearts' was definitely not the return to form her British fans had been expecting and that 'Perhaps everyone is waiting for [album track] 'The One' to be released before they part with their cash.' However, Kylie's new song was responsible for beating her own UK personal best, becoming her 14th consecutive Top 10 hit single since 2000's 'Spinning Around'. She had previously clocked up 13 successive Top 10s from 1988 to 1991.

The Kylie Show

An ITV Production / 46 minutes / First broadcast (UK) 10 November 2007

Creative Director – William Baker / Directed by Simon Staffurth / Produced by Lee Connolly / Sketches written by George Jeffrie and Bert Tyler-Moore / Edited by Reg Wrench / Musical Director Steve Anderson

Starring Kylie

With special guests Dannii Minogue, Simon Cowell, Jason Donovan, Joan Collins, the Crazy Horse Girls, the Royal Philharmonic Orchestra and Matthew Horne (as *Paul*) and Luke Evans (as *soldier*)

Track listing: Can't Get You Out of My Head, 2 Hearts, Tears on My Pillow, Wow, No More Rain, Got to Be Certain, The One, I Believe in You, Sensitized, Cosmic

Exactly six years after she had boosted ITV Saturday night viewing figures with *An Audience with...*, Kylie came back with a bigger bang to promote her new album 'X'. Less contrived than her first special, *The Kylie Show* still made a virtue of her singing voice, warm personality and magnetic stage presence. Guy Freeman, ITV's controller of music, spoke glowingly of the production: 'We are delighted to be bringing Kylie back to ITV in what will become the must-see television event of the autumn.'

The experience proved to be a thrill for Kylie herself, who worked closely with her creative director William Baker on the entire look of the special. 'Working with ITV on this special has been an incredibly exciting experience,' she told *TVTimes*. 'My creative team and I are preparing a fabulous evening with a mixture of old songs, new songs and lots of surprises thrown into the mix!'

The special was recorded at the famous London Studios on the South Bank on 4 and 5 November 2007 and broadcast in the UK just five days later. The programme was a slickly produced homage to the variety shows of yesteryear. 'When I was growing up I used to love the glamorous TV specials – Sonny and Cher, Judy Garland, Raquel and of course, Cilla!' said Kylie at the top of the show. 'So when I was offered a show of my own, well, what could a girl say?'

As with her showbiz predecessors Kylie's special was a hearty mix of music and comedy. Obviously having got her acting bug back from filming *Doctor Who* over the summer, Kylie threw herself headfirst into some very self-deprecating, and extremely funny, skits, playing on the twisted tabloid perception of her private life. The 'real' Kylie is a foul-mouthed, horse racing-addicted harridan who likes wearing a prosthetic arse, punching her sister and swearing in front of nuns.

The Kylie Show opens with a chauffeur arriving at Kylie's Chelsea mansion to take her to the studios. The horrified driver discovers the star semi-conscious on the floor, surrounded by empty wine bottles and half-eaten takeaway food. Dressed in her tatty *Neighbours* dungarees, Kylie is nodding off halfway through the Scott and Charlene wedding video, which is playing on her flat-screen TV. 'Bouncer, is that you?' she mumbles. From this rather unexpected beginning the rest of the comedy revolves around Kylie's eccentric backstage antics as she prepares for the big show.

First off, Kylie bumps into Jason Donovan, busy promoting his autobiography but unable to recognise his most famous ex-girlfriend. 'I was your co-star in *Neighbours* and we had the big wedding and everything,' implores Kylie. 'More to the point we actually dated for a few years so you must remember!' It's fun to see the *Neighbours* sweethearts acting together for the first time in nearly 20 years and making a mockery of a *News of the World* claim that the two performers now 'hated' each other. Even funnier is Kylie's dressing-room scrap with sister Dannii. 'You have always resented me haven't you?' shrieks Dannii, 'because I'm the pretty one!' Their catfight is straight out of a classic *Dynasty* episode with feather boas being used as garrottes and Kylie being hurled head first into a clothes rail. When Dannii's *X Factor* boss Simon Cowell casually strolls in he nabs the best line of dialogue: 'No introductions necessary,' he says to a bedraggled Kylie. 'The family resemblance is striking. You must be Dannii's mum!' For that Kylie rightly rewards him with a Ramsay Street right hook.

Actor Matthew Horne, best known for his roles in BBC sitcom *Gavin and Stacey* and *The Catherine Tate Show*, takes the role of Kylie's effeminate stylist Paul. He sneakily loves dressing up in her stage costumes (namely the D & G catsuit from the *Showgirl Homecoming Tour*) and being indiscreet about her beauty secrets. 'It's more like being a plasterer's mate than a wardrobe assistant,' he bitches. So, the comedy is an unexpected delight, but the real reason six million UK viewers switched on to *The Kylie Show* was to see her performing.

The special opens with a futuristic performance of 'Can't Get You Out of My Head' with Kylie dressed in a retro 'Destiny of the Daleks' outfit among a sea of waving hands, followed by the laid-back 1970s groove of her latest single '2 Hearts'. Here Kylie's in Betty Grable mode, a forces' 40s sweetheart playfully tossing her suspended microphone and oozing sex. The wartime theme runs through a torch-song rendition of 'Tears on My Pillow', a prodigious song choice and one that works surprisingly well. Kylie plays the role of Suzie Wong, red rose nestling in her jet-black hair, and serenading a theatre of uniformed servicemen. She enjoys a romantic smooch with a handsome corporal, played by Luke Evans, fresh from his lead role in the West End revival of the musical *Rent*, reimagined as *Rent Remixed* by William Baker in October 2007, in which Kylie's voice is heard on an answer-phone. 'It was terrific fun to do,' recalls Luke, 'but with me trussed up in the military outfit and Kylie in vintage Valentino we didn't have much opportunity for movement!'

Unquestionably, William Baker's creative staging is almost picture perfect. Kylie effortlessly slips from one stylised era to another, equally at home as a Japanese disco dolly on a freaky fashion catwalk ('Wow'), as Debbie Harry drenched in a 1980s laser show ('No More Rain') or as a raven-haired temptress in fishnet stockings swinging about on a bucking bronco ('Sensitized'), bringing to mind her notorious Agent Provocateur advert. Unlike her previous ITV special, Kylie doesn't perform in front of a celebrity crowd. In their place are a gaggle of anonymous Kylie fans, stick-thin models and über-trendy clubbers creamed off the top tier at BoomBox. The only time Simon Staffurth's direction disappoints is when he employs these pretentious fashion victims to dance next to Kylie during her fabulously brassy version of classic hit 'Got to Be Certain', where they provide a most unwelcome and annoying distraction.

Far more impressive is Kylie in Grace Kelly-mode singing a spine-tingling slowed-down version of 'I Believe in You' in a hall of mirrors, one of the most sensitive and vulnerable TV performances she has ever given. However, highlight of the entire special has to be Kylie's breathtaking performance of new album track, 'The One', considered by many fans as the debut comeback single Parlophone should have insisted on. Joined on stage by the near-naked Crazy Horse Girls from Paris, Kylie does an incredible soft-focus performance bathed in pastel shadows and eerie hypnotic circles. The six identical backing dancers, who parade to the mesmerising electro-beat in g-strings and tassle-tipped bras, are like a 1970s throwback to Soho's Raymond Revuebar and could have easily come straight out of a British sex comedy like *Erotic Fantasies* or *What's Up Superdoc!*

Kylie's TV extravaganza, later screened in Australia in February 2008, ended with a big version of 'Cosmic' backed by the Royal Philharmonic

Orchestra, but it was the coda snuck in after the end credits which provided the biggest shock of the night. Backstage, Kylie is winding down in her dressing room. Grabbing the back of her head she yanks off her rubber face to reveal ... the legendary Joan Collins! 'Oh, I can't keep this up much longer,' the septuagenarian diva sighs wistfully.

'X'

Released November 2007 (UK)
Parlophone / Mushroom Records
Produced by Kish Mauve (track 1), Cutfather and Jeberg (tracks 2 and 9), Richard 'Biff' Stannard and Calvin Harris (track 3), Bloodshy and Avant (tracks 4 and 12), Cathy Dennis and Guy Chambers (track 5), Calvin Harris (track 6), Richard 'Biff' Stannard and the Freemasons (track 7), Greg Kurstin (tracks 8 and 11), Richard 'Biff' Stannard (track 10), and Eg White (track 13)
Highest chart position #4 (UK), #1 (Australia)

Track listing:
'2 Hearts'
'Like a Drug'
'In My Arms'
'Speakerphone'
'Sensitized'
'Heart Beat Rock'
'The One'
'No More Rain'
'All I See'
'Stars'
'Wow'
'Nu-di-ty'
'Cosmic'
Bonus tracks: 'Rippin' Up the Disco' (downloadable from CD), 'Magnetic Electric' and 'White Diamond' (iTunes bonus), 'King or Queen' and 'I Don't Know What it Is' (Japan only), 'All I See' feat. Mims (USA only)

Kylie's tenth studio album (hence 'X', the Latin numeral for ten), and her first since her battle with cancer, was also her first to be available as an exclusive iTunes digital download from 21 November 2007, its 'physical' release following five days later. Recorded in London, Stockholm and Ibiza, and originally entitled 'Magnetic Electric', Kylie resisted the temptation to make her 'comeback' too personal. 'I just want to sing about the disco, which might seem flippant, but it would have been wrong to have an album that was too far one way or the other,' Kylie told *Madison* magazine. 'I wanted to deliver something that was, in a sense, what people would expect. Something you can listen to when you're getting ready to go out, or when you're out. But I also have songs like 'Cosmic' or 'No More Rain', where it acknowledges my past two years, but that's not something I wanted to dwell on.'

Kylie is indeed right back in the disco on several standout tracks, including the brain-thudding Eurythmics-style 'Like a Drug' with its hard as nails lyrics ('Damn right, I got my radar on you...') and featuring a sneaky sample of Visage's hit 'Fade to Grey'. The walloping dance tunes continue with 'Heart Beat Rock', with Calvin Harris' fiery staccato synth tearing through the song like an angry laser beam. Harris comes up with the goods again on slithery future-single 'In My Arms', with biting electro beats and a great hands-in-the-air chorus. 'Wow' (or more accurately 'Wow-wow-wow-wow') is classic Kylie pop at its most exuberant, but best of all is 'The One'. A re-working of an obscure 2006 club track called 'I'm the One', this supremely catchy techno-lite floorfiller positively sparkles all over and gives Kylie the rare opportunity to sing about Michelangelo. 'How gay is that?' Kylie laughed.

She also gets sexed up on the almost avant-garde 'Speakerphone', where the singer commands: 'Drop your socks and grab your mini-boombox.' But, sadly, the twitchy 'Nu-di-ty' is more whimsical than lascivious, especially when Kylie starts popping zippers and referring to her man's 'thing'. The R'n'B-flavoured 'All I See' is the album's biggest surprise, a fast-paced, yet tender, Usher-style love song which may have sat more comfortably on the 'Body Language' album, but presses all the romantic buttons here.

Despite what Kylie said she wanted to achieve with her new album, 'X' was still criticised in some corners of the music press for being 'too anonymous' and 'picking the wrong songs', especially as she revealed she had jettisoned collaborations with Daft Punk, Mylo, Goldfrapp, Boy George and Groove Armada. In January 2008, in Australia's *Herald Sun*, she was forced to defend her choice of tracks again. 'I didn't want every song to be about being ill,' she stressed. 'I wanted to do what I do, which is mostly feelgood music. My conclusion is that if I'd done an album of personal songs it'd be seen as 'Impossible Princess Part 2'.'

The album's three concessions to autobiography are 'Stars', 'Cosmic' and 'No More Rain', the latter describing Kylie's thoughts on recovering from her illness: 'Got a second-hand chance, gonna do it again. Got rainbow colours and no more rain.' Kylie wrote the song towards the end of her treatment, dreaming of playing live again to her fans. 'As I was coming out of it and feeling like, "OK, I can start looking forward to other things," I wrote the chorus,' she said, 'and was trying to project what it would be like to be on stage again.'

Incidentally, the track 'Like a Drug' on Kylie's 'X' album should not be confused with her cover of Roxy Music's 1975 hit 'Love is the Drug', a Bryan Ferry-Andy Mackay composition which she recorded for the 2007 BBC Radio 1 tribute album 'Established 1967'.

X-amining Kylie:
David Tennant in Conversation with Kylie Minogue

A BBC Radio 2 Production / 56 minutes / First Broadcast 27 November 2007 (UK)

Directed and Produced by Malcolm Prince / Presented by David Tennant

Track listing: '2 Hearts', 'Wow', 'White Diamond' (live version), 'Cosmic', 'Stars', 'In My Arms', 'Speakerphone', 'The One', 'All I See' and 'White Diamond' (studio version)

Hot on the platform heels of the UK release of 'X', Kylie was rewarded with her very own BBC Radio 2 special. In the preceding weeks Kylie's promotional machine had seen her co-presenting *The Jo Whiley Show* and guesting on *Steve Wright in the Afternoon*, but here was a programme devoted entirely to Kylie discussing her career and new album with her *Doctor Who* co-star David Tennant.

Before Kylie was invited into the Doctor's surgery for a thorough examination, Tennant (reverting to his Scottish accent) posed a very long question: 'She's everywhere – on the big screen and in music stores. She's on television and even your local perfume counter. She might even be in your underwear drawer, but do we know everything about her? Is there any more that she's willing to reveal?'

The unrehearsed feel of the interview wound its way around Kylie presenting some of the new tracks from 'X', punctuated with Tennant cheekily ribbing his guest. He was particularly baffled by the trendy names of Kylie's new producers and writers – Bloodshy and Avant, Cutfather, Babydaddy, 'Biff' Stannard and Eg White. (When Kylie casually mentions Calvin Harris, the co-producer of 'In My Arms', Tennant rejoiced: 'Finally a name you can make sense of!') Kylie discussed the writing and recording of 'X' and picked her favourite tracks, including '2 Hearts' 'Do you know that Time Lords have two hearts?' asked Tennant. 'Is the song about me?'

She also touched on her Ibiza moment for 'Wow' and 'Stars', which referenced her battle with cancer. 'The darker it is the brighter the stars shine,' she revealed. Tennant was careful not to probe Kylie too deeply about her illness, a topic other interviewers have dwelt upon. 'It's been difficult the last few weeks,' she confessed, 'but for each person I have to mention it to, they don't understand that I'm talking about it all day. It's a tricky one because it's such a deep subject, not only for me but for a lot of people, [so] that I can't skim over it. Some people think of celebrities as being infallible, indestructible. But at the base of it we're all the same, and I'm thankful for that.'

Kylie also talked about the post-cancer recording of 'White Diamond' with Scissor Sisters and her decision not to include it on the 'X' album. As a treat to her fans Kylie allowed Tennant to play the previously unavailable studio version of the track. Kylie also discussed the *White Diamond* movie, her public persona, how proud she is of sister Dannii on *X Factor*, her love of *The Muppet Show* and her forthcoming range of bed linen, fabrics and cushions ('Kylie at Home'). Also, as a radio exclusive there was an excerpt from the *Doctor Who* episode 'Voyage of the Damned'. Kylie was embarrassed to admit she had little prior knowledge of the classic series: 'I wasn't an über-fan, but knew enough to be interested. I knew it would be a lot of fun and a good step back into acting. I loved it!'

The chemistry between Kylie and Tennant prompted the question whether they should be given the breakfast slot. In fact, Kylie's dalliance with BBC Radio continued at 1.00 pm on Christmas Day when sister

THE TIMES

15.12.07

KYLIE WHO?
**BEHIND THE SCENES
WITH THE TIME LORD**
BY CAITLIN MORAN

MAGAZINE

PLUS **GIFTS FOR YOURSELF** ★ FOUR WRITERS GO HOME ★ BECKHAM'S NEW STRIP station Radio 1 let her have a go at DJ-ing. *Kylie Minogue's Christmas Special*, a pre-recorded two-hour programme, had the star playing festive tunes and several of her favourite tracks from the previous 12 months, by the likes of Just Jack ('a lovely chap'), Justin Timberlake (whom she affectionately called 'Timbers'), Mark Ronson, The Kaiser Chiefs, Leona Lewis, The Killers and Robyn ('I absolutely love her'). Kylie also revealed her admiration for Dolly Parton and what her average Melbourne Christmas is like (a game of Scrabble, prawns on a Bar-B-Q and a 'whirly-whirly' in the pool, apparently). In the second half of the programme Kylie's special guest was none other than David Tennant. And on Boxing Day a revised version of her Radio 2 special with Tennant was broadcast as *Re-X-Amining Kylie*, including additional discussion of the *Doctor Who* Christmas episode.

Doctor Who 2007 Christmas Special: 'Voyage of the Damned'

BBC TV / A BBC Wales-Canadian Broadcasting co-production / 71 minutes / Episode first broadcast (UK) 25 December 2007

Directed by James Strong / Produced by Russell T Davies and Julie Gardner / Written by Russell T Davies / Edited by Llana del Giudice

Starring: David Tennant (*The Doctor*), Geoffrey Palmer (*Captain Hardaker*), Clive Swift (*Mr Copper*), Gray O'Brien (*Rickston Slade*), Russell Tovey (*Midshipman Frame*), Debbie Chazen (*Foon van Hoff*), Clive Rowe (*Morvin van Hoff*), George Costigan (*Max Capricorn*), Jimmy Vee (*Bannakaffalatta*), Bernard Cribbins (*Wilf Mott*), Bruce Lawrence (*engineer*), Nicholas Witchell (*reporter*), Paul Kasey (*Heavenly Host*) and Kylie as *Astrid Peth*

On 22 April 2007 the *News of the World* claimed irrefutably that Kylie would be starring in the Christmas episode of *Doctor Who*. The newspaper wrote that she had already met executive producer Russell T Davies in secret and had discussed the forthcoming role. An 'insider' was quoted as saying, 'She is flattered to be asked to be in such a classic TV show. The Doctor Who team are delighted they've got someone as sexy and high profile as Kylie.'

Gossip went into overdrive, with *Sun* journalists claiming Kylie would be cast as a baddie, and more specifically a 'sexy Cyberwoman'. This was obviously a vain stab in the dark based on the fact that Kylie had featured dancers wearing Cybermen helmets on her recent *Showgirl Homecoming* tour. A week later Russell T Davies made a categoric denial of the *Doctor Who* rumour. 'Don't be stupid,' he laughed. 'I haven't even written the script yet, and a woman like Kylie is booked up two years in advance.' However, on 12 May Kylie herself admitted to her participation in the show. Almost bubbling over with excitement at the news, she told *InStyle* magazine: 'Yes, I'm doing it! My gay husband is so excited about it! But I'm not going to play a villain.' A further seven weeks went by before the BBC finally confirmed her part in the Christmas special, 'Voyage of the Damned'. In the meantime internet fanboys had been working themselves up into a lather of excitement.

'This had been planned ever since the press launch of *Doctor Who* series three in the spring of 2007, which Kylie's stylist William Baker attended,' confirmed producer Phil Collinson. 'The arrangements started months in advance, because Kylie's got a year-long schedule which is more intricate than Operation Desert Storm!' A fan for three decades, Baker had casually mentioned that Kylie should be in *Doctor Who*, unaware of the consequences of what he was proposing. 'I think I agreed to it before she actually did,' joked Baker.

Luckily for her eager stylist, Kylie did eventually agree, even with Davies not knowing exactly how her character would evolve. The producer revealed in an interview for *Doctor Who Magazine* that having Kylie guest starring in the series could have far-reaching consequences. 'Of course, she's iconically huge,' he said, 'and this episode will get seen by more people than any other *Doctor Who* episode ever; it will travel around the world. It'll be phenomenal. There will be bunches of gay men in Utah, who've never even heard of *Doctor Who*, sitting watching it cos Kylie's in it!'

It was eventually announced that Kylie would be playing a character named Astrid, a silver service waitress aboad the Titanic, but quite *which* Titanic was debatable. When Kylie first arrived on set there was a frisson of excitement among cast and crew. 'They all think they're going to marry her,' Davies revealed. 'Even the gays. *Especially* the gays.'

Filming commenced in great secrecy on 9 July 2007 with studio work in Cardiff and some location work completed at the Swansea

Exchange and neighbouring Morgan's Hotel. Still dressed in her black mini-dress, frilly apron and foxy leather boots, Kylie had the pleasure of being mistaken for a real waitress. A pensioner hobbled over to Kylie and asked for refreshment. 'Excuse me, love,' she whispered. 'Is it too late for a cup of tea?' As expected, Kylie saw the funny side and pointed the lady in the right direction for a cup of Earl Grey and an eclair. For a star as big as Kylie to appear in such a high-profile series was a very special event, especially considering she hadn't acted in a leading role for several years. 'She's as big a legend as *Doctor Who* is, if not bigger,' commented the Doctor himself, David Tennant. 'It's like two icons colliding with each other!'

Actor Colin Baker, who had previously played the title role during the 1980s, visited the set in Cardiff and immediately recognised Kylie's desire to prove herself. 'She was clearly relishing the opportunity to demonstrate her acting prowess on television again,' he told the press. Working alongside Tennant and veteran guest stars like Clive Swift, Bernard Cribbins and Geoffrey Palmer was an extremely happy experience for Kylie. 'I was a little nervous,' she confessed. 'But being amongst such wonderful actors, and playing opposite David, who's divine, made me determined to do my absolute best. My first day on set was like stepping back in time. I felt really at home being back in the world of TV and acting. It felt very liberating to be a character and not *Kylie*.'

Mixing elements from *The Poseidon Adventure*, the classic 1977 *Doctor Who* episode 'The Robots of Death' and maybe even a dash of Kylie's *Showgirl* tour, 'Voyage of the Damned' creates a disaster movie of epic, intergalactic proportions. Within minutes it becomes apparent that Tennant has not materialised his time-travelling TARDIS aboard the real Titanic but a vast spaceship of the same name, cruising millions of miles above the Earth. ('Bad name for a ship,' mutters the Doctor.) Crammed with wealthy holidaymakers from across the galaxy, the guests are hoping to experience a 'traditional Earth Christmas', but what they get is more 'sinister night' than *Silent Night*.

Kylie's Astrid is a disillusioned waitress who stares listlessly from the space cruiser's portholes, yearning for a more glamorous life, and who finds a kindred spirit in the stowaway Doctor. 'She is a dreamer,' explained Kylie. 'Her dream is to travel and in the Doctor she sees someone who's living the life that she has dreamt of. And there's that hint of possibility which I imagine she'd kind of lost faith in.' Having dispensed with a long line of glamorous female assistants, the Doctor is subconsciously looking for a new travelling companion and Astrid could well be next in the queue. 'You could imagine them sailing off into the sunset together,' said Tennant. 'Astrid could stay with the Doctor for a long time, if it wasn't for that album and international tour...'

When the beleaguered captain of the Titanic (Geoffrey Palmer) betrays his crew, his vessel comes under fire from devastating meteors and the robotic 'Heavenly Host' start detaching their halos and calmly murdering people. The heroic Doctor is forced to take control and lead a motley band of survivors to help. In the grand tradition of disaster movies you see people from all social backgrounds attempting to pull together, including cute alien 'talking conker' Bannakaffalatta. When the Doctor's abilities are called into question, he is forced to fight back with some iconic Russell T Davies dialogue: 'I'm the Doctor. I'm a Time Lord. I'm from the planet Gallifrey in the constellation of Kasterborous. I'm 903 years old and I'm the man who's going to save your lives and all six billion people on the planet below. You got a problem with that?'

Astrid *definitely* hasn't got a problem with the new man in her life. She is instantly smitten. The Doctor paints a picture of exciting interplanetary adventure ('No tax, no bills, no boss...') which Astrid cannot resist, and he readily agrees to take her with him, once they escape from the burning spaceship, that is. Concordant with Davies' reimagining of the Doctor as a totally irresistible, quietly sexual, character, Astrid too falls under his sensual spell. 'So you look good for 903,' she says. 'You should see me in the mornings!' he jokes. 'OK,' she replies, rather too keenly.

The chemistry between Tennant and Kylie is obvious from the outset and their performances compliment each other beautifully. The rich, visual backstory of *Doctor Who* has echoes of Kylie's real life as a performer. The Doctor's ability to regenerate, his life spanning centuries in different costumes and with different faces, mirrors Kylie's evolution as a modern-day pop star. Amusingly, in the 2006 *Doctor Who* episode 'The Idiot's Lantern' the Doctor actually references the real-life Kylie on screen. 'It's never too late as a wise person once said... Kylie, I think!'

Kylie's performance is, considering the space-age setting, believable, compassionate and brave; she is even ultra-efficient in despatching the less-than-angelic robotic Host. Unfortunately, the Doctor's relationship with Astrid is to be short lived. When they encounter the real menace lurking on deck 31, the megalomaniac Max Capricorn (basically a head in a glass box on quad bike tyres, and by modern *Doctor Who* standards a very substandard baddie), courageous Kylie climbs into a forklift truck and pushes him into the fiery chasm at the heart of the stricken vessel, falling to her death at the same time. She makes the ultimate sacrifice. It's an unusually bittersweet ending for a Christmas special, especially when the heartbroken Doctor attempts to bring Astrid back to life but succeeds only in releasing her into the cosmos as stardust. When Kylie dissipated into tiny atoms and floats out of a porthole you could almost hear millions of Kylie fans blubbing into their Christmas Campari and Cokes.

Half an hour after the climax of 'Voyage of the Damned', BBC3 screened an episode of the companion show *Doctor Who Confidential*. The 56-minute 'Kylie Special' went behind the scenes, with footage of Kylie filming on location in Cardiff's St John Street, doing a cheeky publicity shoot with Bannakaffalatta and being photographed by William Baker for the *Radio Times* front cover with David Tennant. The special also featured interviews with Tennant, Baker, and Kylie herself. 'It's been an absolute blast,' she says excitedly. 'I really had trouble wiping the smile off my face!'

Kylie's unbridled enthusiasm for the project, and an unprecedented amount of publicity, helped 'Voyage of the Damned' not only become the second most-watched TV programme of Christmas Day, peaking at 13.8 million viewers (only narrowly beaten by a predictably unseasonal instalment of *EastEnders*), but also the second most-watched show of 2007. It was also the most successful *Doctor Who* episode since 1979, when Tom Baker was in residence. The press were almost unanimously positive about Kylie's performance, particularly the *Times* which, rather amusingly, called her 'merry and squeezable'.

But does Kylie's lead role in 'Voyage of the Damned' signify her return to acting? 'She did *Doctor Who* because I think that's the way her thoughts are heading,' surmised Russell T Davies during the episode's press launch at London's Science Museum. 'She's missed acting and she fancied the discipline. You forget she has been in *Neighbours*, so is used to knocking out an episode a day. I'd cast her again like a shot!'

OFFICIAL
KYLIE
MINOGUE
CALENDAR
2007

✩　✩　✩

Kylie concluded a triumphant 2007 headlining the Nobel Peace Prize concert in Oslo on 11 December. She opened the prestigious show with '2 Hearts' followed by 'Can't Get You Out of My Head'. Four days later she was appearing on the live final of ITV1 talent show *The X Factor*, alongside her sister, and resident judge, Dannii and a very appreciative Simon Cowell. Kylie duetted with eventual winner, Leon Jackson, on the jazzy version of 'Better the Devil You Know', but the press was more obsessed with her all-in-one black lace bodysuit.

Then came a pre-recorded New Year's Eve appearance on the acclaimed *Jools Holland's Annual Hootenanny* on BBC2, where Kylie sang two numbers accompanied by the host and his Rhythm and Blues Orchestra (including the torch song interpretation of 'I Should Be So Lucky') while celebrity guests (and former co-stars) David Tennant and Dawn French looked on, slightly the worse for drink. The climax of Kylie's evening was a duet with Paul McCartney on his single 'Dance Tonight'. Newly presented with an OBE, Kylie hit it off with Sir Paul in unexpected style, much to her obvious delight. 'She's awfully good,' commented the beaming ex-Beatle.

'Wow'

Released February 2008 (UK and Australia)
Written Karen Poole, Kylie Minogue and Greg Kurstin
Produced by Greg Kurstin
Highest chart position #5 (UK), #11 (Australia)

Additional tracks: 'Cherry Bomb', 'Do It Again' and 'Carried Away'
Video directed by Melina Matsoukas

With an album and an upcoming tour to promote in 2008, Parlophone announced that 'Wow' would be the second British single from 'X'. The song is a glittering return to disco form, a gloriously sanguine Daft Punk-esque homage to an unnamed man in Kylie's life. 'Every inch of you spells out desire...' she coos. Wow indeed!

Opening with some beautifully deranged piano work, the song suddenly explodes into life and straight onto the dancefloor.

Kylie herself described the track as 'outrageously club-tastic', but it very nearly didn't happen. Frazzled after recording 40 or so tracks for possible inclusion on her new album, Kylie, along with her co-writers Karen Poole and Greg Kurstin, travelled to Ibiza where they rented a sun-kissed villa on the south-west edge of the island. Looking out to sea, Kylie couldn't fail to notice the volcanic rock named Es Vedrà rising from the sea, reputed by islanders to have spiritual and magnetic powers. Four hundred metres high, with almost vertical cliff sides, Es Vedrà looks more like a cathedral than a rocky outcrop, especially at sunset. Kylie's first impression of the magnificent view from her villa was, quite simply, 'Oh, wow!' 'The three of us were writing together and I wanted a song with a title that you say every day,' explained Kylie. 'I suggested the word 'wow' because that's all I said when I stared out to sea!'

Kylie premiered 'Wow' live on *The X Factor*, receiving a standing ovation from the judges and particular praise from an embarrassed Sharon Osborne, obviously uncomfortable after making several bitchy remarks about Dannii a week earlier on *The Graham Norton Show*. It was reported that Kylie had been seething after hearing what she said. After Kylie's primetime performance, 'Wow' immediately entered the UK download chart, fully two months before its official release, eventually hitting the #1 spot on the UK club and airplay charts.

Kylie also gave an unsurprisingly camp performance of 'Wow' at the 2008 BRIT Awards on 20 February at Earls Court flanked by dancers dressed in, what can only be described as, 'Power Ranger' costumes. Kylie won 'Best International Female Artist' (the latter being the seventh time she'd been nominated in that category) and was presented with her award by a beaming David Tennant.

'In My Arms'

Released February 2008 (Europe) / May 2008 (UK and Australia)
Written by Kylie Minogue, Paul Harris, Julian Peake, Richard 'Biff' Stannard and Adam Wiles
Produced by Richard 'Biff' Stannard and Calvin Harris
Highest chart position #8 (Germany), #10 (France)

Additional tracks: 'Cherry Bomb', 'Do It Again' and 'Carried Away' (Europe only)
Video directed by Melina Matsoukas

Providing some variety in Kylie's single schedule, Parlophone simultaneously released 'In My Arms' in mainland Europe while 'Wow' hit the shops in the UK and Australia. 'In My Arms' was co-produced by Calvin Harris, the young Scottish supermarket-shelf-stacker-turned-electroclash-purveyor, who hit #8 in the UK album charts with his well-received debut 'I Created Disco' in 2007. Harris' music was brought to an intrigued Kylie's attention and her A & R men suggested a collaboration, although a nervous Harris confessed to 'needing a few drinks' before their first meeting. When the DJ got her into the studio he was impressed by what he saw. 'She's very good with melodies,' he told *Q* magazine. 'There are pop stars who can't sing and have their songs written by other people, whereas she helped write the tunes and sang them perfectly.'

The resulting 'In My Arms' is a chewy, synth-driven pop knee-trembler, much in the same style as Harris' earlier work, and a number that quickly emerged as a fan favourite from Kylie's 'X'. The videos for both this track and 'Wow' were shot back-to-back in Los Angeles during the second week in January, directed by Melina Matsoukas, famed for her work with urban stars Beyoncé Knowles, Jennifer Lopez, Snoop Dogg and Leona Lewis, the latter with the video for her record-breaking 'Bleeding Love'. The video for 'Wow' is best characterised as 'neon Buck Rogers', while the futuristic clip for 'In My Arms' involves Kylie grappling with a giant wind machine. Kylie confessed shooting promos was not as much fun as it used to be and filming two videos at the same time was a labour-saving exercise. 'My patience has gone,' she said. '"You've got it? Right, I'm off." And I'll just keep walking!'

Kylie premiered 'In My Arms' at the NRJ Music Awards in Cannes on 26 January 2008 with an energetic performance dressed in a bizarre, cowl-necked, checkerboard-themed Gareth Pugh dress (which also appears in the video), before Mika presented her with a Lifetime Achievement award. The song got its belated UK release in May 2008.

KYLIEX2008 Tour

Devised and Designed by William Baker and Alan MacDonald / Music Producer – Steve Anderson / Choreography by Michael Rooney / Tour Manager – Sean Fitzpatrick / Wardrobe by Jean Paul Gaultier

6 May-2 August 2008 (Europe and Russia)

After weeks of 'will she or won't she?' debate in the press Kylie finally announced her latest world tour in November 2007. As par for the course, tickets for the British leg sold out in 30 minutes and extra dates were added almost immediately. 'I am putting together a show that is going to be a new and exciting experience for both the audience and me,' Kylie explained on her website. 'The eclectic mix of sounds on 'X' is affording me an opportunity to explore and develop a new live show that will be fresh, exhilarating and innovative.'

Kylie kicks off proceedings in Paris on 6 May, playing 22 dates across Europe and stopping off in the Czech Republic, Romania, Turkey, Greece and even taking in her first promotional visit to Russia. On 26 June she returns to the UK, starting at Belfast then Glasgow, Manchester and Newcastle, culminating with 7 dates at London's O2 Arena (formerly the Millennium Dome). With over 50 gigs spread over four months, several newspapers questioned whether a post-cancer Kylie had the stamina. 'I now do two nights in a row then have a night off,' explained Kylie. 'It's part of my new regime and preserves my heath and sanity, but it's a logistical nightmare for my crew.' An excitable Kylie also warned fans to expect a few surprises. 'It'll be an all-new band and a lot of things are changing,' she said. 'We're all ready for it!'

*   *   *

As Kylie enters her fourth decade in pop she has more than proved her staying power in a notoriously fickle business. She has cleverly avoided the psychodrama of Amy Winehouse, Britney Spears and Whitney Houston as well as sidestepping the excess and abrasiveness of Madonna. She remains as dignified and diverting as ever, remaining true to herself and genuinely grateful for her fan's unwavering faithfulness. Crucially, Kylie still has ambition and the ultimate pop princess undoubtedly has plenty more surprises in store. 'At this time in my life, I feel grateful for all the wonderful experiences I've been lucky enough to have,' she said in 2007, 'and I'm looking forward to those yet to come.'

Thanks for everything, Kylie. It's been fabulous!

Appendix 1

Additional and Promo Singles

'EXCLUSIVO MIX' (1988)
One-sided, Spanish-only 7" single featuring a megamix of Kylie's first four UK singles. Released on Sanni Records.

'ENJOY YOURSELF' (1989)
The jubilant title track from Kylie's second PWL album was passed over as a single in the UK, but a limited 12" promo was pressed by CBS in France. 'Hand on Your Heart' appeared on the B-side.

'DO THEY KNOW IT'S CHRISTMAS' (1989)
Stock Aitken Waterman's well-intentioned but embarrassingly cheesy remake of the 1984 festive classic was released to raise money for the humanitarian crisis in Ethiopia. Under the moniker Band Aid II, a host of Hit Factory stars including Bananarama (who had appeared on the original), Jason Donovan, Big Fun and Sonia were joined by Bros, Lisa Stansfield, Cliff Richard, Chris Rea, Jimmy Somerville and Marti Pellow. Kylie and Jason recorded their vocal contributions separately but were briefly reunited at the London video shoot, the first time they had seen each other since their very public break-up.

'I GUESS I LIKE IT LIKE THAT' (1991)
British white label 12" promo anonymously credited to 'Angel K'.

'DO YOU DARE' (1991)
British white label 12" promo, again credited to 'Angel K', and released to clubs prior to the rave-inspired track turning up on the B-side to 'Give Me Just a Little More Time'.

'NOTHING CAN STOP US' (1994)
Very limited edition UK pressing of Kylie's cover version of Saint Etienne's minor 1991 hit.

'OTHER SIDES' EP (1998)

Limited edition Australian-only EP featuring 'Tears', 'Love Takes Over Me' and the epic 'Take Me with You', issued to coincide with the release of 'Impossible Princess' at HMV record stores.

'TOO FAR' (1998)

Remixed by Brothers In Rhythm for a 12" club promo single. Before Kylie parted company from the deConstruction label, 'Too Far' was considered for the fourth UK single release from the 'Impossible Princess' album.

'DANCING QUEEN' (1998)

Kylie's live cover version of ABBA's 1976 worldwide #1. Extracted from the soundtrack of the 'Intimate and Live' album as a promotional radio-only single in Australia.

'THE REAL THING' (2000)

Australian white label 12" of the lead track from the *Sample People* movie, released exclusively to clubs in Melbourne and Sydney in May 2000.

'BUTTERFLY' (2000)

Taken from the album 'Light Years' and produced by Chicago DJ Mark Picchiotti, 'Butterfly' was originally released to clubs in the UK as a white label in early 2000, before getting a limited promo-only 12" release in the US in the autumn of 2001 with a slew of new remixes.

'FEVER' (2002)

The title track from Kylie's 2001 album was released as a radio-only promo single in Australia in July 2002.

'MONEY CAN'T BUY' EP (2004)

Limited edition American EP given away exclusively to Target retail stores in February 2004. Includes three live tracks recorded during the *Money Can't Buy* concert: 'Can't Get You Out of My Head', 'Slow' and 'Red Blooded Woman'.

'SECRET (TAKE YOU HOME)' (2004)

A Taiwanese-only promo single of the hip hop flavoured track from 2003's 'Body Language' album. Backed by two mixes of 'Slow'.

'SOMETIME SAMURAI' (2005)

Originally intended for inclusion on Towa Tei's 1997 album 'Sound Museum', 'Sometime Samurai' only existed in demo form until 2004 when Kylie re-recorded her vocals. More accessible than 'GBI', the song was co-written by Kylie and features her singing about her then-partner, photographer Stéphane Sednaoui ('Man of the moment, possibly all time'). Released as a promo single for Tei's 2004 album 'Flash', the song became a big airplay hit in Japan.

'OVER THE RAINBOW' (2005)

A live version of Judy Garland's classic 1939 song, recorded on the 6 May date of Kylie's *Showgirl* tour at London's Earl's Court and issued to UK radio stations. The single was released on Christmas Day 2005 as a digital-only single, backed with Kylie's 2000 recording of 'Santa Baby'. As digital singles were not eligible for inclusion in the UK chart until 1 January 2007 there is no official chart position for the release.

'ALL I SEE' (2008)

North American digital download-only single, taken from Kylie's album 'X'. An additional radio version was recorded featuring a rap by New York hip hop star Mims.

Appendix 2

Compilation Albums

KYLIE'S REMIXES (VOLUME ONE) (1989)
Originally released in Japan in March 1989 on the Alfa label, this compilation features nine extended remixes from Kylie's debut album. Later reissued in Australia by Mushroom Records.

KYLIE'S REMIXES (VOLUME TWO) (1992)
A second Japanese volume of 11 extended remixes of songs which had originally appeared on the 'Rhythm of Love' and 'Let's Get to It' albums. Also includes the 12" version of 'Keep On Pumpin' It'.

'GREATEST REMIX HITS 1' (1993)
'GREATEST REMIX HITS 2' (1993)
'GREATEST REMIX HITS 3' (1998)
'GREATEST REMIX HITS 4' (1998)

Four Japanese volumes of over 80 remixes and rarities covering Kylie's formative years with Stock Aitken Waterman. Most notably, volume two contains Kylie's version of 'Getting Closer' (originally a minor UK hit for Sharon Haywoode in 1985) and volume four contains the unreleased 'I Am the One for You' from the 1990 recording sessions for 'Rhythm of Love'. All volumes were reissued with new artwork in Australia on the Mushroom label in 1998.

KYLIE'S NON-STOP HISTORY 50+1 (1993)
An enjoyably haphazard 76-minute megamix featuring a colossal 50 Kylie tracks from the SAW period 1988-92 (including dreamy B-sides like 'Closer' and 'Do You Dare'), plus a bonus of the hard-to-find

Techno Rave Mix of 'Celebration'. Originally remixed and released solely in Japan in November 1993, it was reissued in Australia the following year on Mushroom Records.

'MIXES' (1998)
Released just four months after the UK release of 'Impossible Princess', the shocking pink boxed 'Mixes' collects together nine excellent club versions of 'Too Far' (the single that never was), 'Breathe', 'Did It Again' and 'Some Kind of Bliss' by dance luminaries including the Trouser Enthusiasts, Sash!, Junior Vasquez, Nalin and Kane, and Brothers In Rhythm. The album hit #63 in the UK charts.

'IMPOSSIBLE REMIXES' (1998)
Australian double-album featuring ten dance remixes from 'Impossible Princess'. In addition to the tracks on the earlier British 'Mixes' collection it also includes the scarce TNT Club Mix of 'Breathe'.

'HITS +' (2001)
A British 16-track compilation of material from Kylie's deConstruction years bringing together her six hit UK singles, plus her duet with Nick Cave. In addition there are album tracks, B-sides and several previously unreleased songs, including 'Gotta Move On', 'Difficult By Design' and a chilled-out acoustic version of 1994's 'Automatic Love'. The album made #41 in the UK charts.

'CONFIDE IN ME' (2002)
17 tracks culled from Kylie's two deConstruction albums released on the budget Camden label for the UK market. There are no B-sides, remixes or rare tracks here, but the collection does include Australian single 'Cowboy Style'. 'Where is the Feeling?' and 'Breathe' are conspicuous by their absence.

'GREATEST HITS 87-92' (2002)
Ten years after Kylie's original 'Greatest Hits' album (a worldwide #1), PWL re-issued the collection with a slightly amended track listing and a bonus CD of 11 remixes. Intended to cash in on Kylie's re-energised success with 'Fever', the album infuriated her new label Parlophone. Heavily promoted with TV advertising in the UK (and without consultation with Kylie), the release of this album was a contentious one. A generic photograph of a headless woman dancing in white

knickers and vest was featured on the sleeve, but an enraged Kylie had an alternate cover designed, called 'Vintage Kylie', which could be downloaded from her website, printed and stuck over the top of the offending body-double. The album still managed to reach #20 in the UK charts, with an accompanying DVD release. Most fans seemed to have bought it for the ultra-rare Oz Tour Mix of 'The Loco-motion' and a funky new W.I.P. remix of 'Hand on Your Heart'.

'GREATEST HITS 87-97' (2003)

European double album of Kylie's hit singles, up to and including 'Breathe' (which was actually released in 1998), but excluding 'Where is the Feeling?', 'Some Kind of Bliss' and 'Where the Wild Roses Grow'. Like the 2002 UK 'Greatest Hits', the second disc also features remixes of some of her biggest SAW hits including the original Movers and Shakers 12" Mix of 'What Do I Have to Do' and the legendary Espagna Mix of 'Wouldn't Change a Thing'.

'GREATEST HITS 87-99' (2003)

Released in Australia in November 2003, this excellent 33-track compilation includes all of Kylie's hits in chronological order from 'The Loco-motion' to 'Cowboy Style', but also including 'Dancing Queen' (from the *Intimate and Live* tour), 'Tears' (the popular B-side to 'Did It Again') and 'The Real Thing' (from the 1999 soundtrack to *Sample People*). Also available as a limited edition DVD featuring all the videos.

KYLIE MINOGUE: ARTIST COLLECTION (2004)

A budget compilation on the BMG International label boasting a frankly bizarre, and unflattering, painting of Kylie on the cover. Featuring 14 album tracks, remixes and rarities from the deConstruction era, including the acoustic version of 'Where is the Feeling?'

'CONFIDE IN ME: THE IRRESISTIBLE KYLIE' (2007)

The latest in a long line of Kylie anthologies bringing together material from her deConstruction era. Released in the UK on the budget Music Club label with 33 songs over two discs including album tracks, B-sides and an alternate mix of the Pet Shop Boys-penned 'Falling' from 1994.

Further Reading

Jason Donovan, *Between the Lines: My Story Uncut*
(HarperCollins 2007)

Mark Frith (ed), *Best of Smash Hits* (Sphere 2006)

Chris Heath (ed), *Kylie* (Booth-Clibborn Editions 1999)

Andrew Mercado, *Super Aussie Soaps* (Pluto Press 2004)

Kylie Minogue, *Kylie* (V & A Publications 2007)

Kylie Minogue and William Baker, *Kylie La La La*
(Hodder and Stoughton 2002)

James Oram, *Neighbours: Behind the Scenes*
(Guild Publishing 1988)

Mike Stock, *The Hit Factory* (New Holland 2004)

Pete Waterman, *I Wish I Was Me: The Autobiography*
(Virgin 2000)

Index

Picture Acknowledgments

The pictures on the following pages are copyright Rex Features. Where credited, photographers' names appear after each page number.

BLACK AND WHITE

2 Charles Sykes
8 Ken McKay
10 News Group
14 Nils Jorgensen
37 Newspix
122 Profile Press
133 unknown
182 Richard Young
186 unknown
194 Tom Farmer
204 Ken McKay
239 Chris Alan/BEI
260 Jen Lowery

COLOUR

Section 1
1 Brendan Bierne
3 unknown
4 Brian Rasic
6 Simon Burt
8 unknown

Section 2
1 Richard Young
2 Brian Rasic
3 Brian Rasic
5 unknown
6 Brian Rasic
7 Richard Young
8 unknown

Section 3
1 Andrew Milligan
 2 Richard Young
3 Brian Rasic
5 (top) unknown
5 (bottom) Action Press
6 Ken McKay
7 Nils Jorgensen

Section 4
1 Richard Young
2 Ken McKay
5 Ken McKay
6 unknown
7 (top) Sipa Press
7 (bottom) Jim Smeal/BEI
8 David Fisher